PUBLIC CULTURE IN THE EARLY REPUBLIC

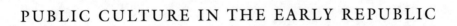

PUBLIC CULTURE
IN THE
EARLY REPUBLIC

Peale's Museum
and Its Audience

David R. Brigham

SMITHSONIAN INSTITUTION PRESS

Washington and London

Editor: Deborah Sanders
Designer: Alan Carter

Library of Congress Cataloging-in-Publication Data

Brigham, David R.
Public culture in the early republic : Peale's Museum and its audience / David R. Brigham.
p.   cm.
Includes bibliographical references and index.
ISBN 1–56098–416–3
1. Peale's Museum (Philadelphia, Pa.)—History. 2. Museums—Pennsylvania—Philadelphia—History. 3. Museum atten-
dance—Pennsylvania—Philadelphia—History. 4. Peale, Charles Willson, 1741–1827. 5. Museum directors—United
States—Biography. I. Title.
AM101.P496B75 1995
069'.09748'11—dc20   94-7705

British Library Cataloguing-in-Publication Data is available

Manufactured in the United States of America

02 01 00 99 98 97 96 95 5 4 3 2 1

∞ The paper used in this publication meets the minimum requirements of the American National Standard for
Permanence of Paper for Printed Library Materials Z39.48–1984.

For permission to reproduce illustrations appearing in this book, please correspond directly with the owners of the
works, as listed in the individual captions. The Smithsonian Institution Press does not retain reproduction rights for
these illustrations individually, or maintain a file of addresses for photo sources.

For

HOLLY

Contents

Acknowledgments

THIS PROJECT has developed from an idea into a dissertation and finally a book through the generous assistance, advice, and critical readings of a number of people. As dissertation advisors, Karin Calvert, Murray Murphey, and Elizabeth Johns challenged me to carefully formulate the research problem, my approach to the questions, and my arguments. Elizabeth Johns deserves a special expression of gratitude for her willingness to read multiple drafts of my manuscript and for her continually insightful commentary. Gary Kulik has also been a steady source of encouragement and a careful reader. I am grateful to David Bjelajac, whose reader report gave me the confidence to attack the revision of my dissertation. Additionally, Chandos Michael Brown, through his reader report, helped to refine many of my thoughts on the social and cultural implications of Peale's program. Numerous others—John Durel, Lois Fink, Ellen Grayson, Amy Henderson, Duane H. King, Penny Lazarus, Amy Meyers, Lillian B. Miller, Robert Blair St. George, David Steinberg, Andrew Walker, and David C. Ward—have generously read and commented upon individual chapters or papers that I have written on Peale, his museum, and the audience for that institution. Additionally, the following people have directed me to citations or offered specific suggestions that proved to be helpful: Rachel Dvoretsky, Jeff Groff, Owen Hannaway, Susan B. Heller, Tony Lewis, Simon Newman, Elizabeth O'Leary, David Rees, John P. Riddell, and Anne A. Verplanck.

Several institutions provided forums in which I had the opportunity to rehearse and refine my arguments before committing them to print. In particular, The Philadelphia Center for Early American Studies (1991), the American Studies Association (1991), the American Association of Museums (1992), the Peale Museum, Baltimore City Life Museums (1992), the National Museum of American Art and the National Portrait Gallery (1992), the Pennsylvania Historical Association (1992), and the American Historical Association (1992), by their informed audiences, furthered my knowledge of the period and my topic.

The learned advice of staff members at numerous research institutions directed me to valuable resources, accelerated my searches, and often furthered my understanding of the documents I encountered. At the Library Company of Philadelphia, I especially appreciated the help of Phil Lapsansky and Mary Anne Hines. Linda Stanley at the Historical Society of Pennsylvania enabled me to study the list of subscribers, which had to be removed from display, and without which a central chapter of this book could not have been written. At the American Philosophical Society, I am particularly grateful to Beth Carroll-Horrocks, Roy Goodman, and David Rees. Doris Fanelli and John Milley contributed to my understanding of the Peale portrait collection at Independence National Historical Park, as well as the history of the buildings. Lillian B. Miller, Sidney Hart, and David C. Ward shared freely their knowledge of Peale and granted me access both to the Peale Papers and to vast files of newspaper items relating to the museum. I am also deeply indebted to the staffs at the City Archives of Philadelphia, the Philadelphia Museum of Art, the Pennsylvania Academy of the Fine Arts, the Huntington Library, the rare book and reference divisions at the Van Pelt Library of the University of Pennsylvania, the Archives and Records Center at the University of Pennsylvania, the libraries of the Smithsonian Institution, the Library of Congress, the Museum of Comparative Zoology, and the Peabody Museum of Archaeology and Ethnology.

The research for this book was completed with substantial financial support. During my first year on the project, a fellowship from the University of Pennsylvania allowed me to define the problem and broaden my knowledge of Peale, cultural audiences, and early national American history. A predoctoral fellowship from the Philadelphia Center for Early American Studies introduced me to a community of scholars with similar interests and allowed me time to conduct much of my primary research. The following year I enjoyed the privilege of a predoctoral fellowship at the Smithsonian Institution, under the sponsorship of the Peale Family Papers at the National Portrait Gallery. At the Smithsonian, I benefitted from the community of scholars at the National Museum of American Art and the National Portrait Gallery, finished my primary research, and drafted the dissertation. I completed the dissertation and completed the book manuscript as a Research Associate in the art division of the Huntington Library, Art Collections, and Botanical Gardens, where my position was supported by The Virginia Steele Scott Foundation.

I am grateful also for the editorial support I received from the Smithsonian Institution Press. Amy Pastan's contagious enthusiasm for my manuscript accelerated my revisions, and her good cheer has made a laborious task into a pleasurable one. Cheryl Anderson and Duke Johns have greatly facilitated the production of this book. Alan Carter's elegant design has enhanced the readability of the book. But I must reserve a special thanks for Deborah Sanders, whose painstaking work as copy editor has significantly enhanced the clarity and flow of the text.

Finally, I could not have undertaken this study without the constant support of my family. My parents provided both moral and financial support, and raised me to believe that I could accomplish a task such as this. My wife, Holly, has helped me through every frustrating moment and shared in the excitement of each turn toward the completion of this book. She has also provided intelligent responses to the many drafts of this book, offered creative suggestions for understanding Peale's images, and tolerated the many nights and weekends that have been lost to this project.

Introduction

CHARLES WILLSON PEALE aspired to exhibit within his museum "a world in miniature," a display that embodied the full range of natural and artificial productions from around the globe.[1] But his museum was more than a static repository of natural history specimens and artifacts. It was a dynamic social site through which Peale helped to define the terms of participation in early national cultural institutions, while his varied audiences sought to shape the museum to meet their distinctive needs.[2] More specifically, Peale set a standard for the extent to which cultural institutions were accessible to people of different social rank, gender, race, political affiliation, and religion. Although Peale proposed that the museum was democratically open, the composition of his audience was significantly limited, especially with respect to social rank, gender, and race. In promoting the museum to his potential audience, Peale defined it broadly as a public benefit, but he also targeted specific audiences by concentrating on the economic, social, scientific, moral, and religious implications of his exhibitions. In turn, his audience members used the museum to identify with particular social groups, to promote their intellectual accomplishments, to market their products, and to establish the boundaries of their community. In these ways, the world in miniature that Peale fashioned was representative of broad cultural patterns in early national America.

Peale's interests in developing public displays evolved from his initial engagement in the painter's trade-practice of keeping a small picture gallery into a more expansive view of a museum as a compendium of knowledge. Shortly after returning from a student trip to London (1767–69), Peale began exhibiting paintings from his own hand in his house in Annapolis, Maryland. Upon moving to Philadelphia in 1776, the artist continued this practice. Peale specialized his picture gallery in 1784 to feature bust-length portraits of men who distinguished themselves in the politics and warfare of the American Revolution. The following year Peale opened a long-running exhibition that he referred to as "my perspective views with changeable effects," an exhibition that evoked a sense of motion through images of landscapes, and literary and historical subjects. In 1786 Peale redefined his exhibition space as a "Repository for Natural

Curiosities,"[3] augmenting his collection of paintings with preserved animals, fossils, and minerals. In this newly conceived museum, Peale—who had apprenticed as a saddler and later trained as a fine artist—expanded his definition of art from just paintings to a broad artisanal category that included handcrafted objects from the New and Old worlds, Western and non-Western civilizations, and present and past. This combination of art and natural history defined the contents of the museum from 1786 until after Peale's death in 1827.

Both visually and verbally Peale claimed for his museum an audience characterized by its breadth. In his late self-portrait and commemoration of the mature museum, *The Artist in His Museum* (1822), Peale delineated, in visual terms, visitors who vary in age, gender, and religion (figures 1 and 2). The young woman in the foreground wears a bonnet that identifies her as a member of Philadelphia's vast Quaker population. Behind her and to the right, a father teaches his son about natural history. The boy holds a book, probably Peale's *Guide to the Collections,* which indicates that the father is also instructing the boy on how to visit a museum. Further back and to the right, the final audience member is a young man whose age is somewhere between those of the other two male figures. The males in the painting therefore span the age categories of youth, young adulthood, and middle age. The figures are both male and female, and they include both Quaker and people whose religion is not specifically denoted. Just as the representatives of Peale's audience in this painting vary in social characteristics, they also respond in different terms, including surprise or awe, learning, and contemplation.[4]

This depiction of varied audience members is consistent with Peale's written claims that, in keeping with the emergence of a republican form of government, American cultural institutions ought to serve a wide range of the public. In particular, Peale argued that the openness of his museum stood in marked contrast to the exclusive admission policies of European museums:

> In Europe, all men of information prize a well regulated museum, as a necessary appendage to government, but in several parts of that quarter of the earth, the means of visiting those repositories, are within the reach of particular classes of society only, or open on such terms or at such portions of time, as effectually to debar the mass of society, from participating in the improvement, and the pleasure resulting from a careful visitation.

Peale thus presented his museum to the state legislature as an institutional form derived from aristocratic precedents, but adapted to fulfill a particularly American and republican goal: a universally educated public. This statement of the museum's mission was linked to a plea for government money, a request that required Peale to ex-

Figure 1. Charles Willson Peale, *The Artist in His Museum*, 1822. Courtesy of The Pennsylvania Academy of the Fine Arts, Philadelphia. Gift of Mrs. Sarah Harrison (The Joseph Harrison, Jr., Collection).

Figure 2. Charles Willson Peale, detail of *The Artist in His Museum,* 1822. Courtesy of The Pennsylvania Academy of the Fine Arts, Philadelphia. Gift of Mrs. Sarah Harrison (The Joseph Harrison, Jr., Collection).

press the public benefits of the museum. But Peale's statement did not simply fulfill this requirement; it was an assertion of his personal commitment. In his private correspondence, Peale affirmed his hope that his efforts would serve the needs of "the unwise as well as the learned."[5]

In keeping with this commitment, Peale extended the museum's hours into the evenings. An early advertisement for the oil-lit openings offered "TO Accommodate those who may not have leisure during the day light to enjoy the rational amusement which the various subjects of the MUSEUM afford" by having the museum "handsomely LIGHTED on TUESDAY and SATURDAY evenings." Peale similarly scheduled evening readings of his natural history lectures to reach audience members who worked during the day. Explaining the repetition of his lectures at night, Peale stated that "some of my friends have not leisure to attend" during the daylight hours. The chandeliers hanging from the ceiling in *The Artist in His Museum* evoke such nighttime lectures and performances.[6]

Peale further embraced diversity among his audience by inviting into his museum workers from all three sectors of the economy: agriculture, commerce, and manufactures or "the mechanical arts." In his "Introduction to a Course of Lectures on Natural History," Peale explained the relevance of natural history for each group:

> The farmer ought to know that snakes feed on field mice and moles, which would otherwise destroy whole fields of corn. . . . To the merchant, the study of nature is scarcely less interesting, whose trafic lies altogether in materials either raw from the stores of nature or *wrought* by the hand of ingenious art. . . . The mechanic ought to possess an accurate knowledge of many of the qualities of those materials with which his art is connected.

The importance of Peale's choice of these categories may be better understood in contemporary terms. Both the media and public ritual defined a healthy economy as one that maintained a balance among these three realms. Moreover, it was commonly argued that a republic maintained its political freedom by developing economic independence in all three areas. Editor Benjamin Franklin Bache promoted these beliefs when he promised in 1790 that his fledgling newspaper, *The General Advertiser*, would inform the public about topics relating to agriculture, commerce, and "manufactures and useful arts." Similarly, public celebrations included toasts to these categories, often complemented by such patriotic songs as "The Plough Boy," "America, Commerce and Freedom," and "The Loom and the Shuttle." Peale's explanation of the benefits to farmers, merchants, and mechanics was, therefore, a republican statement of the economic and political importance of the museum as much as it was a broad appeal to the public.[7]

Peale's advertisements suggest that he intended to make the museum inclusive across gender lines as well. When Peale first offered lectures in natural history (1799–1800), he extended a special invitation to women: "It is my wish to behold ladies among my hearers; for female education cannot be complete without some knowledge of the beautiful and interesting subjects of natural history." Peale adjusted the fee structure to ensure that women could attend the lectures. During the first year, he stated the "Price of a ticket for the season to admit a *Gentleman and Lady*—ten dollars." The following year (1800–1801) the terms were slightly restated: "a gentleman, purchasing a ticket, is entitled to introduce a lady."[8]

Philadelphia had a population of wide-ranging ethnicities, and one observer defined responses to Peale's Museum as expressions of those identities:

> [T]he *French* generally appear to be well informed therein; and do not seem to be at a loss to know the various subjects of the collection, although they are mostly American. That the *English* who view it pretend to know a great deal, yet with a few exceptions really know but little: That the *Germans* appear to be better informed: and that the *Americans* show some knowledge of them, yet it is without pretending to know more than they are really acquainted with.

The pro-French bias in this account probably expresses the political sympathies of the editor and readers of the *General Advertiser* more than it accurately characterizes the behavior of Peale's audience.[9]

Peale's policy of admission seems remarkably broad, yet the terms of participation were not equal for all social groups. In examining *The Artist in His Museum*, cultural historian Laura Rigal found not simply a plurality of people and responses, but also a number of hierarchical relationships. The division of male figures into pupil, learned young man, and teacher characterizes one such ranked set of roles. Whereas these differences are intellectual ones that can be overcome by maturation and education, the picture depicts a more rigid barrier between the sexes. Rigal convincingly argued that the young woman's emotionally expressive response in contrast to the young man's internal reflection establishes gendered expectations of audience behavior. Although the museum may have been widely accessible, Peale defined different terms of participation for various social groups.[10]

Tension between Peale's expressed interest in including women among his audience and his reinforcement of gender hierarchy must be situated in a larger cultural framework. In her study of early national women, historian Linda Kerber demonstrated that, although education of women was encouraged as a matter of republican reform, it did not place young women and young men on equal status. Rather, edu-

cation of women reinforced expectations that girls would mature into traditionally domestic lives. Peale's invitations to women similarly embody a gender hierarchy by placing control of family finances in male hands. Such control is evident when Peale's offer
"a gentleman, purchasing a ticket, is entitled to introduce a lady" is rewritten in a way
that reverses the gender roles: "a lady, purchasing a ticket, is entitled to introduce a
gentleman."[11]

The museum's openness to people of different social ranks was similarly limited.
For instance, Peale accorded special recognition to audience members of prominent
reputation. This practice acknowledged the elevated social status of certain public
men, and served to attract the rest of the population to the museum. In 1787 Peale
invited George Washington to an exclusive showing of the exhibition on changing
perspective views, an event reserved for members of the prestigious Society of Cincinnati. Membership in this elite society was limited to officers of the revolution. In
addition to this offer to the local elite, Peale extended special invitations to visiting
dignitaries. In 1793, Peale greeted the new French minister plenipotentiary Edmond-
Charles Genêt with a free ticket for yearlong admission to the museum. The following year, Peale extended a similar courtesy to scientist and religious philosopher
Joseph Priestley. When Peale succeeded in attracting famous patrons, he promoted his
endeavors through his association with them. In his attempts to sell polygraphs, for
example, Peale solicited and published letters of endorsement from President Thomas
Jefferson and Philadelphia waterworks engineer Benjamin Henry Latrobe.[12]

Despite Peale's assertions that the museum was open to everyone, some contemporaries perceived restrictions to that policy. Of particular note, one anonymous author characterized such constraints as one of the museum's strengths: "The doors of
the Museum have ever been closed against the profligate and the indecent; it has been
preserved, with scrupulous fidelity, as a place where the virtuous and refined of society could meet, to enjoy such pleasures as can be tasted by the virtuous and refined
alone." Praise of this sort seems to contradict Peale's democratic claims for the museum. Was the museum capable of uplifting the public, as Peale claimed? Or did the
museum exclude some lower, unregenerate stratum that was regarded as permanently
"profligate and indecent"?[13]

Peale resolved this tension by insisting that the museum remained accessible to all
who would avail themselves of its intellectual and moral influence. No one was actively
excluded. Rather, those who were not audience members excluded themselves. An incident that took place early in 1797 illustrated this psychological smoothing of an otherwise significant contradiction in Peale's world view. Late in 1796 the city of Savannah suffered a devastating fire. Peale responded by announcing that he would donate

the proceeds from one day's receipts toward the relief of the southern city. The theater and circus also commonly responded to public tragedies through acts of philanthropy, thereby demonstrating their vital place in the community. After the benefit, Peale announced that he and his audience had raised $139.00 for the "sufferers by fire at Savannah." To his account of the event's success, Peale appended an anecdote of a working woman who had the entrance fee but chose not to enter.

> A middle aged woman, with modest address, approached the *Museum* door; her dress bespoke that her wants were supplied by industry; at that moment a small company came forward presenting their tickets of admission; the good woman wished to let them pass, and then most courteously demanded, what was the price of entrance?—Only one quarter of a dollar. There, says she, holding out her hand, with two quarters, *it is my mite,* and was turning away. But, Madam, won't you walk into the *Museum.*—Not now, she replied, there is company enough there without me, and I will find a quarter to pay for seeing it some other day, and retired uttering pathetic benedictions.

The entrance fee was not beyond the woman's means, Peale insisted, as she carried away with her twice the price of admission. She simply chose not to participate in this community effort to rebuild a troubled city. The woman "with modest address" was further distinguished as an outsider by the mention that she "retired uttering pathetic benedictions." If the museum was a cultural analogue to the community at large, such nonparticipants exempted themselves not only from the museum, but also from the larger category of citizenship. By contrast, Peale grouped himself and his paying customers among the community-spirited when he wrote, "I present my grateful thanks to my fellow-citizens, who have enabled me to become one of their agents in an act of humanity."[14]

Thus, Peale addressed his audience with a rhetoric of inclusiveness that, ironically, promoted social boundaries, and the actual composition of his audience reflected this. Not only did the audience consist of a disproportionate number of men and people belonging to the upper ranks of society, but also it was nearly uniform in terms of race. Women did attend exhibits and lectures at the museum, and they recorded their responses in diaries, letters, and published works. Women also patronized the silhouette portrait concession at the museum, subscribed to annual tickets of admission, and donated objects to expand Peale's collections. But in each of these categories of audience involvement with the museum, women were outnumbered by men. Similarly, the occupations and accumulated wealth of Peale's audience members indicate that they were, as a group, substantially better off than a random cross section of Philadelphians would have been. Although a few Native Americans did visit the museum, Peale's audience consisted almost entirely of whites.

These limits were indicative of broader social constraints in the early republic, and public institutions like Peale's Museum both mirrored and reinforced them. Public life centered around the activities of independently operated family businesses, which were typically identified with the name of the male head of the household. Newspapers and city directories announced the names of merchants and mechanics, and enumerated the particular wares that they imported or manufactured. Property tax was assessed to men, signifying their control of land, buildings, precious metal, and all other material wealth. Women typically held these public roles only as widows. That some widows continued the business suggests that they had previously played an integral part in the family economic unit, but were publicly accorded secondary status. The city also housed thousands of laborers, who were more transient and less likely to appear either in city directories or on the tax rolls. Peale's Museum echoed these social patterns in that the working people who were considered, in the contemporary terms, the "lower sort," are much less frequently listed among the audience. Women's names are likewise scarce on the lists.[15] As women seem to have participated in economic life despite their relative absence from public records of business, they probably also attended the museum in numbers greater than museum records indicate. For instance, records of men purchasing multiple tickets to the museum probably indicate participation in the museum (and more broadly in public culture) by women. Members of the lower socioeconomic ranks are similarly absent from Peale's records of audience members. As their absence from the tax rolls does not prove their lack of productivity, their absence from Peale's records may not indicate their exclusion from the museum. One-time admission was the least expensive way to visit the museum and therefore was the most inclusive policy, but the names of such short-term visitors were not recorded for posterity.

Although limited in these ways, Peale's audience represented a wide range of economic, social, and intellectual pursuits, and individuals expressed their particular interests through their participation in the museum. Local writers boosted Philadelphian and American cultural achievement in their support of Peale, whereas foreign travelers maintained the continued superiority of their native land by judging Peale's Museum to be a faint approximation of European museums. Women embraced their central role in the domestic sphere by using silhouette portraits purchased at the museum to document their kinship networks. The respectable ranks of society staked their distinguished social position by affiliating publicly with Peale's Museum as well as with other learned institutions. Donors of objects to the museum promoted their occupational interests by presenting the raw materials and finished products by which they made a living. Manufacturers fought during this period to gain legislative support—copyrights, tariffs, foreign trade restrictions—to promote their emerging industries, and the museum offered an institutional framework for elevating their enterprise to a national cause. Donors of scientific items also capitalized on the fact that a museum held objects up for public view, thereby distinguishing intellectual pursuits as particularly valuable to society. Naturalists contributed specimens that promoted their publications and served as hallmarks of their accomplishments in their field of study. Donors also contributed to the definition of community by adding objects that pronounced the limits to which republican society would be inclusive. In particular, donor-generated exhibits enabled Peale to construct a human world that confronted racial difference, social inequality, criminal transgression, and bodily disfiguration and disease. In such exhibits, Peale and members of his audience resolved for themselves the republican tension between an open society and one that depends upon a ranked order.

The first two chapters of the book explore the ways in which Peale developed his audience. Chapter 1 situates Peale's public engagement with his audience in the context of the museum's contemporary institutions of entertainment and education in Philadelphia. In particular, this chapter interprets the specific connotations of the various ways in which Peale housed and arranged his collections in relation to the uses of space in neighboring structures. In addition to interpreting these spatial contexts, chapter 1 also examines the rhetoric employed by Peale in relation to that used to promote other places of public leisure. Finally, this chapter develops an impressionistic account of the social composition of leisure audiences at Philadelphia's other cultural institutions. Against these spatial, rhetorical, and social contexts, Peale's Museum may be better understood as a business, an intellectual pursuit, and a place of entertainment. As well, preliminary limits may be set for understanding the extent to which republican institutions embraced the full range of society.

The second chapter considers the specific methods by which Peale shaped meanings of his displays for his audience. In prints and paintings, Peale constructed a set of paradigmatic images of the museum. These images promoted the relevance of the collections to religion and science, and to art and nature, and they proposed models of both individual and collective achievement. Peale also addressed his audience in advertisements, published pleas to government bodies, lectures, and public service announcements. In these verbal communications, Peale argued the museum's ability to further the economic, moral, and intellectual needs of the community. Through these varied messages, Peale balanced broad statements of the museum's public contributions with messages aimed at attracting the patronage of specific constituencies.

Chapter 3, through an analysis of the written responses to the museum, shifts the viewpoint from Peale to his audience. This and other measures of audience response to the collections demonstrate that visitors gauged their visits in Peale's terms, as well as in ways that served their own interests. Just as Peale claimed the museum's relevance to numerous purposes, visitors wrote about the economic, political, moral, religious, scientific, and artistic importance of the exhibitions. Writers established independent concerns most dramatically when they criticized Peale's efforts. These negative responses ranged from suggestions for expansion of certain collections to harsh judgments of the aesthetic and historical significance of the portrait collection.

The fourth chapter examines the audience for silhouette portraits, an extremely popular concession beginning in 1802 at the museum. Peale promoted this interactive exhibit in gendered terms, and therefore it is apt for a case study of the ways in which men and women were invited to participate in the museum. Peale proposed that silhouettes were especially attractive to women, and indeed surviving silhouettes demonstrate that a large audience of women purchased these souvenirs during their museum visits. Whereas Peale believed silhouettes to be important as an external index to inner character, a number of his audience members used them to document family connections. Because four identical portraits were produced at a sitting, audience members could exchange silhouettes among family and friends. As such, silhouettes became a kind of social exchange medium, serving particularly the domestic sphere, a domain that was encoded as female.

Chapter 5 shows how subscribers to annual tickets of admission were participants in the process of public affiliation. In contrast to the silhouettes and their private and female orientation, subscription was a public practice and consequently a primarily male activity. Through subscription, audience members gained more than unlimited access to the museum. Subscription and other forms of association were important ways of proclaiming one's connection to social networks, political positions, and cultural refinement. Peale's subscribers collectively spanned the social spectrum from the lower margins of the middling ranks to the economic, political, and intellectual elite. For the already distinguished members of society, subscription reinforced their elevated social position. For younger men and those striving to improve their rank, subscription became a symbolic means of presaging future advancement.

The final two chapters consider audience members who donated artifacts and natural history specimens to Peale's Museum, thereby actively participating in its expansion. Chapter 6 discusses donors of minerals, natural resources, and manufactures, and it demonstrates how the museum served both the material and intellectual interests of Peale's audience. Although Peale had a modest interest in such collections, and Rubens—the son entrusted to manage the museum after his father's retirement in

1810—developed a deeper affinity to mineralogy, these collections were built primarily through gifts from audience members. Many of these donors had a direct stake in the items they donated. For instance, mine owners gave metal ores from their land, manufacturers contributed raw materials and finished products, and scientists added minerals relating to their research.

Chapter 7, the final chapter, surveys donors of Native American and non-Western objects, and donors of other objects that expressed difference from mainstream American society. In these collections, too, donors expressed personal interests. For example, some American military officers who subdued Native American unrest and others who conducted expeditions in the western territory contributed to the museum collections. In addition to expressing attitudes about interracial contact, Peale shaped these exhibits into a broad statement of human order. The overall message was that humanity should live in harmony, but that hierarchical relationships are natural. Peale's exhibits conveyed that, although individuals might advance themselves through emulation of the respectable men of society, the best course for happiness and longevity is through resignation to one's station in life. For all audience members, this arrangement of artifacts invited the question, What is my place in this world in miniature, and, more importantly, in the world at large?

1. Contemporary Institutions of Education and Entertainment and Their Audiences

THE LOCATIONS of Peale's Museum and the rhetoric Peale used to promote it provide a basis for comparison to contemporary cultural institutions in Philadelphia. Because Peale cultivated an image of the museum as a serious educational enterprise, links are immediately apparent to the American Philosophical Society, the University of Pennsylvania, and the Library Company of Philadelphia. But Peale attracted his audience also by highlighting the entertainment value of his displays and demonstrations in language that he shared with promoters of the theaters, circuses, wax works, and itinerant amusements in the city. Defining these varied associations is a crucial first step to understanding Peale's attempt to develop varied audiences, ranging from Philadelphia's well-educated, politically empowered, and economically advantaged to the multitude of mechanics and their families. But these associations also hint at potential limits to Peale's and other cultural entrepreneurs' audiences—limits in terms of religious affiliation, place of residence, social rank, gender, race, and political partisanship. These limits to participation in cultural institutions hint that, in an age of optimism about developing a broad community, significant social constraints persisted.

Between 1786 and 1827, Peale housed his collections in three distinct sites, which signaled alternative identities to the public: the museum as a typical family-run business, as a learned institution, and as an expression of national character. From 1786 to 1794, Peale kept his museum in the outbuilding to his house on the southwest corner of the intersection of Philadelphia's Third and Lombard streets. This location offered a domestic context to the budding museum, an image projected in a nostalgic painting by Rubens Peale of the home of his youth (figure 3). The long span of buildings is identified by a sign that reads "PEALES MUSEUM." The gambrel-roofed building has its gable end fronting Lombard Street and is followed by the skylit gallery and the moving picture room, all running parallel to Third Street. The tall house that rises above the museum buildings indicates that the Peales preside over this family business. Clean socks, shirt, and trousers hang over the fence to dry, emphasizing the domestic over the professional character of life there. Among the nearby occupants during these years were a coach maker, a baker, a grocer, and a mast maker. As city directories

13

Figure 3. Rubens Peale, *The Old Museum*, 1858–60. Courtesy of The Pennsylvania Academy of the Fine Arts, Philadelphia. Bequest of Charles Coleman Sellers.

demonstrate, houses included both residential and business quarters. Like other eighteenth-century families, the Peales lived and worked in the same place.[1]

Charles Willson Peale more firmly claimed the domesticity of this neighborhood in his engraving *The Accident in Lombard-Street*, published in 1787 (figure 4). The Peale house figures prominently as the building on the corner at the left side of the print. In the foreground, a young girl raises her hands to her head in dismay as she looks down at the pie she has just dropped in the street. In addition to the loss of her baked goods, the girl suffers the taunts of chimney sweeps and the din of barking dogs that approach from left and right. In contrast to the girl's failed errand, a woman at left carries a pie in two hands and a woman at right carefully manages a child in her arms. A pair of couplets inscribed at the bottom of the print reinforces the visual narrative:

> The pye from Bake-house She had brought
> But let it fall for want of thought
>
> And laughing Sweeps collect around
> The pye that's scatter'd on the ground

Whereas Rubens's painting of the Peale house and museum balanced the personal and professional, this print presents the neighborhood primarily as a domestic space. Only the baker's sign on the residence three houses away from Peale's and the horse-drawn cart further down the street suggest commercial activity. Upon entering this space to visit Peale's Museum, the print suggests, visitors encountered rows of neatly kept homes, family-run shops, and clean streets populated by men, women, children, and animals.[2]

In 1794 Peale moved his collections and family into Philosophical Hall, home to the American Philosophical Society, gaining for the museum the specific respectability of this learned society and the broader context of public life at the heart of Philadelphia. By 1794 the American Philosophical Society already had a fifty-year history and enjoyed the distinction that Philadelphia's most distinguished scientist, Benjamin Franklin, had been its founder. Peale joined a noteworthy group of tenants at Philosophical Hall. The University of Pennsylvania had recently moved out of the hall to new quarters on Fourth and Arch Streets. The College of Physicians of Philadelphia also met in Philosophical Hall and continued to do so after Peale's move there. Thus, Peale's Museum entered into fellowship with the most prominent institutions of in-

Figure 4. Charles Willson Peale, *The Accident in Lombard-Street*, 1787. Courtesy of the Library of Congress.

tellectual activity and academic purpose in Philadelphia. Philosophical Hall added to the museum the weight of science, reason, and objectivity.[3]

In contrast to Peale's former residential neighborhood, his new environment was the center of higher learning and political activity. The importance of this public arena was captured in a *View of Several Public Buildings, in Philadelphia,* which illustrated the *Columbian Magazine* in 1790 (figure 5). In this engraving, James Thackara and John Vallance delineated, from left to right, the Episcopal Academy, Congress Hall, the State House, Philosophical Hall, the Library Company of Philadelphia, and Carpenter's Hall. The grand scale of these buildings and the surrounding expanse of lawn gave visitors a vastly different impression from that of the ordinary streets of the museum's previous location. Impressive towers, cupolas, weather vanes, balustrades, and chimneys surmount these public structures, distinguishing them from the simple chimneys and dormers that adorn the homes in *The Accident in Lombard-Street.* A visit to Peale's Museum on Lombard Street would have been as routine as a visit to the baker's house three doors away, but entrance into Philosophical Hall would have been a remarkable occasion.[4]

In 1802 Peale moved into the Pennsylvania State House, better known today as Independence Hall, claiming for the museum an identity as a national institution. This was not a new role for the museum, but rather an affirmation of the patriotic note on which his gallery of Revolutionary War hero portraits began in 1784. In the contem-

Figure 5. James Thackara and John Vallance, attrib., probably after Charles Willson Peale, *View of Several Public Buildings, in Philadelphia,* from *Columbian Magazine,* v. 4, January 1790. The Library Company of Philadelphia.

porary depiction *View of Several Public Buildings,* the central location and larger size of the State House relative to Philosophical Hall suggest that Peale's move there in 1802 constituted an elevation in the museum's status. In addition to housing the city and state governments, the State House was known as the site where the Declaration of Independence was signed and first read publicly and where the United States Constitution was written. Through its identification with these events, the building came to symbolize the birth of the nation, and this reputation validated Peale's Museum as a bastion of American culture. Between 1802 and 1811, Peale maintained his museum in both Philosophical Hall and the upper floor of the State House. This dual location lent credibility to Peale's presentation of the museum as both a serious educational institution and a national enterprise. Peale also maximized his profits through this arrangement, since it allowed for separate admission charges to the popular mastodon exhibit in Philosophical Hall (fifty cents) and to the core collection in the State House (twenty-five cents).[5]

What the *View of Several Public Buildings* obscures is the proximity of public leisure sites to these more official and academic institutions. Just one block west on Chestnut Street, Peale's neighbors included Ricketts's Circus and Oellers's Hotel on the south side of the street and the New Theatre on the north side. Oellers's Hotel frequently hosted fashionable events including concerts and balls. Although Peale actively developed his affiliations with the intellectual community, his public promotion of the museum also linked him to Philadelphia's public amusements.[6]

While Peale communicated meaning to his audience through his choice of buildings in which to exhibit his collections, he more directly addressed the public through newspapers, broadsides, and pamphlets. In his promotional literature, Peale often used key phrases to convey broad messages. These phrases operated for the audience as a kind of shorthand, since they were already well known through the promotions of other institutions of entertainment and education. Moreover, they reveal assumptions about economic priorities, social distinctions, and moral beliefs that were central to life in the early republic.[7]

One principle that Peale shared with fellow educators was that his exhibits should advance "useful knowledge." This phrase expressed a pragmatic approach to education, and especially favored the economic returns of cultural inquiry. Adherents to the concept of useful knowledge also pronounced immoral the wasteful pursuit of knowledge for its own sake. The assumption was that people of a wide range of social ranks would benefit from this type of education, since only the elite could afford to acquire knowledge that did not lend itself to practical application.[8]

Peale formalized his commitment to useful knowledge outside the museum through his longtime affiliation with the American Philosophical Society. Benjamin Franklin invoked this principle in 1743 in his "Proposal for Promoting Useful Knowledge among the British Plantations in America." The phrase still echoes in the full name of the society: The American Philosophical Society Held at Philadelphia for Promoting Useful Knowledge. Peale's election to the society followed just two weeks after his first announcement of the museum in the *Pennsylvania Packet* on July 7, 1786. Eighteen months later, Peale was elected one of three co-curators of the society, an office he shared until 1811 with University of Pennsylvania professors Benjamin Smith Barton, Robert Patterson, and Robert Hare, Jr.; Swedish Church minister Nicholas Collin; Pennsylvania Hospital physician Thomas Parke; inventor Robert Leslie; and others. His fellow curators were just a few of the educated peers whom Peale met through the philosophical society and upon whose support he counted to bolster the reputation of the museum. Peale and the museum also benefitted through his responsibilities at the society. Among other duties, Peale and the other curators maintained the society's library and its cabinet of mechanical models, fossil bones, minerals, and various items of scientific and historical significance. Pierre Eugène DuSimitière, the first museum operator in Philadelphia, preceded Peale in the American Philosophical Society, being elected a member in 1768 and a curator in 1776, 1779, and 1781. The society's cabinet and DuSimitière's American Museum both served as models of collecting, organization, and display upon which Peale improved in building his Philadelphia Museum.[9]

Peale's categories of display were consistent with contemporary ideas about a public school curriculum that would advance useful knowledge. Under the heading "a comparative view of the UTILITY of different branches of EDUCATION," one anonymous author counted as useful subjects spelling, mathematics, geography, natural history, political history, "*practical* branches of metaphysicks," French, German, and "the arts of promoting national happiness by the means of free government, agriculture, commerce, and manufactures." Natural history exhibits were central to Peale's presentation. As well, Peale argued that his collections of minerals, preserved animals, American manufactures, and native manufactures from around the world promoted the three types of production believed to be essential to a self-sustaining economy: agriculture, commerce, and manufactures. On the other hand, this anonymous writer named astronomy, logic, "speculative" mathematics and metaphysics, Latin, and Greek as "entirely useless in the pursuits of the greatest parts of mankind." These latter subjects were a matter of social distinction more than of real value, this writer charged. Translating this assessment into fiscal terms, he compared useful education to hard money and to "bank notes, which are very valuable and easily transferred from place to place, to the great emolument of society, without trouble or expense." Meanwhile, useless pursuits "are like family plate, valuable in themselves, but proper only for persons of a certain rank" or "may be justly compared to old continental money," devoid of value. By invoking references to the evils of social ranking, this author positioned himself as a republican reformer, an identity which Peale also fashioned for himself.[10]

Peale's repeated support of useful knowledge amounted to a moral plea that his audience members devote themselves to increasing their productivity. An unidentified essayist furthered the argument that such pursuits by an industrious middling population were not only "useful" but also "just":

> Men of leisure, who have patience of investigation, may, perhaps, employ themselves in useless enquiries, without producing any hurtful effects: indeed they may happen to strike upon some discovery from which benefit will result. But where such an ardour of curiosity prevails, as to induce people to researches, from which no practical advantage is derived, it disqualifies them for active pursuits in life.
>
> It should be an established rule with every person who reads to enquire of himself, when he lays aside his book, whether he has gained any ideas at all, and whether they be just and useful. To read, and yet to acquire no ideas, is, at any rate, a destruction of time: but the mere loss of time is not so pernicious, as to catch sentiments that are fallacious or trifling.

Only "men of leisure" have the luxury to expend time for the acquisition of knowledge that has no further application. This observation implies that the middling sort, who learn in order to advance their "active pursuits in life," contribute more to society than their wealthier fellow citizens. One goal of the museum, then, was to address a broad public with a message that the acquisition of useful knowledge was a social responsibility.[11]

While his application of the phrase "useful knowledge" aligned Peale directly with educational reformers and the American Philosophical Society, his promotion of the museum as "a constant source of instruction as well as amusement" offered his audience broader associations. Early national educational reformers shared Peale's interest in combining instruction with amusement. Burgiss Allison, founder of the Bordentown Academy in New Jersey and a patron of Peale's Museum, explained his own similar philosophy of education in a letter to Benjamin Rush:

> With regard to amusements, certainly much may be done to unite the *utile* with the *dulcs*, and it must be evident to every person of the least reflection, that if we can contrive to amuse whilst we instruct, the progress will be more rapid and the impression much deeper. But to connect instruction with the very amusements, during relaxation from the discipline of school hours, is surely of the utmost consequence, and therefore worth attempting. With an

eye to those things, I have gone to some expense, to furnish myself with a variety of materials calculated thereto; such as geographical, historical, technographical and natural history cards, geometrical blocks, dissected maps, tour of Europe, &c. amusements in optics, magnetism, electricity, &c. some entirely new, and some in use heretofore; which have never failed to afford entertainment and information at the same time; and I have had sufficient proof, that rendering the exercises of oratory more agreeable, by mixing something of the dramatic kind with their orations, gives them a relish for the study, a desire of excelling, and an animation in the pursuit, with which I could never inspire them when engaged in nothing but plain speaking; or when nothing of Play was connected with their business, or amusement with their study.

Allison's mode of education and Peale's concept of the museum blurred the boundary between learning and leisure.[12]

Just as educators hoped to attract audiences by claiming to amuse, leisure promoters hoped to sell their products by promising to instruct. Literary scholar and cultural historian Cathy Davidson argued that, as a genre, novels were regarded as morally suspect in post-Revolutionary America. But the claim that a work amused and instructed defined the consumption of novels as redeeming. When Royall Tyler promoted his new children's book to his publisher, he argued that "a book which will amuse while it instructs children will sell in this country." This assertion both forestalled criticism about the wastefulness of certain types of reading and offered an appealing alternative to strictly didactic books. In embracing this language, Peale was equally explicit about his hopes that this approach would attract the visitors he needed to support the museum: "As this is an increasing Museum,* it will be a constant source of instruction as well as amusement, and may therefore meet with a cheerful enocuragement [*sic*], which it needs, by the frequent visits of the citizens."[13]

Identifying the museum as a leisure offering was risky for Peale, since the boundaries of morally acceptable nonwork activity were still being negotiated during the 1790s. To avoid the censure of contemporary critics, Peale and fellow operators of public amusements promoted their offerings as forms of "rational amusement" or "rational entertainment." In 1794 Peale announced himself "EVER solicitous to render his MUSEUM still more and more an object of rational entertainment, and subservient to the interests of useful science." Similarly, the opening of Ricketts's Circus in 1792 was hailed with the expectation that "the citizens of this metropolis will experience considerable gratification from this new field of rational amusement." To justify this claim, the manager offered lessons to men and women in the care, handling, and riding of horses. Another writer asserted that "while we see morality blended with amusement (such as is exhibited in Don Juan) it will be in vain for stoicism to preach against mankind, partaking of such amusements [as the circus]."[14]

Peale's choice of language was an important signal to his audience, because his promotions shared key phrases with legal codifications of socially beneficial leisure. Legal debates over the social implications of public leisure date from 1774, when the Continental Congress prohibited certain nonproductive activities as extravagant. Among the articles of the colonial association for the "non-importation, non-consumption, and non-exportation" of British goods, the following restrictions were stated:

> We will in our several stations encourage frugality, oeconomy, and industry, and promote agriculture, arts, and the manufactures of this country, especially that of wool; and will discountenance and discourage every species of extravagance and dissipation, especially all horse racing, and all kinds of gaming, cock fighting, exhibitions of shews, plays, and other expensive diversions and entertainments. And on the death of any relation or friend, none of us, or any of our families will go into any further mourning dress than a black crape or ribbon and necklace for Ladies, and we will discontinue the giving of gloves and scarfs at funerals.

Anxiety about dissipation recalls the concerns of educational reformers, who characterized nonuseful or frivolous reading as a distraction from the "active pursuits of life" and as "the destruction of time."[15]

Whereas the Continental Congress implemented these restrictions as a means of preventing anticipated economic scarcity, the Pennsylvania legislature later codified the suppression of extravagance in moral terms. In 1779 and again in 1786, the General Assembly passed laws limiting the number of taverns and banning the profanation of the sabbath, cursing, gambling, drunkenness, dueling, and, most controversially, the theater. However, throughout the 1780s Lewis Hallam, a would-be theater manager, petitioned the state legislature to reverse its position on the theater. In 1789, partly through Hallam's exertions and partly through the post-Revolutionary transfer of legislative power away from the Quakers, the theater was legalized. In the 1790s an observable process of liberalization of public entertainment occurred, expanding the number of acceptable leisure forms and loosening the terms by which leisure was justified.[16]

Among the key phrases used by the Pennsylvania legislature to justify reinstating the theater in 1789 were the very ones Peale employed to attract his audience, most importantly "rational amusement." The authors of the 1789 law maintained the moral terms of debate set by their opponents, but argued that the theater was capable of uplifting the audience rather than promoting its downfall. As the law stated, "by permitting such theatrical exhibitions as are capable of advancing morality and virtue, and polishing the manners and habits of society," the Assembly upheld the standards of a righteous society. The law more directly addressed the reservations of those who feared "that theatrical representations may be abused by indecent, vicious and immoral performances being exhibited on the stage, to the scandal of religion and virtue, the destruction of good order and decency in society, and the corruption of morals." The legalization of the theater was subject to the restriction that three high public officials be empowered to license performances, forbid suspicious ones, and punish actors and agents who violated the moral intent of the law. Drafters of the law also responded to the belief that leisure distracts people from their productive lives, and defended the rights of citizens to enjoy any "rational and innocent amusement, which at the same time, that it affords a necessary relaxation from the fatigues of business is calculated to inform the mind and improve the heart."[17]

As the theater controversy marked a liberalization of public amusements in Philadelphia, the language used to promote them expanded as well. Morality, rationality, and usefulness remained important terms of justification, but elegance and fashion became new criteria for attracting customers. During the theater controversy, elegance was among the contested characterizations of entertainment. Adopting the persona of the devil, "Blacklegs" wrote to the editor of the newspaper that if the theater remained legal, he would open a house of gambling to "all the bucks in town" and "many of the ladies of the baut-ton." If that project escaped reproach, his friend would establish a place of prostitution called "the Temple Of Venus." Justifying his reasoning, this personification of evil explained, "I hope the party in favour of plays will succeed, for elegance begets elegance and even rusties may be polished by attending places of genteel resort."[18]

Shortly after the controversy passed, Ricketts announced in a newspaper advertisement that, in constructing his new circus building, "no expence or attention has been spared to render his Amphitheatre commodious and elegant." An observer praised the circus-goers as "a more constant and fashionable" audience than that of any of Philadelphia's other "public entertainments." Embracing similar terms, a critic complimented the patrons of Bush Hill Gardens for their good taste in supporting "this elegant place of amusement." Peale, too, shifted his appeal, when he billed the museum as a "rational amusement, and fashionable lounge." Peale thus maintained his commitment to the traditionally educational and moral program and acknowledged simultaneously the now positive connotations of elegance.[19]

The debate over the theater did more than develop a language for defending leisure activities; it also divided the public into opposing groups. These divisions threatened Peale's and other cultural entrepreneurs' ability to build an audience. Anti-theater sentiment brought together Quakers, Protestant clergymen, and hinterland residents on one side, and pro-theater, non-sect-specific, urban Philadelphians on the other. With the Pennsylvania vice law set to expire in 1794, people rallied support for their positions in late 1793. The Quakers distributed a broadside to the young people of their faith, warning against "reading Plays, Novels, Romances, and such like delusive and corrupting Performances, which have a natural Tendency to lessen your Esteem for, and Delight in the Holy Scriptures." The Quakers also petitioned the Pennsylvania General Assembly, claiming that with the revival of the theater in Philadelphia, "infidelity, profligacy, and licentiousness, have been lamentably manifested." In their view, the theater was "obviously poisonous and corrupting to the sentiments and morals of the young and inexperienced, and others who frequent them, impressing their minds with delusive, irreligious, romantic and lewd ideas." Perhaps most powerful, though, was the intimation in the petition's opening paragraph that the recent outbreak of yellow fever, the first since 1747, was caused by the spread of vice. Rather than a medically explicable phenomenon, the Quakers maintained, the yellow fever epidemic was a divinely ordained scourge. Only by eliminating the offensive institutions of entertainment, an act of communal atonement, could Philadelphians hope to avoid further retribution at the hands of a wrathful God.[20]

As a promoter of a public amusement, Peale must have been discomforted when Philadelphia's prominent Protestant ministers joined the Quakers' fight against the theater. Episcopalian, Presbyterian, Baptist, Methodist, Lutheran, Moravian, and Associate clergymen bore witness to "Divine Providence in the late distressing calamity [yellow fever] which has been experienced in this city." Removal of the theater, they proposed, would "prevent the numerous injuries to which our citizens are thereby exposed in their morals, their health, their property, and their general happiness." The petition also advocated that the legislative body should defer "to the Supreme Governor of the Universe," and subordinate their power "to his providence, his laws, and his ordinances." If such arguments had been extended to Peale's displays, the results could have been devastating. That Peale understood the possibility of such a linkage may be discerned in his advertisement for his exhibit on changing perspective views: "There is nothing in the Exhibitions, that can possibly offend the most rigid Religionist."[21]

Because Peale's Museum was an urban institution, opposition to the theater from the hinterland was less foreboding than resistance by the city's Quakers and clergymen. Still, Peale once made the claim that the museum was supported by "Chiefly strangers," and that residents, knowing that they could visit at any time, did not often avail themselves of the museum. Hundreds of petitioners from Philadelphia and its environs—Northern Liberties, Southwark, and Delaware County—joined south-central Pennsylvanians from Franklin County in the fight against the theater. The journal of the state's House of Representatives recorded numerous other petitions in favor of a vice law, without specifying their position on the theater question. These petitions arrived from as near as Chester County, and from as far as York County some 100 miles away and Washington County at the opposite end of Pennsylvania. Taking exception to these outside voices, "Mentor" reminded the legislators that "every member must reflect, that he sits as a representative of the whole state and that in determining a question which only respects the city of Philadelphia, the sentiments or instructions of the inhabitants of Chester, or Fayette, ought not to prevail, over the voice of those who are immediately and exclusively interested." The 1793 reprinting of the editorial by "Mentor," originally published during the 1789 struggle over the legalization of the theater, was evidence of the recurrent division between city and hinterland. "A Citizen" likewise dismissed the relevance of the anti-theater efforts of non-Philadelphians: "The people of this city might as well say they should have no husking matches, raffling parties, or dancing frolics, as they should say we shall have no theatre."[22]

The theater debate also divided the public according to economic concerns. The most vocal proponents of the theater were those materially interested in its continuation. The New Theatre had been built through a stock issue of one hundred shares at three hundred dollars each, bringing the monetary stakes of the controversy to thirty thousand dollars in capital. The subscribers to these shares reminded the General Assembly members of their own words from the law that made their theatrical institution possible:

> This assembly being desirous to promote the interest of genius and literature, by permitting such Theatrical exhibitions as are capable of advancing morality and virtue, and polishing the manners and habits of society; and it being contrary to the principles of a free government to deprive any of its citizens of a rational and innocent entertainment, which at the same time, that it affords a necessary relaxion from the fatigues of business is calculated to inform the mind, and improve the heart.

Pointing out that the stockholders and managers of the theater would suffer extreme losses if the theater was again banned, they argued that such a law would be "unjust, impolitic, and fruitless." Because building the theater had depended on the establishment of contracts and the proposed law would nullify those legal relationships, the law would be unjust and unconstitutional. As this would undermine civic confidence "in the sanction and inviolability of the laws of the land and the constitution," it would be impolitic. Based on the concept of the social contract, such a law would be fruitless, since the people would not feel bound by such an unfair restriction on their liberties and rights to property. Among the other pro-theater submissions to the General Assembly, New Theatre managers Thomas Wignell and Alexander Reinagle presented a memorial in defense of their enterprise.[23]

As the proprietor of a museum, Peale shared the perspective of the theater's shareholders. From this elevated social position stemmed a kind of paternalism for the less privileged among the audience. "Philanthropos" argued that the people considered the "lower sort" in their time would clearly benefit from the continuation of the theater. Surely drinking and other "low & vulgar vices" would gain favor if the theater were abolished, a shift that "may naturally be attributed to the want of some public & general amusement to draw the attention of the lower class of citizens. Cock-fighting, horse-racing, and every other species of low gambling will be resorted to by the populace if some more rational amusement is not publicly allowed." In the ironic "Protest or Counter-Petition" that was signed by "Sallad, Chairman" and purported to represent the interests of theater managers, performers, writers, and employees, "an old lady" made the case playfully:

> The play-house supports us, by giving many opportunities in the upper boxes which we cannot get else-where. Besides I have great compassion upon those poor diseased wretches and worn-out Venuses who attend the doors, waiting their fortune among the vulgar. Something ought to be done for them if the theatre should be no more—the dear theatre! that repository of elegance and grandeur! that polisher of manners.

The complaint of prostitution among the lower sort at the theater was frequent in anti-theater arguments, and attempts to eliminate this baneful practice continued long after the theater was safe from legislative proscription.[24]

Just as social stratification was evident in the rhetoric about public amusements, it was likewise apparent in the division of space at leisure sites. The least-valued seats at Philadelphia's two theaters (figure 6) in the 1790s were the highest ones; the middling ones were on the floor; and the best seats were in the intermediate two tiers of boxes. The circus, too, ordered its audience, though in just two levels rather than three. "Patty Puzzle" related a viewer's social status to his or her place in the spatial hierarchy, as she pondered where the critic sat at the theater.

> I often fancy I hear your voice in the gallery, but if you were to sit there, you would look down upon the performers, and I am sure you are too well-bred a beast for that. If you were in the pit, you would loook [*sic*] up to them, and in that case you would be more civil than you are; so, I conclude you are above that; and I can't think you would trust yourself in the lower boxes, for then they would be even with you.

Figure 6. W. Ralph, engraving after S. Lewis, *Inside View of the New Theatre, Philadelphia,* 1794, 11.4 × 19.4 centimeters, United States, active 1794–1808. Museum purchase in memory of Mrs. John Innes Kane, 1948–89. Courtesy Cooper-Hewitt, National Design Museum, Smithsonian Institution/Art Resource, New York. Photo by Ken Pelka.

Though this is a playful inquiry, it points to the more serious relationship between the way one participates in public leisure and one's place in a rank-ordered society.[25]

Entertainment establishments also ranked audiences through multiple levels of admission charges, a practice shared by Peale. In 1791 at the Old Theatre (which, until the New Theatre was opened in 1794, was known as the Theatre on Cedar Street or the Theatre in Southwark), admission to the boxes cost seven shillings six pence, to the pit five shillings, and to the gallery three shillings nine pence. People attending the circus where admitted to the boxes for one dollar and to the pit for fifty cents. On a separate occasion, the fees at the circus were stated in pound units: seven shillings six pence for boxes and three shillings nine pence for the pit. Thus, Peale's fifty-cent admission charge to the mastodon exhibit was equivalent to the cheapest ticket offered by the circus or the theater. His lower fee was half the price of the least expensive ticket to either of the other entertainments. To this two-part fee structure, Peale added another tier—tickets of annual admission—which created an elevated third category of patrons. Peale's fees suggest that the museum was more accessible financially than the

alternative entertainments offered at the circus and the theater. Yet, like his fellow promoters of leisure, Peale created a hierarchy of admission fees that probably divided his
audience members according to their economic means. In 1810 a Moravian woman
recorded her visit to the museum with a party of friends. In her diary she noted that
her group desired to see the mastodon skeleton but decided the fee was too high. Such
divisions may be understood in the broader context of the earnings and expenditures
of ordinary Philadelphians. Billy G. Smith's careful study of the budgets of working
people (laborers, mariners, cordwainers, and tailors) indicates that Peale's admission
fees were probably prohibitive to many members of the skilled and unskilled labor
forces in Philadelphia. Cathy Davidson's findings confirm that inexpensive novels,
comparable in price to middle-priced theater seats, were beyond the means of the
lower sort.[26]

Editorial discussions about attendance practices further illuminate the parallels between participation in public leisure and the enactment of social distinctions. In 1791
one writer proposed to Old Theatre managers Lewis Hallam and John Henry the institution of half-price admission to the farce for those "who for want of *leisure,* or *in-
clination,* would not go at an early hour." "A Real Friend to the Drama" quickly opposed this idea, "for at the performance of the Farce, the peaceable orderly part of the
audience would be troubled with the grating noise and din of a set of rude fellows,
who, after getting drunk during the play, would, upon paying the trifling sum of one
fourth of a dollar, stagger into the house, *Buck-like,* and by a continued scene of riot,
prevent those from enjoying the entertainment, who had paid the full price for admittance." Perhaps such observations on the Old Theatre, combined with their own
experiences, prompted the managers of the New Theatre to enlist the aid of patrons
in preserving the gentility of the space: "Ladies and Gentlemen are requested to send
their servants to keep places by 5 o clock, and order them, as soon as the company are
seated, to withdraw, as they cannot on any account be permitted to remain." Although
this request suggests the orderly replacement of the common with the fashionable
prior to show time, subsequent reports of conflict among social unequals describe an
ongoing drama in the audience.[27]

Violent outbursts most graphically demonstrated the boundaries among the social
ranks in different parts of the theater's audience. Addressing Old Theatre managers
Lewis Hallam and John Hodgkinson as "Gentlemen," "A Frequenter of the Theatre"
distanced the managers and himself from the unruly "boys of the Gallery." This middling writer complained about the disorderly behavior that pit dwellers suffered at the
hands of socially inferior gallery occupants. As evident in the distribution of the audi-

ence in the *Inside View of the New Theatre,* the spatial arrangement inverted the social order by situating the least expensive seats above the middle-priced ones.

> Those who frequent the *Pit,* have in a particular manner been the objects of their ill treatment. No sooner does a person enter it than he is summoned in a peremptory tone to *doff* his hat to those *respectable blades* in token of his *inferiority,* which if he does not immediately comply with, the vociferating lungs of a hundred *Stentors* declare he must be punished for so flagrant a violation of *their imperious commands,* and then apples and pears, sticks and stones are hurl'd at him without mercy, while scurrility and abuse are as freely poured upon him as could possibly be at *Billingsgate;* nor do they stop there, but during the whole of his sitting in the house, he becomes a marked object at whom every scoundrel aloft endeavors to vent his malice by *spitting* and emptying *beer bottles* on him, tho' very frequently the innocent suffer equally with the guilty; & they who complaisantly bowed to the insolent demands of these *Gallery despots* find their cloaths ruined and their persons bruised, as well as those who independently refuse to submit to those unreasonable and unjust demands.

This complaint cast the lower sort ironically as "respectable blades" and in classical terms as "Stentors," in politically potent words as "Gallery despots," as well as in racially charged terms as "Bucks and Bloods." The writer evoked the unseemly character of the situation by referring to the London fish market Billingsgate, and to the acts of spitting on, dumping beer on, verbally abusing, and throwing objects at the socially respectable.[28]

Peale's complaints about audience members touching and defacing exhibits indicate similar concerns about the lower sort. Addressing his son Rembrandt, Peale wrote:

> You know how much we have [been] pestered by persons going down from the Museum in ringing the bells, it is completely cured by my writing in large letters, facing them in their de[s]cent. "None but the Rude and uncultivated ring the Bells going down." I wish I could also prevent visitors from puting their fingers on the Glasses and frames in the different parts of the Museum, they dirty the glass and destroy the brilliency of the gilding. The standing on our covered benches is another dirty custom, could I be often in the museum I should prevent it as I sometimes do taking out my Handkerchief and wiping & brushing after them, without uttering a sylable. I have just thought that I might put into conspicuous places, frames on containing requests that Visitors may not scratch their names on the Chama's [shells], Pensil or nor mutilate the Casts, sully the Glass or frames with their fingers, nor stand on the covered benches, as Stepes are provided to raise them to the sight of high Objects, that it must be obvious to every thinking being that these rules are necessary to preserve the articles of a Museum formed for the instruction and amusement of the present as well as future generations.

From this letter, Joel J. Orosz, a historian of museums, concluded that "Peale's concept of education was essentially a didactic effort to control the lower classes." Like his contemporaries who complained about the behavior of disruptive theater audiences, Peale became concerned about the behavior of some museum visitors and the safekeeping of his collections and he began regulating visiting habits. Glass was placed in front of natural history displays, low railings were added to protect the glass, and signs were posted to discourage continued breeches of decorum. Thus the museum taught science through its displays, but also structured the limits of proper behavior.[29]

Leisure practices helped to define gender differences, just as they informed and shaped distinctions of social rank. In his series of letters entitled "Advice to a young lady," Reverend John Bennet proposed the appropriate bounds of a young woman's recreation. Bennet repeated such familiar notions as relaxation restores energy for work and amusements should not preoccupy one's life. Insofar as this advice recalls the argued benefits of the theater and reading, Bennet's proposal was not limited by gender. However, Bennet also submitted that a woman's sphere of entertainment was more appropriately private than public: "A woman's amusements should, as much as possible, be domestic: and her walls will present many excellent opportunities of such a nature." Among the activities appropriate to a woman outside the home were "exercise in the open air" and "attention to a garden." Particularly suspicious to Bennet were tea parties and social visits, surely vehicles of "gossoping and scandal." "A group of beautiful females are not, unfrequently, seen together, without one single person of the other sex to share the enjoyment; and it is, I conceive, in mixed companies alone, that conversation has its proper interest, flavour or improvement," Bennet wrote.[30]

However, Peale and other promoters of leisure hoped to maintain large audiences and were unwilling to eliminate half of their potential viewers from their money-making entertainments. For instance, in 1799 and again in 1800, Peale extended specific invitations for women to attend his lectures on natural history. Other entrepreneurs described the specific appeals of their programs to women. Ambroise & Company, for example, advertised its fireworks display by noting that an interlude, "'the agreeable tie of love', with its variations, a favorite piece of the fair sex," would be presented in the course of the entertainment. Women, the primary consumers of novels, were encouraged to attend a benefit performance at the theater for a novelist and her husband, Mrs. and Mr. Rowson: "Those ladies who have perused with pleasure Mrs. Rowson's elegant novels, the Trials of the Heart, Charlotte, Victoria, the Fille de Chambre, &c. will avail themselves of this opportunity of evincing their sense of her very laudable endeavours to contribute to the entertainment and improvement of their sex."[31]

Advertised claims of the decorous nature of various amusements singled women out as a special category of audience members who possessed a heightened moral and emotional sensitivity. Upon the opening of the Philadelphia Lyceum as a forum for debate on contemporary issues, the announcements promised that discussions would proceed "without danger of offence to the delicacy of either sex." When a representation of a chase of the Lapland ram was offered, the following assurance was offered: "The LADIES will be satisfied to see these Amusements, this kind of CHACE being only a picture of reality, in which care has been taken to introduce nothing repugnant to humanity." When exhibiting his painting *Danaë,* which featured a nude female, Adolph Wertmüller set aside Mondays "for the accommodation of Ladies exclusively." Although Wertmüller's segregation of his audience by gender was meant to preserve decency, some critics theorized that mixed company was more apt to prevent indiscretions. For instance, the British traveler Sir Augustus John Foster attributed graffiti "in a female hand upon the legs of statues of the gods Cupid and Mercury" at Peale's Museum to separate visiting hours for the sexes.[32]

Whereas audiences for public entertainments in Philadelphia spanned differences of class and gender, albeit on unequal terms, they were more nearly homogeneous in terms of race. Ventriloquist John Rannie proposed a special performance for "coloured people," but he postponed this offer indefinitely. The Washington Museum in New York City explicitly excluded "people of colour" from its evening hours. Ironically, Peale's popular concession of cut paper silhouette portraits depended on the labor of his onetime slave Moses Williams, but extant silhouettes reveal that African-Americans were not among the sitters (as discussed in chapter 4). Occasional notices of Native Americans attending the circus and the theaters suggest that such occurrences were extraordinary. In 1796, Ricketts announced that "Indian Warriors, from the Northern States" and Anthony Wayne, the general celebrated for subduing Indian resistance to Americans on the frontier, would attend the circus on the same evening. Later that year, the *Philadelphia Gazette* noted a chance meeting of visiting Native American chiefs at Peale's Museum, an encounter that resulted in a treaty among traditionally enemy peoples. Several years later, Choctaw chiefs, traveling through the principle cities on a treaty-signing trip, were announced as anticipated guests at the Old Theatre. Such advertisements, when they preceded attendance, turned the announced guests into spectacles; the audience itself became part of the entertainment. Not only Native Americans but also women and celebrities drew such attention. One person, identified as "Z.," called upon the circus proprietor to improve the lighting in the amphitheater so that men could better view the beautiful women, "who always add the great lustre to every scene either in public or domestic entertainment." Similarly, the announcement that George Washington would attend a performance was hoped to fill the house. Greatness, beauty, and exoticism were all social distinctions that producers of leisure hoped to transform into profit.[33]

Because museums, theaters, and circuses catered to white audiences, the representation of race at these sites provides a meaningful context for conceptualizing racial difference in early national America. Peale displayed wax figures of Native Americans along with native manufactures from around the world. In 1803 the Old Theatre billed "Othello the Grand African," who performed "his astonishing feats on the Slack Wire." According to author Bernth Lindfors, the ascription of special abilities to people of African descent mystified racial difference and helped to perpetuate racial stereotypes. The spectacle of white men dressed as Native Americans, such as Peale's wax figure of Meriwether Lewis clothed in Shoshone costume, ritualized control over racial difference. The circus promoter Ricketts rode his horse "in the Character of an Indian Chief, With his Bow and Arrow, and other Implements of War" on the occasion of "A Party of Indian Chiefs" expected in his amphitheater. Sometimes Native Americans actually played the Indian characters, thereby authenticating the stereotypical images of horsemanship and warfare. Emphasizing the supposed savagery of Indians and innocence of white women, the circus performed "a Representation of the Death of Miss McCrea," a theme conveyed in John Vanderlyn's well-known painting, *The Death of Jane McCrea,* of 1804. On one visit, when the Tammany Society invited them to a meeting in Philadelphia, Native Americans encountered a very different stereotypical view of themselves. This group considered them to be "natural men"— that is, a primitive, innocent, and peaceful people capable of coexisting with Anglo-Americans.[34]

Early national leisure practices also divided audiences according to political affiliation. Historian Simon Newman demonstrated that national holiday celebrations were particularly subject to these divisions. Although both parties honored Washington's Birthday and the Fourth of July, Newman argued, the former holiday had stronger resonance for Federalists and the latter for Democratic Republicans. Parades and festivals in honor of French independence, Jefferson's inauguration day, and the Louisiana Purchase also associated revelers with Democratic Republican partisanship.[35]

Political splits were also expressed at the theater and the circus in terms of American allegiance to either Britain or France. The threat of war heightened the salience of this issue. As the Adams administration seemed dangerously close to siding with England against France, Democratic Republicans vehemently criticized the abandonment of the republic's Revolutionary War ally. This rhetoric culminated in the arrest of Benjamin Franklin Bache, publisher of *Aurora. General Advertiser,* one of Peale's two most frequent vehicles for promoting the museum during the 1790s, under the Alien and Sedition Acts. Promoters of public amusements expressed their partisanship through their choice of programs. At the height of this controversy, one writer warned that "the managers of the Theatre ought to beware how they suffer the Theatre to be converted into a political engine." Several days later, one angry theatergoer characterized the controllers of the theater as the "Anglo Monarchical Tory party." Reflecting heightened political partisanship, two circuses emerged in 1798. One reminded audiences of British betrayal with representations of traitor Benedict Arnold and his British conspirator John André. The other was called the Federal Summer Circus, echoing party alliance in name and in practice. For instance, an advertisement stating that John Adams would attend this circus probably served to target a partisan audience. But exclusive political alliances were not profitable for long; the *Aurora* noted the diminished theater audience in 1799. Controversy along political lines quieted soon thereafter, and did not reemerge at the theater until the War of 1812. Peale honored political culture in the museum through his portraits and special evening illuminations, but he avoided entering the fray. For instance, Peale expressed his Democratic Republican sympathies when he illuminated the museum during the Louisiana Purchase Jubilee, but tempered his partisanship with Rembrandt Peale's *Apotheosis of Washington* (figure 7) as his choice of transparencies. On the occasion of the Fourth of July in 1808, with Jefferson's embargo in place and the threat of war, Peale displayed transparencies of Washington and Jefferson, with the message, "Peace to the World." Similarly, the portrait gallery recognized the achievements of such Federalist heroes as Alexander Hamilton, John Jay, and Timothy Pickering, and such Democratic Republicans as Thomas Jefferson and Thomas Paine.[36]

The environment in which Peale opened his museum was one that divided potential leisure audiences in many ways. The extended controversy over the theater demonstrated the potential for religious opposition to public amusements. Perceptions of immorality at the theater also invited criticism from the hinterland. Peale's insistence that the museum offered moral education was one way in which Peale assuaged such potential critics. Arguments about the nature of property and legal rights signaled the special stakes of the economically advantaged in the formation of early national public leisure. The physical structures and fees charged for admission to these places of amusement further expressed the ranked order into which early national society was forming. Physical conflicts among theater audiences, however, demonstrate that although such ordering may have reinforced social hierarchies, at times it resulted in conflict. Peale's democratic invitation to all people and his simultaneous concern over the improper behavior of certain visitors may be situated precariously within

Figure 7. David Edwin after Rembrandt
Peale, *Apotheosis of Washington,* 1800.
National Portrait Gallery, Smithsonian
Institution, Washington, D.C.

these socioeconomic tensions. Although women attended public entertainments, their status as a separate audience points to their unequal place in the social hierarchy. The exclusion of African-Americans from audiences and the exhibition of Native Americans suggest that the terms of participation and the content of entertainments sustained racial marginalization in this period. Political controversy in the early national period further threatened the stability of leisure audiences. The next chapter expands upon Peale's public efforts within this fractious context to build an audience with varied interests and diverse places in the social fabric.

2. Peale's Public Presentation of the Museum

FROM THE FOUNDING of the museum in 1786, Peale expressed its purpose through visual representations, as well as in written newspaper advertisements, broadsides, statements addressed to government bodies, lectures, short articles, and pamphlets. In contrast to Peale's private correspondence and diaries, these visual and verbal statements constituted his public efforts to shape meanings of the museum for his audience. Taken together, they demonstrate that Peale extended multiple layers of meaning to his different audiences. Peale presented the collections in several ways, as fanciful, religiously significant, or scientifically important, and each of these broad themes was likely to appeal to a particular constituency. As discussed in chapter 1, Peale also presented the collections as a storehouse of utility and a source of moral education. Through this strategy of wider meanings, Peale built an audience that consisted of people with broad interests. Another important dynamic revealed within these public promotions of the museum was the alternating role of Peale: he was portrayed either as the manager of a collective effort or as the sole creator of the institution. This dynamic is essential to understanding the place of cultural institutions in early national America. Was the museum, like any other business, dependent upon its ability to attract customers within the marketplace? Or was it in some sense created by the community to express shared values, and therefore worthy of public subsidy?

Peale advertised the museum primarily through Philadelphia's newspapers. By submitting most items to at least two newspapers, Peale maximized local distribution. Both Charles Willson Peale and Rubens Peale, who managed the museum from 1810 to 1822, favored the *Pennsylvania Packet* and the *General Advertiser*. Publisher Benjamin Franklin Bache produced the *General Advertiser* for readers in Philadelphia, and distributed another edition to the hinterland. Peale hoped to gain additional publicity through the reprinting of his advertisements in other cities. "It will be obliging in the Printers, friends of science, in the other states as well as this," Peale pleaded in a 1794 request for donations, "if they will give the above a place in their newspapers." As Peale had hoped, he gained some free notice in Baltimore, Charleston, and Washington, among other places. Although most of Peale's advertisements were published in Philadelphia, the coastal trade, the stagecoach system, and the official United States mail transported Philadelphia newspapers to other port cities and from there outward to rural areas. Contemporary travel accounts, typically written by foreign visitors and published abroad, and the geographic diversity of donors further suggest that the museum maintained national and even international constituencies.[1]

Peale's newspaper campaign spanned the political spectrum, but favored his own political identity as a Democratic Republican. The *Pennsylvania Packet* was regarded as a Democratic Republican newspaper, though less partisan than the radical *General Advertiser*. By the end of the first decade of the nineteenth century, the two newspapers were in conflict over the state constitution issue. The *Aurora. General Advertiser* favored the radical wing of the party and *Poulson's American Daily Advertiser*, successor to the *Packet*, sided with the moderates. By 1802 Peale received encouragement from and placed advertisements in the Federalist *Gazette of the United States*, although it was far less frequently Peale's choice for promoting the museum. The editors of the Federalist *Gazette of the United States*, *The Port Folio*, and *Porcupine's Gazette* all poked fun at Peale's Museum—a kind of recognition in itself—and the former two promoted the museum as well.[2]

By presenting the museum as beneficial to the public, Peale probably gained some free access to the newspapers. In 1794 Peale announced, for instance, that he would maintain a register of "discoveries, inventions, improvements, schemes, observations, experiments, projects, hints or queries, relating to the arts or sciences," which would, he wrote, "soon contain and be the means of disseminating a vast fund of useful knowledge, and promote that spirit of enquiry and invention, for which the people of the United States are already so justly distinguished." In explaining that birds and snakes ought not to be killed because they eat worms and mice that devastate crops, Peale proposed the usefulness of natural history to agriculture. Peale also offered his interests in inventions, models of which were on view at the museum, as public benefits. He characterized his designs for stoves and chimneys as safer and less expensive than conventional heating methods, and suggested that introducing them to the public would reduce the threat of urban fires and broaden access of this basic need to the poor. For his bridge innovation, Peale claimed ease of construction, potential longevity, and reduced expense relative to other designs. In promoting John Isaac Hawkins's polygraph, a letter-writing machine that produced two identical manuscripts at a time, Peale hailed the possible labor saved by this device.[3]

Characterizing the museum as a public benefit was also central to Peale's strategy for requesting government sponsorship. Peale submitted his memorials, as such applications were called, to the newspapers in order to recruit public support. The rhetoric in these statements typically moved beyond the benefits of a particular exhibit to broad statements of the museum's worth to society. Preparing to approach the state government, Peale told his Board of Visitors and Inspectors that the museum would one day "become the basis of a great national magazine of those subjects in nature" that he planned to collect. Quoting Richard Pulteney's translation of Linnaeus, Peale hoped to provoke the museum-goer "to the consideration of what he ought to be, as an *intelligent and moral being*." In requesting aid from the Pennsylvania legislature in 1795, Peale argued "the national importance of his Museum" in that "the promotion of knowledge" is essential for preserving "the virtue of the people." As Peale became discouraged with the apparent unwillingness of the state to assist his finances, he threatened to move the museum out of Philadelphia in these terms: "when it shall be known, that I am willing to accept a proper provision to render my Museum a Public Establishment, some other city in the Union will rejoice in receiving my labours." When Peale was granted the use of the Pennsylvania State House in 1802, he described the museum as "an institution, which promises to become not only a lasting benefit to the citizens of Philadelphia, but to the public in general."[4]

In contrast to the statements of purpose that accompanied his addresses to government bodies, Peale's advertisements more often featured the new and interesting displays that were constantly being added to the museum. Animal exhibits included a golden pheasant given to George Washington by the Marquis de Lafayette, a moor hen, a pelican, a collection of birds from Sweden, an orangutan, an anteater, a porcupine, a "sea devil" (giant ray), a two-headed snake, a lion, and a large turtle. After their installation in 1801, the mastodon remains were featured in an extended advertising campaign. Among the inventions that Peale put on display were the models of his stove and bridge designs, John Isaac Hawkins's "physiognotrace" and polygraph, and, after 1816, the gaslights made by Benjamin Kugler to illuminate the museum. Portraits painted by Rembrandt Peale, primarily in Paris, were advertised as special attractions in 1808 and 1811. Wax figures by Charles Willson Peale displayed Native American, African, and Chinese costumes beginning in 1797, and an exhibit of "Eastern Armor" opened in 1805. Objects from the Lewis and Clark Expedition were announced early in 1810. Inside the museum, however, Peale primarily addressed his audience through images and displays of artifacts and natural history specimens, rather than with words.[5]

In the first visual representation of his budding museum, a ticket of admission engraved in 1788 (figure 8), Peale conveyed important elements of his program: nature and art as the broadest categories in the collections; animals grouped by their environment and presented as though alive; natural history promoting secular knowledge

Figure 8. Unidentified artist, Ticket of admission, 1788. Collection of Elise Peale Patterson de Gelpi-Toro. Photograph courtesy of Hirschl & Adler Galleries, Inc., New York, New York.

and the service of God; and the museum as an entrepreneurial venture. In this simple composition, the arc of the central banner leads the eye from a pair of playful monkeys at upper left to a hyena that turns toward the viewer at the foot of the tree, then to a reptile (an alligator or crocodile) whose long body aligns with the horizon, a shell and a small bird, a pelican eating a fish at right, and, from the pelican's tail, up the tree to an exotic bird perched in a limb. The slightly open mouth of the reptile reaches up toward the pelican's prey, suggesting food-chain relationships. Behind the animals on the ground, a body of water stretches into the shallow distance; thus, the scene offers trees, ground, and water as habitats. Several indistinct birds at center right, above the pelican's head, extend the domain of natural creatures to the air. At top center, a book inscribed "Nature" radiates the light of knowledge. The banner advertises, "The Birds & Beasts will teach thee!," a paraphrase from the Book of Job, adding a religious quality to the possibly secular book of nature. The main message on the banner also announces that the contents include both nature and art, a dual emphasis that Peale maintained throughout the life of the museum. Finally, the stated admission charge of twenty-five cents characterizes the business aspect.[6]

Clearly the image was not a literal rendering of the museum's arrangement, but Manasseh Cutler—a minister, amateur scientist, and historian who visited Philadelphia—responded in 1787 to the installation in terms that are recognizable in Peale's engraving. Cutler listed several minerals and soils at the base of the principal display. A small pond and sandy beach provided a context for numerous shells and marine and amphibious animals preserved in lifelike attitudes. The beach and tree furnished habitat display spaces for various birds, while a bear, a deer, a squirrel, and other quadrupeds occupied a nearby mound of earth. In all, Cutler assessed the display as a

group of "natural curiosities . . . arranged in a most romantic and amusing manner."
Moreover, his account was not a "particular account of the numerous species of fossils and animals, but only their general arrangement." As Peale's engraved ticket of admission was emblematic of the concepts embodied in the displays, Cutler's more elaborate verbal enumeration was also just an evocation of the entire installation.[7]

Nearly twenty years after completing this engraving, in 1806–8 Peale depicted himself in the act of collecting and presented himself as the manager of a collective enterprise (figure 9).[8] Peale defined these roles for himself in *The Exhumation of the
Mastodon,* a painting that commemorates the recovery of two nearly complete fos-
silized skeletons of the extinct mastodon. The painting thus conveys a narrative of a
specific event and projects two broader messages about Peale's role at the museum
and the nature of that institution.

Peale accomplished the sense of collective action through the formal arrangement
of his canvas. The apparatus for carrying water out of the pit dominates the center of
the canvas and defines the basic compositional units. Five poles converge at the top of
the machine to create the most conspicuous triangular forms, which the tents at left
and center repeat. Water dumps from the buckets into a sluice that empties toward the
right side along the horizon, creating a triangular arrangement of the buckets, the
sluice, and the ground. A retaining wall of logs at bottom left, three round half bar-
rels at bottom center, and the log turning in the water all echo the circular form of the
large wheel at center. The beams supporting the pulley system at right form a rectangle that frames Charles Willson Peale, while the rectangular bridge at bottom right
leads the viewer's eye to the Peale family members positioned behind the large drawing of mastodon leg bones. Because the rectangular sheet of paper was rolled and then
unrolled, it combines circular and rectilinear forms to create an undulating curve,
which is then repeated in the variegated outline of the pit.

Repetition of the shapes established by the machine develops a sense of the people
and the machinery as a collective unit, working in concert to achieve the excavation.
Two individuals inside the large wheel run on a treadmill to turn the cables that lift
the buckets of water from the pit, representing the most direct connection between
people and machines. Two other figures exert their energy in circular motion to turn
the crank that lifts one round barrel at a time from below. Peale's sons Franklin and
Linnaeus stabilize the log that keeps the buckets on course by extending a pole into
the water along a diagonal that nearly parallels the left leg of the main triangular structure. Workers ankle-deep or knee-deep in water shovel marl onto the first rectangular
platform, which two more figures move to the next level, and a final man lifts onto the
ground, the team forming another triangle. The men seem to move in synchronized

Figure 9. Charles Willson Peale, *The Exhumation of the Mastodon*, 1806–8. The Peale Museum, Baltimore City Life Museums.

motion in this systematic digging effort, and the step-by-step human process echoes the mechanized removal of water. This sense of collective action is extremely significant, because it is representative of the way the museum's collections were built. Although Peale did go on such high-profile collecting trips as this one, he relied upon his audience to donate birds, quadrupeds, minerals, and Native American and non-Western artifacts. In some cases these donations merely supplemented his own collecting efforts; in other instances they were the principal means of expanding his holdings.[9]

In verbal communication with his audience, Peale recognized that the museum was a collective production. This verbal contact took the form of requests for donations and acknowledgments of objects received as gifts. When in 1792 Peale specified the categories of objects he hoped would be given to the museum and recruited a Board of Visitors and Directors for guidance, he applauded "the generous patronage" he had already received. A later request for donations began, "MR. PEALE is highly sensible of the obligations he is under to the gentlemen of several states, distant as well as near, who have kindly assisted him with such curious articles as they possessed for advancing his Museum." As Peale started to gather subscriptions for his proposed catalogue of the natural history specimens in the museum, he offered "sentiments of the sincerest gratitude for the distinguished patronage which he has received from his fellow citizens and many respectable foreigners." Even more compelling than these general expressions of thankfulness were the lists of donors and their contributions to which Peale frequently devoted his newspaper publicity.[10]

In *The Exhumation of the Mastodon,* Peale paid homage to one very important donor, Alexander Wilson. Even though Wilson was not present at the excavation, Peale included a portrait of Wilson facing forward with his arms folded against his chest, on the left side of the canvas. One explanation for this addition is that Wilson frequently donated bird specimens to the museum. Like the laborers in the pit, Wilson contributed his efforts toward expanding the museum's collections. Wilson obtained specimens with which to illustrate his multivolume work *American Ornithology* in two ways: by hunting them and by observing the birds preserved at Peale's Museum. The relationship was mutually beneficial, as Wilson donated many of the birds he shot to the museum. Wilson also recognized Peale in a generous dedication to his published study of ornithology. Peale's inclusion of Wilson does not make sense in the specific narrative of the mastodon exhumation, but it does fit with the broader themes of collecting and the collaborative effort in creating the museum.[11]

Both in his self-portrayal in *The Exhumation of the Mastodon* and in his role of co-ordinating contributions from his audience members, Peale presented himself as the manager of a collective enterprise. That Peale placed most of the figures in shallow space renders them nearly the same size as himself in the exhumation painting, yet his physical inactivity distinguishes him from the vigorously engaged laborers who perform the many tasks. Peale's down-stretched arm gestures managerially along a diagonal to a shirtless man lifting a bone from the water, a modest step toward the goal of a complete skeleton. The leg of the machine next to the successful digger and the leg of the mastodon point vertically to the space occupied by Peale's brother James, who directs the viewer with his downturned arms and open palms back to the latest find. The triangular visual path created by the positioning of Charles Willson Peale, the digger, and James Peale is one of the many in the painting. Peale controlled the painted scene by creating these patterns, just as he orchestrated the event by employing men and borrowing cash, equipment, and tents.[12]

Peale ordered the pictorial space not only with the excavation workers but also with family members who, like naturalist Alexander Wilson, were not in fact at the site.

Rembrandt Peale, the male figure to the right of Charles Willson Peale, was the only family member actually at the excavation. To Rembrandt's right, Peale added sons Rubens in hat and spectacles and Raphaelle holding the unrolled portion of the scroll. Perhaps their assistance in collecting, preserving, and displaying the objects in the museum earned them a place in the picture. Family connections alone seem to justify the addition of five more pairs of family members—deceased wife Elizabeth speaking sternly to son Titian between the two leftmost poles; brother-in-law John Stagg, Jr., and sister-in-law Margaret DePeyster Stagg to their left; current wife Hannah and Rembrandt's wife Eleanor, between their husbands; daughter Sophonisba and son-in-law Coleman Sellers under the umbrella; and daughters Sybilla and Elizabeth in front of Rubens.[13]

The drawing that Peale holds in his left hand signifies his roles as artist and naturalist. According to his diary, Peale executed a full-scale drawing of mastodon leg bones during the first of two trips to Newburgh, New York, in 1801. New York and then Philadelphia newspapers announced in the autumn of 1800 that "the bones of a huge animal" had been found in the marl pit on John Masten's farm. In Peale's painting, Masten climbs up a ladder from the hole at bottom center. Peale traveled to Newburgh, where he first asked to draw the bones that had been excavated. After offering to purchase the bones and asking for permission to dig for the rest of the skeleton, Peale halted the drawing project. When coupled with the narrative of his diary, then, the drawing stands as Peale's transition from observer to collector and owner of the bones. In addition to the specific reference to the drawing executed in Newburgh, Peale may have intended a second meaning for the scroll he included in *The Exhumation of the Mastodon*. The story of the museum's origin includes a commission in 1783 for Peale to make a series of drawings depicting a group of mastodon bones found at Big Bone Lick on the Ohio River in 1766. Peale's brother-in-law Nathaniel Ramsay, the story goes, saw the bones in the artist's studio, and declared that such natural specimens would form the basis of a very interesting collection, one that would draw more public interest than Peale's picture gallery. As a dual reference to the 1783 commission and the 1801 excavation, the drawing bridges the beginning of Peale's career as a collector and his greatest triumph in that role. His inclusion of two wives—one deceased and one living—signals Peale's willingness to compress various moments in time, a leap that is necessary for this interpretation.[14]

Peale's self-conscious self-representation as artist helps to articulate pictorial conventions that offer alternately rational and spiritual explanations for the event that takes place. Among the many interesting movements enacted by the figures in this painting, Peale's and his daughter Sybilla's most directly exemplify this duality of meaning. Whereas Peale's hand gestures toward the earth, Sybilla's directs the viewer toward the heavens. Perhaps the most famous analogous pair in a multifigured canvas is Plato and Aristotle in Raphael's *School of Athens* (figure 10). Plato the idealist favors divine truth, whereas Aristotle the empiricist seeks natural principles. Of course there are many dissimilarities between these two groupings of figures. Peale and Sybilla do not stand together; they are not the central figures; and Peale's palm faces up, in contrast to Aristotle's downturned hand. However, Peale's earlier *Self-Portrait with Angelica and a Portrait of Rachel* (figure 11) employs comparable iconography. Angelica touches Peale's brush with one hand and points heavenward with the other. Through these gestures, Peale presents his artistic talents as divinely inspired.[15]

The water and storm similarly function within *The Exhumation of the Mastodon* to convey literal components of the excavation narrative and to invoke a biblical metaphor. On a literal level, the painted scene replicates the conditions in which Peale worked. Lightning in the background at right center threatens the progress of the excavation, and the imminent rain may rebury the bones before Peale can dig them out. In his diary, Peale recorded that the walls of the water-filled pit kept caving in, and that

Figure 10. Raphael, *The School of Athens*, 1509–11. Vatican Museums, Rome.

Figure 11. Charles Willson Peale, *Self-Portrait with Angelica and a Portrait of Rachel,* ca. 1788. The Museum of Fine Arts, Houston; The Bayou Bend Collection, gift of Miss Ima Hogg.

occasional rain, thunder, and lightning interrupted the project. On a grander scale, the storm echoes the contemporary characterizations of the mastodon as an "antediluvian" creature. Commenting on Peale's mastodon exhibit, travelers William Newnham Blane and John M. Duncan explicitly connected the animal's disappearance to the biblical flood narrative. Pictorially, the pit of water stands as a mere vestige of the deluge that once covered the earth's surface and destroyed all life not preserved on Noah's ark, including the entire species of the mastodon. By extending this biblical analogy, Noah is the type for Peale; an endeavor at which Noah failed—the preservation of the mastodon—was one at which Peale eventually succeeded.[16]

Peale's painting *Noah and His Ark* (figure 12), executed for the museum in 1819, presents the next major paradigm for his project: a Christian imperative for collecting and preserving each species of God's creation. In a letter requesting permission to copy the original painting by Charles Catton, Jr., Peale praised its composition and added, "I cannot do justice to the merit of the Picture by attempting a description of it, therefore I shall for bear further particulars, and only say, that it is a Museum in itself, and a subject in the line of the fine Arts, the most appropriate to a Museum. . . ." Although the composition was not of Peale's conception, it bears some relation to the preceding two representations of the museum. Whereas the light of knowledge shines from the book of nature in the 1788 engraved admission ticket, light bathing a dove, Noah, and a lamb signifies the grace of God in this canvas. An abundance of marine animals, reptiles, birds, and quadrupeds, exotic as well as domestic ones, repeat the categories exemplified only sparsely in the ticket. Peale was not alone in comparing his natural history collections with Noah's collection. In 1787 clergyman Manasseh Cutler understood the museum in those terms: "Mr. Peale's animals reminded me of *Noah's Ark,* into which was received every kind of beast and creeping thing in which there was life. But I can hardly conceive that even Noah could have boasted of a better collection." The elderly Noah in the painting is aided by his wife, his three sons, and his sons' wives, just as Peale's collecting effort is assisted and attended by his wives and children in *The Exhumation of the Mastodon*. Like the aged Noah, the seventy-eight-year-old Peale shared the goal of gathering into one view "a world in miniature."[17]

The next major rendering of the museum, *The Long Room,* a watercolor and ink drawing by Titian Ramsay Peale II and Charles Willson Peale, describes the space and contents within the vocabulary of empirical observation (figure 13). That the elder Peale began drawing *The Long Room* with the assistance of a perspective machine contributes to the sense that this image accurately records the interior of the museum in the State House just five years before his death. This mechanically facilitated drawing

Figure 12. Charles Willson Peale after Charles Catton, Jr., *Noah and His Ark,* 1819.
Courtesy of The Pennsylvania Academy of the Fine Arts, Philadelphia. Collections Fund.

orders the space strictly according to one-point perspective, accentuating Peale's application of Linnaean taxonomy to hierarchically present the stacked, compartmentalized displays of preserved animals. The Linnaean arrangement of the collections expressed Peale's belief in the essentially rational order of nature, and the perspectival drawing emphasized the rationality of the museum's displays. Whereas the engraved admission ticket may indicate, in Manasseh Cutler's words, "a most romantic and amusing" arrangement, *The Long Room* exemplifies scientific classification of natural history specimens. Rather than the Christian understanding of the collections that the painting *Noah and His Ark* offers, *The Long Room* presents the museum as a purely secular institution.

Through close attention to detail, which contributes to the sense of empirical truth, Titian Peale and his father rendered specific canvases, busts, and natural history mounts distinct and identifiable in *The Long Room.* Two rows of portraits line the

Figure 13. Titian Ramsay Peale II and Charles Willson Peale, *The Long Room,* 1822. The Detroit Institute of Arts, Founders Society Purchase, Director's Discretionary Fund.

upper portion of the south wall, and a single row of larger portraits—painted by Rembrandt Peale in 1808 and 1810 in Europe—adorns the west wall. Four tiers of glass-covered cases filled with birds preserved in positions that replicate their living postures cover the south and west walls below the portraits. In addition to the glass, a single step and a low railing protect the specimens from overly curious museum-goers. A shallow case of Native American artifacts leads the visitor through the doorway at left into the next room. At right, perched atop the cases of minerals, fossils, and insects, busts of physicians, scientists, and generals sculpted by William Rush and Jean Antoine Houdon grace the north side of the room. Displayed on the ends of the mineral cases, Peale's painted views of Germantown, Pennsylvania (1815–19), including the farm and gardens at Peale's country house, Belfield, add landscape to the categories of art on display. Deeper into the room, the stanchions display a tree of hummingbirds under a glass dome and a specimen of basalt from the spectacular Irish land formation known as Giant's Causeway. A half-length portrait, *Miss Harvey, The Albiness* (1818) (figure 14), faces the viewer from below the red drapery. Benches mounted on the outside of the cases invite visitors to sit and view the array of birds. Natural light flows into the gallery from the windows at right during the day, and the lamps overhead illuminate the museum in the evening. Between the first and second cases at right, the organ built by John Lowe in 1807 enlivens evening entertainment. Although the source of each object may be discovered through study, the painting gives no information on maker, collector, or donor. In contrast to the commemoration of the collecting process in *The Exhumation of the Mastodon*, the depiction in *The Long Room* is of the collections as a finished product.[18]

In his masterwork, *The Artist in His Museum* (figure 1), Peale positions himself unambiguously as the sole architect of the museum. Both the relationship among the figures and the title of the work advance Peale as the master of the space. Through the laws of perspective and his placement in the foreground, Peale towers over the audience members set deeper in space. This hierarchy between creator and viewers contrasts markedly with the friezelike arrangement of *The Exhumation of the Mastodon*. Whereas the exhumation scene acknowledges the participation of Alexander Wilson and Peale's sons as collectors who helped to build the museum, the self-portrait includes only one maker and a small group of audience members. He creates; they view his achievement. By eliminating the busts by William Rush and Jean Antoine Houdon and the organ by John Lowe, Peale represents himself as sole creator of this institution. Only the paddlefish and its inscription to Robert Patterson, a detail relegated to the far left margin of the canvas, acknowledge the importance of donations to the development of the collections. Peale's place either as the manager of a collective enter-

Figure 14. Detail of watercolor by Titian Ramsay Peale II and Charles Willson Peale, *The Long Room*, 1822, showing Charles Willson Peale's work, *Miss Harvey, The Albiness*, 1818. The Detroit Institute of Arts, Founders Society Purchase, Director's Discretionary Fund.

prise or as the sole creator of the museum was not simply a matter of properly crediting group or individual accomplishment. Upon this distinction hinged the definition of the relationship between Peale's Museum and the community.[19]

What Peale had at stake in this debate was the museum's status, whether it was to be considered a public institution worthy of government subsidy or a private institution dependent on its own revenue. By convincing the state legislature of the museum's role as a public benefit, Peale was permitted in 1802 to move his museum into the State House. But that privilege was opened for public debate in 1810, when the General Assembly considered the conditions for transferring ownership of the State House to the corporation of Philadelphia. Because Peale had moved his collections into the upper floor of the building just eight years earlier, this was an anxious moment for him. Peale suggested that the legislature transfer the building from the state to the city on the condition that the local government finance the addition of new wings onto the State House. The lower floor would store public records in fireproof rooms, while the upper floor would create additional exhibition space for the museum. Peale's memorial to the state legislative body, presented by state legislator William J. Duane, son of the editor for the *Aurora. General Advertiser,* claimed the museum as "the most instructive school for the naturalist, botanist, mineralogist, chemist, anatomist, artist, mechanist, manufacturer, agriculturalist, antiquarian and lover of the fine arts." Among its social contributions, the museum offered "emphatic and sublime lessons of wisdom, morality and taste." Such a grant would render the Philadelphia Museum "useful, not merely to the inhabitants of that city, but to those of the state, and even of the United States." Defense of the plan indicated resistance to the characterization of the museum as a public institution: "It has been objected that the public should not be called upon to provide a building for the accommodation and profit of an individual, and that there is no propriety in connecting this establishment with the offices."[20]

Controversy in 1816 over the amount of rent that the Peales would pay to the city for continuing use of the State House more explicitly and protractedly defined the issue in terms of whether the museum was a public or private institution. Counting museums as "moral embellishments" and Peale's Museum as "one of the oldest and fairest ornaments of our city," a memorial written in favor of Peale asserted that "it would be quite superfluous to intrude upon the attention of a body of enlightened citizens, any observations on the value of such institutions." Peale's offer included the guarantee of the museum's permanence in Philadelphia, the alternatives being the possibility of its dispersal or removal to another city. The proposal for reduced or excused rent met with vehement opposition. An article headed "Let Justice Be Done" stated that the city's proposed rent of sixteen hundred dollars, an increase from the previous charge of four hundred dollars was reasonable for a museum that enjoyed an annual income of between seven and ten thousand dollars. "A Friend to Propriety" pointed out that a publicly owned museum deserves public subsidy, "but as long as it [Peale's Museum] is, in every point of fact, a *Private Institution,* and intended for *private emolument,*" Peale should pay suitable rent. "E." framed the museum as a business rather than as a public institution in arguing, "The Corporation of Philadelphia is not rich, nor is there any more justice in taxing the Citizens for *housing* Mr. Peale and his articles of trade, than there would be in buying an establishment for Patrick Lyon, Peter Pollin or any other useful citizen provided they should threaten to leave us without Fire Engines or handsome Boots, &c. &c. &c." If in requesting government aid, Peale "did not feel it necessary to delineate with precision its public and private nature because political and economic theory allowed a blurring of these categories," as historians Sidney Hart and David Ward have argued, his opponents perceived no such ambiguity. To them, the museum was a private entrepreneurial venture first and a public benefit second.[21]

The rent controversy and the related debate on the museum's position as public or private also brought forth clearly divided views of the museum as created through the singular efforts of Charles Willson Peale or the collective contributions of a large body of donors. Peale entertained both versions of the museum's origins. Peale's request for state money in 1795 honored the notion that the museum developed "by his own persevering industry, and the support and encouragement of his fellow-citizens." However, later appeals to the state and local governments, written by both Peale and his supporters, relied increasingly on the model of the museum as the result of Peale's extraordinary hard work. In his 1800 request for public assistance, Peale claimed that "by his long and individual labours, he has reared a fabric which he need not blush to say, Philadelphia ought to be proud of." Peale's memorial to the city government in 1810 listed the state's grant of space in the State House and "the activity and zeal of its proprietor" as the factors central to the museum's success. "Liberal Justice," downplaying the importance of past state patronage, stated that "this museum is the work of *one man*" and a monument to his "unexampled industry, perseverance and ingenuity." The 1816 memorial said that the collections were "accumulated during the long and laborious life of a single citizen." The word "during" places the collecting activity contemporary to Peale, although not necessarily through his sole agency, whereas the phrase "long and laborious life of a single citizen" more singularly credits Peale. The shift from a social version of the museum's growth toward a more biographical account corresponded ironically with a rise in public sentiment that the museum was undeserving of government support. As the museum was increasingly perceived to be Peale's personal achievement, it was also more clearly understood to be a private enterprise.[22]

Peale's public addresses to his audience—in print, imagery, and display—demonstrated a recognition that the museum depended upon various constituencies, even though his encyclopedic approach made his collections appear to have come from one source. He promoted the collections as varied from art to nature, and offered various strategies for appreciating the displays: to serve economic, social, intellectual, or spiritual concerns. Moreover, the museum exemplified several issues that were important to early national life. The museum's ambiguous status as a public or private institution engaged an issue that was crucial to the allocation of public money, and which remains salient to governmental subsidy of cultural institutions. Similarly, discussion over whether the museum embodied Peale's individual accomplishments or a collective effort was an important concern in an emerging capitalist society. Peale maintained that reciprocal benefit, rather than competition and struggle, could follow participation in economic, social, or cultural exchange.

3. Written Responses to Peale's Museum

ALTHOUGH PEALE was the most conspicuous promoter of the museum, audience members contributed to its public meaning and significance by publishing their responses to the collections. These responses to the museum were published in city directories, guidebooks, and travel accounts. Additionally, visitors recorded their experiences at the museum privately in letters and diaries. They described, interpreted, and evaluated the exhibits, the manner of presentation, and the spaces that Peale and his museum occupied. The audience's engagement with political, religious, moral, and economic concerns demonstrates the breadth of interests among the members and the range of understandings of the institution's significance that they developed. Responses that echoed the language Peale himself used to promote the museum indicate the shared interests of Peale and a segment of his audience, whereas negative assessments and misinformation demonstrate independent concerns. This chapter represents only individuals within the literate population who took the time to record their impressions of the museum and other cultural institutions. Because most of the accounts discussed in this chapter were either published or written for publication, the representative group is further limited to those who had access to some form of the print media. Because of these significant constraints, the interpretations that follow should not be taken as the full range of contemporary responses to Peale specifically or to museums in general.

The particular print media in which responses were published provide a useful means of categorization, since the formats of these publications helped to shape their content. Local authors published their understandings of the museum in city directories, guidebooks, and newspapers. Travel writers typically prepared their impressions of American cities for publication in Europe, extending Peale's fame to an international audience, but often in the derisive tone common to this genre. Private papers, many now published in historical and genealogical journals, offer responses that reflect the social position, occupation, and intellectual interests of Americans, both famous and ordinary.

The compilers of Philadelphia directories and guidebooks were consistently sympa-

thetic to Peale's enterprise, and they treated the museum as one of the city's ornaments. The early directories typically listed Philadelphia's inhabitants alphabetically or,
less commonly, by address in the body of the volume, and appended the names of
elected officials, the officers of civic organizations, and descriptions of the city's cultural institutions. The mere inclusion of Peale's Museum among these institutions implied a considerable level of endorsement, which the written evaluation of the museum's contents and purpose confirmed. James Hardie in 1794 and Thomas Stephens
in 1796 offered grand praise for Peale's emerging museum of art and natural history.
Hardie celebrated Peale's heroic efforts as a patriotic accomplishment, proclaiming,
"He has paved to the American nation, an easy access to the proper subjects of the natural history of our country; an object of great importance, and which, without his exertions, would be almost inaccessible." With similar enthusiasm, Stephens pronounced the museum, "perhaps, the most valuable collection of the subjects of
Natural History to be met with in this country."[1]

Philadelphia guidebooks declared the advanced development of the city by enu-
merating its institutions of civic order and public service. James Mease presented his
account of the city's rise and progress in his 1811 publication, *The Picture of Philadelphia*. As with the city directories, the decision to include Peale's Museum in this account of the city's "increase and improvements in arts, sciences, [and] manufactures"
was itself a statement of support. Subsequent guidebooks extended his affirmation by
updating the growing size of the collections. For example, in the 1811 guidebook,
Mease reported that the birds in the museum collection numbered more than 1,000,
the 1824 guidebook claimed the number of specimens to be 1,100, and the 1835 edition of Mease's book increased the count to 1,284. Thus, Peale's Museum was not
simply a fixed entity that reflected the growth of the city; rather, it participated in the
spirit of progress through its own expansion.[2]

Travel writers offered a foreign counterpart to locally authored guidebooks. Primarily published for European audiences, though also avidly consumed in the United
States, travel books assessed the economic and political character of the nation, the
natural resources, the social divisions and manners of the people, and the writer's encounters with the natural and constructed landscape. Peale's Museum usually appeared among discussions of Philadelphia's public buildings or cultural institutions,
and notice of it varied in length from a brief mention to several pages. Because their
authors were not American and their principal audiences were European, these travel
books did not automatically confer praise upon their subjects. In place of the local bias
exemplified in the Philadelphia directories and guidebooks, foreign travelers often
showed an opposite bias in their written comparisons of Peale's Museum and other

American institutions to the European versions of such institutions. European responses to the museum range from John Bernard's claim that "no traveller has entered this city without awarding the proprietor his due meed of praise" to John M. Duncan's observation of "a good deal that is worth seeing, mingled with many miscellaneous monstrosities which are not worth house-room."[3]

The biases of travel writers also included aristocratic perspectives on republicanism, the critical vision of reformers, and the hopefulness of emigrants seeking a better life. Aristocratic commentators upon the museum included Sir Augustus John Foster, Charles Waterton, and Karl Bernhard, the Duke of Saxe-Weimar-Eisenach. Foster, a disaffected British diplomat on assignment to the United States at the outbreak of the War of 1812, was particularly dismissive of Peale's accomplishments. "Having alluded to the museum I cannot say much for it," Foster grumbled, "all that I remember of its contents being the bones of a large mammoth that had been found in the back country and put into shape at Philadelphia, as well as raised on a frame, so as to appear thirteen feet high." Reformers such as Frances Wright and James Silk Buckingham concentrated their efforts on social change, both here and abroad. Despite Peale's self-identification with contemporary reforms in education and other social causes, these writers were not consistently sympathetic to the museum. For instance, Frances Wright was committed to Democratic Republican politics, the party to which Peale had publicly declared political allegiance. Yet instead of perceiving in Peale an ally, she attacked the museum for locating in the politically hallowed State House. James Flint, Ludwig Gall, and Emanuel Howitt wrote for the benefit of would-be emigrants from their native countries. Whereas Flint and Howitt offered mixed reviews of the museum, Gall embraced the collection as "perhaps the largest private collection of natural history in the world" and appraised the evening entertainment as "completely satisfying."[4]

Newspapers provided another important avenue for responding to cultural institutions. The museum was discussed in Philadelphia newspapers most often in letters to the editor, which move beyond the descriptive and enumerative functions of directories, guidebooks, and travel accounts to engage in arguments. Rather than occurring at random intervals, these editorials often coincided with Peale's requests for government funding. In 1790 and again in 1794, published letters signed "A Lover of Nature" boosted Peale's unsuccessful pleas. The 1794 letter was specific in linking its praise to Peale's request for public money, stating, "the Legislature will do a very popular act by granting to Mr. Peale the moderate loan he requests." But the public subsidy of cultural institutions was not universally approved. As noted in the previous chapter of this book, in 1810 and again in 1816, Peale was opposed by citizens who believed that private enterprise should not be underwritten with public money. Peale's supporters in these battles signed themselves "Liberal Justice," "Philadelphus," and "A Citizen," and his opponents identified themselves as "Let Justice Be Done" and "A Friend to Propriety."[5]

The significant relationship between Peale's attempts to obtain public money and the frequency of editorials about the museum reflects the largely political character of early national newspapers. Philadelphia's editors typically devoted much of their four-page sheets to political news, including regular excerpts from the journal of the legislative branch of the state and federal government. This public record was augmented by rhetorical flourishes from the editor and readers, defining distinct partisan identities for each newspaper. For instance, the *Aurora. General Advertiser* was a radically Democratic Republican sheet, whereas *Porcupine's Gazette* and the *Gazette of the United States* were aggressively Federalist. Interestingly, although these political orientations informed the writers' stances on political issues—appointments during the Jay Treaty controversy, Matthew Lyon's fitness for Congress, the Alien and Sedition Acts, and the Embargo—they did not predetermine the writers' views of the museum. Peale's Museum entered this political forum directly when its proprietor petitioned the city and state governments, and metaphorically in debates over issues not immediately related to the purpose of the museum.

The museum's public role as a repository for valued objects made it a useful metaphor in several rhetorical exchanges among political factions. For instance, the Federalist *Gazette of the United States* proposed the donation to Peale's Museum of a supposedly rare literary production by its Democratic Republican rival: "An Aurora of last week, containing no lies nor any scandal or calumny." A more complex political reference to Peale's Museum appeared in print during the controversy over the Jay Treaty, a nonaggression agreement with England that Democratic Republicans believed was biased against the French. In the midst of this debate, Sharp Delany, the collector of the Port of Philadelphia, was challenged in the Democratic Republican newspaper for limiting the appointment of the new inspector of the port to those politically loyal to President George Washington and the Jay Treaty. "Longinus," an opponent of this policy quoted, in the following manner, Delany's rejection of one such application for the post:

> Mr. Harrison should procure a recommendation of his attachment, &c. to the Government, as it cannot be thought or expected any person *would* or could be an officer of Government—opposed to *its measures*—*the measures* taken by many in opposition to the treaty *comes* under my meaning; and I am confident many of my acquaintance *has* embraced opinions respecting it, that on reflection they will find wrong minded.

Rather than questioning Delany's fairness, "Longinus" attacked the collector's weak command of the language by emphasizing his grammatical errors. "Longinus" further belittled Delany by proposing ironically that "as we have no Royal Society here as yet to initiate the Collector into, I would recommend it to Mr. Peale as an object worthy his Museum, unless indeed he could prevail upon the author himself to add to his cabinet of curiosities." This statement was devised to undermine Delany, but it also informs a contemporary perspective on Peale. "Longinus" recognized that cultural institutions reflect the political character of the nation. By emphasizing the word "Royal" in Royal Society, "Longinus" expressed distaste for the form of rule that the revolution recently rejected. Peale's distance from this elitist model was implicitly supported. But the suggestion that the museum is an appropriate place for such a dubious literary curiosity and its characterization as a "cabinet of curiosities" simultaneously devalued the museum.[6]

As French–English tensions mounted in the late 1790s and American entrance into war seemed imminent, Congress empowered the president to limit the rights of the press and aliens with the passage of the Alien and Sedition Acts in 1798. The following anecdote, written less than one month before the Naturalization Act was passed, indicates the uncertain political climate and the role of Peale's Museum as the repository for esteemed American political values:

> I have just returned from *Peale's Museum,* and have seen a Medal, on one side of which, is the head of General Washington—his name inserted round it; on the reverse the Arms of the United States with a motto, *Liberty and Security;* and on the trilled edge the following; *An asylum for the oppressed of all nations.* The gilding of this Medal is a little worn off and evidently shews base metal beneath.

If the medal commemorated the soundness of American liberty, its erosion announced the decay of that ideal. Similarly, the discovery that it was not made of pure gold but consisted simply of gilding over cheap metal suggested that the American claim to political virtue was a sham.[7]

During Peale's tenure at Philosophical Hall, the museum's proximity to the seat of state and federal government provided a useful comparison in another political controversy. Heightened partisan tension erupted into physical violence on the floor of the United States House of Representatives between Federalist Roger Griswold and Democratic Republican Matthew Lyon. Lyon had gained the reputation of a renegade the previous year when he refused to wait upon John Adams in a ceremonial response to the president's address to Congress. Lyon argued that such a display was not appropriate in a republican government. Adopting the advertising format developed by Peale and other promoters of animal exhibits, the Federalist paper *Porcupine's Gazette* described the politician as a natural curiosity called the "Lyon Of Vermont!!!" The *Aurora* reprinted the bogus advertisement, changing the language to applaud the congressman's integrity. When Griswold and Lyon moved from insults to physical altercation, a new mock advertisement linked the episode more directly to the museum. The notice proposed the publication of "a Dissertation on the nature of *preserving impertinence,* and the method of forcing a man to listen to an insult. This will be followed by an essay on *spitting at a mark,* with some observations on *tongs, canes, & broken heads.*" The notice further instructed, "For farther particulars enquire next door to Mr. Peale's Museum in Philadelphia, where a specimen of the work may be seen every day." This juxtaposition of Congress and Peale's Museum creates two ironic inversions that establish the humor of the commentary. First, the location of Congress next to Peale's Museum inverts the importance of Peale relative to his distinguished neighbor. Second, the museum's foundation upon the principle of natural order stands in marked contrast to the disorder that had come to characterize congressional proceedings.[8]

Travel writers also responded to the museum in political terms, especially after Peale added a nationalist context to the display by moving into the State House in 1802. John Melish observed the Revolutionary associations that had been connected with the building: "The State-House is remarkable as being the place from whence the independence of the United States was first proclaimed." Whereas Melish's discussion of the State House appeared separately from his account of the museum and his prose is quiet in tone, Frances Wright was incensed by her perception that Peale was desecrating this politically sacrosanct building:

> The State-house, state-house no longer in any thing but name, is an interesting object to a stranger, and, doubtless, a sacred shrine in the eyes of Americans. I know not but that I was a little offended to find stuffed birds, and beasts, and mammoth skeletons filling the place of senators and sages. It had been in better taste, perhaps, to turn the upper rooms of this empty sanctuary into a library, instead of a museum of natural curiosities, or a mausoleum of dead monsters.* I might have judged that the citizens felt less respect for this venerable building than had been pleasing to me, had not every friend or acquaintance that ever passed it with me, paused before it to make some observation."Those are the windows of the room in which our first Congress sat." "There was signed the declaration of our independence." "From those steps the declaration of independence was read in the ears of the people." Ay! and deeply must it have thrilled to their hearts. 'Tis a fine moment to recall; one that swells the bosom, and makes us proud of our nature.

> *The lower rooms are more appropriately occupied by the courts of law.

Peale promoted the museum as a national asset and presented his portrait collection as an expression of the nation's greatness in the political and cultural spheres. But to Wright the museum was not worthy of association with the building emblematic of the political origins of the American republic.[9]

In addition to seeing the museum in a political light, audience members also described and evaluated the institution in scientific, artistic, historical, religious, moral, and economic terms. In selecting these categories, visitors participated in the range of discourses adopted by Peale in promoting the museum. The division of the collections into works of nature and works of humans established the basis for scientific and artistic responses. Peale's application of Linnaean order, his unfinished catalogue of the natural history specimens, and his visual representation of the museum as a bastion of empirical study all advanced scientific understandings of the collections. Because of his identity as a portraitist and his preference for ornamental over simply functional native artifacts, Peale developed an artistic layer of meaning for the museum. Peale added historical meaning to the portrait collections by publishing biographical accounts for each portrait subject. Through descriptions of the preserved animals as celebrations of the Creation, visual representation of Noah's Ark, and biblical quotations in verbal promotions, Peale offered a Christian context for the displays. By framing public leisure as "rational amusement" and arranging the collections to embody social values such as order and harmony, Peale identified the museum with contemporary concerns about moral education. Peale's interest in "useful knowledge" expressed the economic potential of his museum. Visitors identified with these varied strains of thought, and they wrote their critiques of the museum in these terms. Rather than as merely derivative prose, however, these responses should be seen as part of an ongoing dialogue between Peale and his varied audience.

As a result of Peale's scientific presentation of the collections, the museum developed a scholarly audience. Robert E. Schofield, a historian of science, has demonstrated that American naturalists often listed Peale's Museum in their acknowledgments. Moreover, their texts and illustrations reflected study of the specimens preserved in the museum. Peale cultivated his scientific audience through correspondence, by which he requested information, specimens, and public recognition. In the United States, Peale wrote to such notables as Benjamin Franklin, Thomas Jefferson, and Benjamin Henry Latrobe. In Europe, he addressed Joseph Banks, Georges Cuvier, and Jean-Baptiste Lamarck, among others. Perhaps most impressive is that Cuvier's classification of the mastodon, popularly called the "mammoth," depended upon Peale's excavation of two complete skeletons.[10]

In the local context, Peale's science-minded audience included those affiliated with the American Philosophical Society, those associated with the Academy of Natural Sci-

ences of Philadelphia, and those whose occupations were founded upon scientific education. For example, James Mease's sympathy for the museum reflects not only the
guidebook genre, but also his professional identity as a physician and his membership
in several public institutions with missions that complemented the museum's. Having
earned his M.D. degree at the University of Pennsylvania, Mease had training in natural history and chemistry. Mease also shared Peale's institutional membership in the
American Philosophical Society, where he served as an officer and presented scholarly
papers. In addition to writing the guidebook, Mease published on various subjects relating to the museum's collections, including geology, medicine, agriculture, and
other useful knowledge.[11]

On a more basic level, visitors acknowledged Peale's scientific aspirations for the
museum by recognizing that the collections were arranged according to Linnaeus and
other proponents of classification. Manasseh Cutler's discussion in 1787 of the "natural curiosities . . . arranged in a most romantic and amusing manner" clearly precedes
Peale's interest in scientific classification. In 1794 Peale moved to Philosophical Hall,
formally adopting a more scholarly presentation of the museum. That year James
Hardie announced in the city directory that the museum "is now arranged with the
greatest order and judgment, agreeably to the mode prescribed by *Linnæus.*" Hardie
elaborated upon the hierarchical system to which Peale's Museum adhered, explaining that it presented humankind first, then "brutes," followed by birds, "Serpents and
other Amphibious Animals," fishes, "the tribe of insects and worms," and lastly, minerals and fossils. James Mease confirmed the continuing importance of Linnaeus to
the arrangements in 1811, and demonstrated that the hierarchy was adhered to in
greater detail than Hardie had indicated: "The first order, rapacious birds, begins in
the upper row, at the east end of the room, and extends nearly to the centre: each succeeding order beginning eastward, and extending to the west." Mease also indicated
that the minerals were presented according to the system devised by mineralogist
Richard Kirwan, demonstrating that Peale's displays also exemplified systems devised
by specialists. The trend toward the application of specialized studies continued, according to an 1824 city guidebook, which stated that Peale's arrangement of the
mammals and birds was based on Linnaeus's system, the minerals on Parker Cleaveland's, and the shells on Lamarck's. Several years after Peale's death, James Mease
praised the arrangement of the insect collection, because it was "in geographical divisions." Peale's shift toward the use of specialized studies is significant because it
demonstrates that the museum was in step with the contemporary trend toward pro-
fessionalization in American science. However, this trend was probably an important
contributor to the museum's eventual decline. No longer would the encyclopedic mu-

seum, the "world in miniature," suffice as scientists developed specialized fields of study and, later, disciplines.[12]

The museum itself was subject to a different kind of classification, since writers of directories, guidebooks, and travel books tried to group their subjects into coherent units. In the city directory, James Hardie placed the museum under the heading "Scientific Societies," and he preceded it with the American Philosophical Society and the College of Physicians of Philadelphia. Immediately after the museum, Hardie listed the circus, invoking the category "Places of amusement," to which Peale's exhibits seemed to belong equally. On the other hand, James Mease, in his guidebook, grouped the museum with Philadelphia's other art establishments, the Pennsylvania Academy of the Fine Arts and the Society of Artists.[13]

Peale's portrait collection was a bridge between the scientific and artistic presentation of the collections. On the scientific level, the portraits represented the highest class of natural beings in the Linnaean system and therefore occupied the uppermost portion of the exhibition space. James Hardie recognized this aspect of the display as consistent with Peale's application of Linnaean taxonomy, stating that "according to this system, *man* is placed at the head of the animal creation; and it is by good and faithful likenesses, that different individuals are handed down to posterity with the greatest precision." Hardie's interest in quality moves the discussion from scientific to artistic concerns in the paintings.[14]

For many visitors, artistic merit was the most important criterion for evaluating the portrait collection, though their assessments varied widely. Manasseh Cutler praised the excellent likenesses achieved by Peale and judged them to be generally "executed in a masterly manner." James Flint praised the concept of a line of portraits of distinguished men, "but," he added, "the execution of the picture is bad." Emanuel Howitt granted that "by the standard of the American school," Peale's portraits are "very decent." Howitt's faint praise, being limited to a comparison with American art, which he apparently held in low esteem, amounted to a politely stated but rather damning critique. William Newnham Blane offered sharper criticism: "The proprietor unfortunately happens to be a painter, and has disfigured it [the museum] with some wretched specimens of his art."[15]

Evaluation of the historical significance of the portraits hinged upon Peale's selection of sufficiently noteworthy subjects for inclusion in the gallery. Jeremy Belknap endorsed Peale's choices when in 1785 he described the portrait subjects as "the most eminent persons in the civil and military lines in America." Belknap's letter was addressed to Manasseh Cutler, who later concurred that Peale had captured "portraits of the principal American characters who appeared on the stage during the late revolution, either in the councils or armies of their country." As Peale expanded the portrait collection, critics suggested that he lost focus. Emanuel Howitt described those honored in the gallery as "numerous celebrated and demi-celebrated men," whereas William Newnham Blane dismissed them more completely as "pretended portraits of worthies, born only to be forgotten."[16]

Peale represented the human figure also in full-sized wax models, which visitors similarly evaluated for their artistic and historical significance. As likeness was an important consideration for viewers of the two-dimensional portraits, it was a source of amazement for some viewers of the wax models. Manasseh Cutler was particularly amazed when he beheld Peale's self-portrait in wax. Although Cutler had not met Peale prior to this encounter, his escort, Dr. Clarkson, was already acquainted with the artist. A boy led the two men into the museum, where they were asked to wait for Peale. They came upon Peale's wax self-portrait, which was posed in the act of drawing on ivory, and which they believed was the man himself. The men were startled as they moved away from the wax figure and encountered Peale stepping toward them. Cutler's amazement was increased when Peale later stood next to the wax model:

> My astonishment was now nearly equal to that of Dr. Clarkson; for, although I knew what I saw, yet I beheld two men, so perfectly alike that I could not discern the minutest difference. One of them, indeed, had no motion; but he appeared to me to be as *absolutely* alive as the other, and I could hardly help wondering that he did not smile or take part in the conversation.

The incident echoes the narrative of an earlier episode involving Peale's double portrait of his sons Raphaelle and Titian I, the *Staircase Group*. According to tradition, George Washington mistook the image for the boys themselves and bowed to them as he passed.[17]

In 1797 Peale added a group of wax figures of Native American, Asian, and African types, which one audience member evaluated in terms of quality and historical significance. Emanuel Howitt in 1819 criticized the wax figures as being in a state of decay and proposed that a well-kept exhibit of this type would gain the appreciation of viewers. But Howitt reserved his strongest language for his pronouncement that a proper exhibit of Native American artifacts would stand as "a monument of national odium" and a "record of Christian violence." This was not simply an opportunity to study the physical and cultural differences of the world's races, but to embody in wax a representation of the decimation of native peoples. To some extent, Howitt's perspective on American history expressed his religious identity as a Quaker and the emphasis on nonviolence in the teachings of that sect.[18]

For many visitors, religious beliefs were central to their written responses. Charles Coleman Sellers discerned a deistic interpretation of the museum in the Comte de Volney's exclamation, "This is the house of God! Here is nothing but truth spoken!" In contrast, several members of clergy and laity alike recorded more conventional Christian understandings of the importance of natural history. Both Nicholas Collin, a Swedish Lutheran minister, and Sister Catherine Fritsch, a Moravian, praised the religious content of the wall labels at Peale's Museum. Collin argued that "the sublime inscriptions in the Museum have for several years borne testimonies of his [Peale's] zeal." Before her visit to the museum, Fritsch "had honored the name of Mr. Charles Willson Peale: but now more than ever—since he has hung on the walls scripture texts—in oval frames—beautifully engrossed—as silent reminders to the unthinking that there is a God who has created all things." Manasseh Cutler, a Congregational minister, likened the exhibits to Noah's Ark, a comparison that Peale later appropriated by exhibiting a painting of this subject (figure 12). In 1799 "A Clergyman" proposed that Peale's lectures on natural history contributed to the appreciation of the Creator. The study of nature, the anonymous clergyman asserted, "elevates the soul to the AUTHOR OF ALL, and thus eminently promotes PIETY:—For who can admire the WORKS and not the MAKER?"[19]

Reverend Nicholas Collin, a consistent patron of the museum, wrote a six-part series the following year, proclaiming the religious and other significance of Peale's exhibits and lectures on natural history. In the first installment, Collin pronounced "the direct promotion of Religion" as Peale's greatest contribution. Collin perceived in nature the work not only of the Creator, but also of "an All powerful, All wise, All-good Ruler." Collin addressed himself to the religiously committed members of society who believed that the Bible alone should inform their understanding of God: "Ask the beasts, and they shall teach thee; and the fowls of the air, and they shall tell thee; and the fishes of the sea shall declare unto thee. Who knoweth in all these, that the hand of the Lord hath wrought this? In whose hand is the soul of every living thing, and the breath of all mankind" (Job 12.7). This is just one of a series of passages that Collin quoted to support his claim that the Bible calls upon the faithful to learn from nature. Significantly, this is the chapter and verse Peale paraphrased on his engraved ticket of admission in 1788 (figure 8). The second part of Collin's essay furthered his position "that both reason and the scriptures enjoin the study of nature as a religious duty." Collin argued that misperceptions of God's Creation could be clarified through science, the study of which would result in better appreciation of His plan:

A Museum stored with specimens of quadrupeds, birds, fishes, amphibia, insects, animals, &c. from all parts of the terraqueous globe, is a miniature of it; and a temple which no thinking person can frequent without adoration of the Creator. When proper instruction improves these devout sentiments, they will cause a deeper impression and higher elevation. Mr. Peale has done this, and will do it with particular care in the Lectures proposed.

In the third section of his argument, Collin proposed that the natural hierarchy evident in Peale's displays conveyed a lesson that greater beings bear the Christian burden of caring for lesser ones. Collin also perceived a set of natural laws, ordained by God, of "rewards and coercions." In this system, all human actions have consequences in this life, which parallel a graver set of eternal consequences. The responsibilities associated with the highest position in the natural hierarchy were elaborated upon in the fourth part of Collin's argument. The final two parts of the essay advanced the economic benefits of nature and proposed the significance of natural history to doctors, as well as to "politicians, philosophers, historians, and poets." Collin's commitment to Peale's work and the language that he used to promote the museum in this three-thousand-word essay—the longest contemporary response to the museum—exemplify his dual role as religious leader and amateur scientist.[20]

Consistent with their correlating the museum with religious education, visitors also evaluated the museum as a place of moral education. For Peale, this component of the museum's mission was very important in the first decade of its operations, when Quakers and Protestant clergy lined up against the immoral effect of public leisure activity, especially the theater. Not surprisingly, then, Nicholas Collin developed a model of moral living that he perceived through the natural example of animals. He found precedents in nature to establish "laws for the support of order and justice," "friendship," "parental affection," "filial reverence and love," and "connubial affection." Collin also perceived lessons in nature to overcome personal financial ruin, disease through excessive consumption of alcohol, and discomfort and illness through irrational subservience to fashion.[21]

In relating nature, morality, and social order, Peale's audience members differed on their perception of the role of education. For the author of a contemporary Philadelphia guidebook, the moral and religious lessons offered at Peale's Museum reinforced social distinctions:

[T]he whole of the intellectual and pecuniary resources of Charles Willson Peale have been devoted, with unceasing ardour, to the accomplishment of the design of conveying instruction and amusement to his fellow citizens, and of advancing the interests of religion and morality, by the arrangement and display of the works of nature and art. The doors of the Museum have been ever closed against the profligate and the indecent; it has been preserved, with scrupulous fidelity, as a place where the virtuous and refined of society could meet, to enjoy such pleasures as can be tasted by the virtuous and refined alone.

The moral content of the exhibits, this author stated, was beyond the comprehension of the "lower sort." Indeed the very act of attending the museum was a mark of distinction. High social standing preceded a visit to the museum, and an intelligent response to the displays confirmed one's right to that position. An alternative understanding of Peale's plan may be discerned in the didactic tone of Collin's description of a system in which the lowly may be elevated through the teachings of God in nature. In this model, education reduces and even eliminates social boundaries, and the museum is an instrument for realizing such transformations.[22]

Moral responses to the museum also inform early national gender expectations and the evils of fashion in particular. In "A Dialogue on Mr. Peale's Museum," published in the *General Advertiser* in 1792, a group of female visitors reflected upon how the museum freed them from such vices as vanity and extravagance. After viewing the splendid natural coloration of birds and insects, the women were humbled into forswearing future extravagant expenditures and displays of clothing, jewelry, and cosmetics. Young men, too, were supposed to dispense with all "buttons, buckles, ruffles, and whatever fripperies of male vanity" upon their encounter with "the magnificent attire of the Peacock, the Swan, and Powees." To "Anacreon," who irreverently declared, "For my part I prefer any bonny lass, blonde or brunette, with paste or rouge, with bishops and cushions, or in naked simplicity, to all the gimcracks of Peale," "Theocles" responded with a warning that closed the dialogue:

> You will sooner or later feel the evil consequences of a vitiated moral taste; try therefore to correct it betimes; let me recommend as a salutary medicine, a frequent meditation on the works of your Creator, and conversation with men of sense, and with women of refined sensibility: by this you will deserve an amiable wife, and by her be radically cured of any remaining corruption.

The engagement of contemporary characters—Charlotte, Maria, and Celia—in conversation with the voices of classicism—Strephon, Theocles, and Anacreon—added to the weight of this moral message.[23]

In contrast to intellectual, religious, and moral concerns, audience members also showed interest in the material significance of the collections. Abundance and variety in nature translated into potential wealth, and increased knowledge offered the means to exploit that economic potential. "A Lover of Nature" proposed in 1790, "The United States are blessed by Divine Providence with admirable treasures in all the domains of Nature[;] discovery and improving knowledge of them will continually open new sources of ease, wealth and happiness. . . ." Four years later, an essay bearing the same signature proposed that natural history "brings to light our many treasures in animals, plants, and minerals; suggesting thereby new branches of manufactures and commerce, which otherwise may lie dormant." Nicholas Collin, in the fifth part of his series on the museum, proposed that through improved knowledge of nature's "numerous and valuable articles suitable for nourishment, cloathing, buildings, utensils, and whatever conveniences and pleasures, we shall increase and diversify our stock of happiness, diminish and mitigate the sufferings of life." In reflecting upon the mineral collections at the museum, Emanuel Howitt perceived "a proof of the subterraneous wealth of this continent, whose surface is yet scarcely broken by the miner, but its riches are reserved for the resource and aggrandisement of future generations."[24]

As the breadth of the collections enabled a range of understandings, single objects similarly inspired a variety of responses. The most often and extensively remarked upon natural exhibit at the museum was the assembled fossil skeleton of the mastodon, which Peale installed in the museum late in 1801. In contemporary accounts of this display, writer-observers recounted the history of the skeleton's discovery and excavation, grappled with the enormous size of the animal, considered scientific questions about it as a species, engaged romantic conceptions of natural antiquity, and contemplated its relationship to biblical beasts.

The discovery and excavation of the mastodon bones were important events in the museum's history, and they became emblematic of Peale's construction of the entire museum. Rembrandt Peale penned the official written account, "An Historical Disquisition on the Mammoth" (1803), which Charles Willson Peale later augmented with his visual depiction, *The Exhumation of the Mastodon* (figure 9). Peale's audience incorporated these historical representations into their accounts of the mastodon. James Mease matter-of-factly reported that the bones were "dug up by Mr. Peale in 1801, out of a marle pit in Ulster county, New York." A later guidebook expanded the account and increased the importance of Peale's accomplishments. In place of a "pit," the bones were found in a "morass" in this version. Whereas Mease wrote that Peale simply "dug up" the skeleton, this writer proposed that the successful excavation was achieved through Peale's "great labour and expense, and by the most determined assiduity." The heroic proportions of the task grew in the estimation of the British naturalist Charles Waterton: "The city ought never to forget the great expense Mr. Peale was put to, and the skill and energy he showed, during the many months he spent in searching the swamps, where these enormous bones had been concealed from the eyes of the world for centuries."[25]

The size of the "mammoth" and its scale relative to other animals were themselves cause for comment. Travel writers often borrowed in part or whole, and occasionally exaggerated, the detailed measurements that Rembrandt Peale provided in his "Disquisition." More than the skeleton's absolute dimensions in inches and pounds, visitors found remarkable its extraordinary size in relation to neighboring specimens. Karl Bernhard, Duke of Saxe-Weimar-Eisenach, noted in 1825, "For the sake of contrast, they have put the skeleton of an elephant next the mastodon. Under its foot is the skeleton of a mouse." Francis Hall was more concerned with its proportions relative to those of the human frame, as demonstrated by wax models in the Mammoth Room: "The human stature is, indeed, pigmean beside it." For John M. Duncan, reflection upon this physical difference was cause for awe. "A human being shrinks into insignificance beside the bony fabric of this enormous antediluvian," Duncan wrote in 1818. The great size of the skeleton contributed to a more physical response by a woman in Deborah Logan's circle of acquaintances: "I looked on its enormous remains with astonishment, the bones of the Head were not compleat and are supplied with wood of such a configuration as naturalists think appertains to the rest of its figure, by means of a wire the jaw open's, and displays such an extent that it frightens the Ladies, Mrs. Smyth told me of one that went to Bed after she returned home from seeing it with the terror it inspired." Logan's statement that the exhibit "frightens the Ladies" and even sent one to bed suggests a conventional response by women to encounters with the terrific, a reaction personified by the woman with upturned hands in *The Artist in His Museum* (figures 1 and 2).[26]

To those visitors interested in current scientific discourse, the mastodon's placement next to the elephant engaged contemporary debates about species, not simply scale. An account published in the *Aurora. General Advertiser* just a couple of weeks after the installation of the mastodon was unequivocal in its assessment: "That it was a species of the Elephant no one will doubt, who has seen that animal; for it is evident that from the shortness of its neck, and the enormous size of its tusks, it must have had a proboscis." Robert Sutcliff compared the feet of the elephant and the mastodon, and concluded that the sharp, clawlike feet of the latter animal proved that it was a formidable "beast of prey." John M. Duncan noted that the dissimilarity between the teeth of the mastodon and the elephant suggested to him that the mastodon was carnivorous, whereas the elephant is herbivorous. From the same evidence, the French anatomist Georges Cuvier argued that the extinct species was herbivorous, and reclassified the animal as a mastodon, not a mammoth.[27]

For some visitors, Peale's use of Native American folklore to promote the mastodon linked these native peoples and the skeleton in an idyllic past. Both Charles Willson Peale, in an 1801 broadside, and Rembrandt Peale, in his disquisition, quoted a Shawnee legend to explain why no one had seen a living example of this species. According to the legend, the "Good Spirit" attempted to protect Native Americans from the vicious mammoth. Lightning was used to eliminate the beast and all but one animal, the most destructive of the whole species, were killed. Under siege from the Good Spirit and "maddened with fury, he leaped over the waves of the west at a bound, and this moment reigns the uncontrouled Monarch of the Wilderness in despite of even Omnipotence itself." In this explanation the mastodon is not extinct, but simply living beyond the bounds of civilization, the natural province of Native Americans. Among the travel writers who responded to the mastodon, Robert Sutcliff, Henry Ker, and Carl David Arfwedson retold the legend. Francis Hall noted the proximity of the mastodon skeleton to the wax figures of Native American and other racial types. Through this juxtaposition, Peale may have hoped to extend this link.[28]

Responses to the mastodon skeleton also invited religious reflection upon this largest of all beasts. Searching to explain the extinction of the mastodon, William Newnham Blane offered, "Perhaps we ought to imagine that Noah found it too large and troublesome to put in the ark, and therefore left the poor animal to perish." Blane's choice of the equivocal "perhaps" and his use of the word "imagine" to characterize such a suggestion indicate that this proposition was offered whimsically. John M. Duncan more confidently and earnestly discussed the disappearance of "this enormous antediluvian; for such we may safely call it, notwithstanding of the fashionable scepticism of those who are in all things too philosophical to accept of explanations of natural phenomena from the sacred volume." Duncan sought not only to understand the extinction of the mastodon, but also the presence of other types of fossils on mountaintops. "The deluge is an explanation of all these wonders," he reasoned, "to which the Christian will devoutly and satisfactorily recur, leaving comfortless infidelity to its own pathless wanderings." Duncan also related the word "mammoth" to the "behemoth" described in the Book of Job. Peale invited this biblical allusion in advertisements for the "Behemoth Or Mammoth," though Rembrandt Peale dismissed this linguistic relationship as accidental.[29]

Although the accounts upon which this chapter is constructed were influenced by the conventions of the genre in which they were written, they also depended upon Peale's public presentation of the museum. For instance, Peale and Nicholas Collin quoted from the same chapter and verse in invoking the religious significance of the collections. In writing his guidebook, which was published in 1811, James Mease depended heavily upon Peale's own "Guide to the Museum." In turn, the later guidebooks, *Philadelphia in 1824, Philadelphia in 1830–1,* and the 1835 edition of Mease's book built upon Mease's early work and upon each other. Rembrandt Peale's "Historical Disquisition on the Mammoth" served as another common source for responses to that exhibit. In the introduction to Sir Augustus John Foster's travels, cultural historian Richard Beale Davis pointed out that Foster augmented his notes with published travel information. The typically chronological arrangement of travelers' accounts, sometimes expressed in epistolary form, contributes to the illusion that the prose was based entirely upon observation, whereas the similarities among travels written by different people indicate that the conventions of the genre contributed significantly to the texture of these sources.[30]

Given the limitations of these accounts as conventional writings and the similarity of their authors as educated, wealthy, and even aristocratic people, these authors registered a notable range of affirmative and negative, descriptive and evaluative, and intellectual and affective responses. Their accounts of the museum express a spectrum of interests that echo the categories of understanding promoted in Peale's public definition of the museum's purpose. But visitors did not simply absorb Peale's version of the museum. They dismissed what they perceived to be insignificant. They railed against what angered them, as Frances Wright did in discussing Peale's presence in the State House. Whereas Peale presented the displays of native peoples as evidence of harmony among the races, as will be discussed in chapter 7, Emanuel Howitt perceived a chronicle of violence already committed. Visitors also contradicted each other's perceptions. Assessments of the quality of objects and the importance of the displays vary widely, and reflect provincialism and nationalism at one extreme and anti-American hostility at the other. Nicholas Collin's optimistic expectation that people can be improved intellectually and socially contrasts with the 1824 guidebook's demarcation of the "virtuous and refined" from the lower strata of society. For one writer the museum is a vehicle for social change, and for the other a means of conserving hierarchy. Subsequent chapters explore the role of the museum in the lives of those audience members who did not record their responses in writing. By observing the uses of museum souvenirs and by evaluating the donations that audience members made, a broader conception of Peale's audience may be achieved.

4. The Audience for Silhouettes Cut by Moses Williams

LATE IN 1802 Charles Willson Peale introduced a new attraction at the museum, a machine that quickly and inexpensively produced small silhouette portraits. Thousands of surviving silhouettes attest to the inclusion of women and the virtual absence of nonwhites among Peale's audience. But these simple profile portraits demonstrate more than just the composition of the museum's audience; they also indicate a specialized application of Peale's interest in collecting, arranging, and displaying similar objects. Just as Peale compressed natural and human productions into a "world in miniature," early national collectors of profile portraits systematized their personal worlds in silhouette albums. Because four identical likenesses were produced at each sitting, museum visitors could exchange these personalized souvenirs among their family members, friends, and colleagues. The social experience of being part of Peale's audience thus continued outside the museum.

Peale received the new portrait machine from John Isaac Hawkins, an inventor who adapted the principle of a pantograph to reproduce the outline of a sitter's profile. Peale and the inventor called the device a physiognotrace, a name that conveyed both its action (to trace) and the subject it reproduced (physiognomy). Peale explained the device in an illustrated letter written to Thomas Jefferson early in 1803 (figure 15). By moving a brass knob (marked "C" in Peale's drawing) along the shadow of the sitter's head, the operator transferred an identically shaped, miniaturized, incised outline onto a sheet of paper near the top of the machine. Peale represented the paper with dotted lines and labeled the rectangle "d." Once the tracing was completed, the likeness could be cut from the paper. To facilitate the cutting, the outline was often first traced with graphite. The sheet was then unfolded, and the four portraits were separated from the sheet. The sitter kept the rectangular quarter sheets, each of which had a hollow center outlining that individual's likeness. Peale referred to the central cutout portions as "block heads," which were regarded as disposable. Behind the completed hollow-cut images, silhouette buyers typically pasted or stitched black or blue paper or cloth. The heads were sometimes embellished with a few strokes of ink or watercolor to suggest hair, eyelashes, or costume. Although most silhouettes in public col-

Figure 15. Charles Willson Peale, illustrated letter to Thomas Jefferson, explaining the physiognotrace, January 10, 1803. Courtesy of the Library of Congress, Manuscripts Division, Papers of Thomas Jefferson.

lections today are not framed, their original owners often displayed them in natural wood, black enamel, or gilded frames.[1]

As a concession within the museum, the physiognotrace soon broadened Peale's audience and became a profitable attraction. In the first notice about this exhibit, Peale invited customers "to take the likeness of themselves or friends." One cent was collected to cover the cost of paper, and audience members operated the machine, tracing themselves or someone else. To obtain this inexpensive silhouette portrait, a customer first had to pay the twenty-five-cent admission fee to the museum. Frames could be purchased for an additional twenty-five cents. This was a financially appealing alternative to Charles Saint-Mémin's contemporary offer of twelve "impressions" made with a "physiognotrace" for eight to thirty-five dollars. Writing to sons Rembrandt and Rubens, who were then touring in England with the second mastodon skeleton, Peale extolled the machine's promotional impact: "[I]t has been the best article to draw company, that I ever had, the Idea of getting a likeness at the cost of only *one Cent,* has a happy effect." Indeed, Peale was so enthusiastic about the business potential of Hawkins's latest invention that he shipped one to his sons in England, taking special precautions to protect it from theft. During the summer of 1803, the traditionally slowest season for the museum, Peale credited a steady flow of customers to the physiognotrace. By 1806 the sensation had reduced to the point that Peale wrote, "The Physiognotrace is still going on, but not quite in demand as formerly." Despite this decline in business, the physiognotrace remained an important feature of the museum well after Peale's death in 1827.[2]

The social breadth of this phenomenon may be measured by the vast numbers of silhouettes that were cut at the museum. Reflecting upon the middle years of the museum in his unpublished autobiography, Peale wrote that 8,880 silhouettes were cut in the first year (1803) alone. Sidney Hart and David C. Ward have estimated that 11,620 people attended the museum in 1800 and 16,862 in 1805. If Peale's claim is accurate that 8,880 visitors sat for silhouette portraits, then a significant proportion of those who paid for attendance also had their profiles taken. At another point Peale claimed that silhouettes could be found in almost every household in the nation. Peale's boast expressed his sense of the immense popularity of the silhouettes, though his claim was surely exaggerated. Raphaelle Peale toured the American South with a physiognotrace and advertised his display of three thousand silhouettes from his collection of one hundred thousand, which were presumably the disposable block heads from profiles cut during his travels.[3]

Soon after the installation of the physiognotrace, Peale granted Moses Williams control of operating the machine and cutting out the profiles. Williams was Peale's slave probably until 1802, the last year Peale was assessed a property tax in Philadel-phia for slave ownership and the year the physiognotrace was added to the museum. The coincidence is most likely not accidental. Peale assumed a paternal role toward Moses Williams, a typically affirmative self-identification for an American slaveholder in that period. Just as a father would help a child develop a skill upon which his liveli-hood could depend, a master would help a manumitted slave lead a productive life. Fulfillment of this responsibility served a civic duty as well, since it answered to social anxiety about the place of emancipated slaves in the community. Beginning in 1813 Moses Williams was listed in the city directory as "profile cutter," with the designa-tion of "+" that was used to indicate a person of color. Although Williams had ob-tained his freedom from Peale a decade earlier, he continued to practice his art at Peale's Museum. Peale first advertised Williams's commission for a silhouette at one-sixteenth of a dollar, about six cents, and then raised it slightly to eight cents per sit-ting. Customers maintained the option of cutting their own silhouettes and paying only for the paper.[4]

Despite the constant presence of an African-American silhouette cutter at the mu-seum, Peale's audience remained almost uniformly white. A silhouette portrait in-scribed "Mr. Shaw's blackman" (figure 16) is the lone identified example of an African-American silhouette-sitter. Indeed this man, identified solely in relation to his race and his master, is unique as the only museum visitor documented in this study to be African-American. This limitation in the composition of Peale's audience echoes the racial boundary established at other public entertainments in early national Philadelphia. Furthermore, the exclusion of African-Americans from cultural oppor-tunities symbolically enacted a pattern that was repeated with greater consequence in the economic, social, and political spheres.[5]

While silhouette portraits demonstrate the virtual absence of African-Americans from Peale's audience, they document the inclusion of women. In fact, Peale pro-moted the physiognotrace in gendered terms, noting women as likely purchasers of these simple portraits:

> A smaller and more beautiful size of Profiles may now be taken by the Physiognotrace in the Museum—and while ladies are getting their charming faces delineated, gentlemen may be amused in examining the Birds, of which there is now a classical catalogue in handsome frames over each case—not only the Linnæn but also the English and French name: with cor-respondent numbers annexed to each subject.

Peale's specific identification of silhouettes with women suggests limited expectations for their engagement with the collections. In the above advertisement, for instance,

Figure 16. Moses Williams, attrib., *Mr. Shaw's blackman,* after 1802. The Library Company of Philadelphia.

Peale located women's interests in a museum attraction that he elsewhere described as a reflection of vanity, whereas he reserved for men the more elevated, intellectual domain of natural history.[6]

Despite Peale's claims that silhouettes were a female form, male subjects constitute the majority of extant profiles. Out of a large collection of silhouettes at the Library Company of Philadelphia (1,182 examined for this study), nearly two-thirds (63 percent) represent male sitters and slightly more than one-third (37 percent) represent females. That proportion remains nearly constant for profiles cut at the Peales' Philadelphia and Baltimore museums, and for those cut by such artists as Augustus Day, T. P. Jones, Martha Ann Honeywell, John McConachy, and Isaac Todd. Thus, a cultural form designated as female meant that women had access to it, not that they constituted the majority of its participants.[7]

With regard to the breadth of the museum's audience, silhouettes contributed also to Peale's ability to reach out across religious lines, particularly to Quakers. John Michael Vlach, in his study *Plain Painters,* noted that Quakers issued formal strictures against ownership of portraits specifically and pictures in general. But Vlach also observed that many Quakers flouted these prohibitions by purchasing silhouette portraits of themselves. Similarly, the Quakers voiced opposition to the theater as a form of public leisure that promoted immorality. Peale escaped censure from Quakers and other religious spokespeople partly by recruiting support from prominent clergymen, such as Nicholas Collin. The addition of an exhibition with specific appeal to the Quakers must have been a welcome means of maintaining their support.[8]

Just as existing collections of silhouettes suggest that different social groups achieved various levels of access to the museum, the ways the silhouettes were used indicate that they also carried distinct meanings for their diverse users. Peale was especially interested in the theories of Johann Caspar Lavater, a Swiss clergyman who believed that one's character could be read from the essential physiognomic evidence contained in a silhouette portrait. Peale subscribed to this notion when in 1806 he sent to Thomas Jefferson silhouettes portraying members of a visiting Native American delegation, including *Waconsca* (figure 17). In the accompanying letter, Peale wrote in terms that echoed Lavater: "Some of these Savages have interresting Characters by the lines of their faces." However, Peale did not elaborate on the traits he discerned in these silhouettes, and it is unclear if Jefferson shared Peale's perception. But it is clear that Peale found in these visitors an opportunity to conduct an experiment with a group of heads he regarded as clearly different from his own.[9]

Peale pursued his interest in the physiognomic importance of silhouettes by collecting the disposable block heads, and by beginning an album for their study (figure 18). In his *Essays on Physiognomy,* Lavater described the process of taking a "shade" by candlelight, which if done with care would yield an accurate profile. With the mechanical assistance of the physiognotrace, Peale must have felt equipped to advance

Figure 17. Moses Williams, attrib., *Waconsca,* 1806. National Anthropological Archives, National Museum of Natural History, Smithsonian Institution, Washington, D.C.

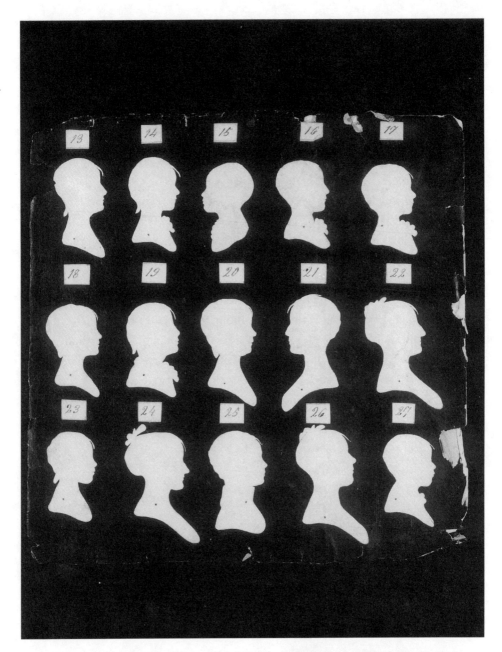

Figure 18. Page of "block heads" assembled by Charles Willson Peale in his *Profile Book*, dated January 22, 1803. American Philosophical Society, Philadelphia.

Lavater's theory. The potential for error in tracing the profile would be greatly reduced by the new drawing machine. The aspiring physiognomist, Lavater proposed, should collect a number of silhouettes and classify them according to the shape of the forehead. For Peale this proposal offered an opportunity to apply new technology to the development of a system of human classification to complement the Linnaean arrangement by which his other displays were ordered.[10]

Like Peale, some audience members also carefully gathered, ordered, mounted, and labeled their silhouettes into bound books that held two or four images on a page. Because Moses Williams and other silhouettists folded each sheet of paper into quarters, they cut four identical portraits from each sitting. In the portrait of an unidentified woman (figure 19), the four likenesses were never separated from the sheet. Multiple production facilitated exchange among friends and family, much in the same way that multiple prints from a single negative later invited the more widespread assembly of family photograph albums.[11]

That kinship was central to the arrangement of silhouettes connects these albums to the domestic sphere, reinforcing Peale's perception of this type of portraiture as a

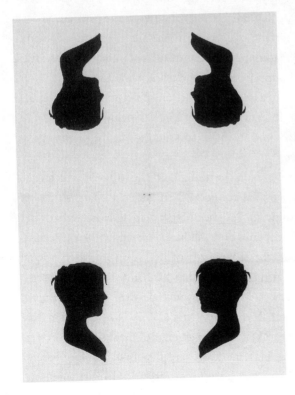

Figure 19. Unidentified artist, *Unidentified Woman*, 1805–15. Four identical silhouettes, demonstrating that multiple portraits were produced at a single sitting. The Library Company of Philadelphia.

female cultural form. But this gender orientation does not mean that only women collected silhouettes, as was demonstrated by the finding that men, more frequently than women, sat for profiles. For instance, an album at the Historical Society of Pennsylvania appears to be the collaborative effort of Patience Marshall Tyson and her husband Isaac Tyson. The Marshalls hailed from Philadelphia, and the Tysons came from Baltimore. Coincidentally, Baltimore was the site of a second Peale Museum, opened by Charles Willson Peale's son Rembrandt Peale about a decade after the physiognotrace first entered the Philadelphia Museum. In addition to silhouettes cut at the Peale museums in Philadelphia and Baltimore, the Tysons pasted into their album profiles by other artists, published stipple engravings, and a graphite drawing. Familial connection was more important than the silhouette's origin from Peale's Museum or any artist's hand. Patience Marshall Tyson's silhouette is the first cut profile in the album and her husband's follows several pages later. The remaining pages alternate between clusters of Patience's and Isaac's relatives, modulated by sitters whose familial connection is uncertain.[12]

Just as Peale assumed a paternal role toward Moses Williams, the Tysons asserted the place of an African-American domestic worker within their family by including his portrait in their silhouette album. The graphite drawing *"Bill" Waiter of Patience Marshall* (figure 20) shows the sitter in profile, as if posed for a silhouette portrait. However, in contrast to the hollow-cut outline of a conventional silhouette, the drawing includes a delineation of Bill's facial features. Ironically, instead of humanizing the figure, the addition of features has the opposite effect of making him ridiculous. Rather than possessing the individual dignity of a believable portrait, Bill's portrait has the exaggerated appearance of a caricature. It seems likely that Bill was included in the album as a benevolent statement of his place within the Tyson family, but the stereotypical representation undercuts the gesture.[13]

The selection of many of the silhouettes in the album and the order in which they appear clearly depended upon their familial connection to Patience Marshall Tyson (1771–1834). Among her favorite subjects, Patience Marshall included images of her sisters and grouped them with their husbands and children. Placing her blood relative first, Patience arranged on one page the silhouettes of her younger sister Abigail (1773–1847) at upper left, followed at right by Abigail's husband, Joseph S. Morris, and below them their daughter, Mary S. Morris. Patience devoted two subsequent pages to her next younger sister, Sarah Marshall Morris (1777–1824), Sarah's husband, and four of their children (figure 21). The arrangement of these silhouettes similarly reflects the family structure. The placement of Abigail's portrait before Sarah's indicates their relative ages, since Abigail was born four years prior to Sarah. Follow-

Figure 20. Unidentified artist, *"Bill" Waiter of Patience Marshall,* before 1814. Page from a silhouette album assembled by Patience Marshall Tyson and Isaac Tyson. Silhouette Collection, Perot Collection, The Historical Society of Pennsylvania, Philadelphia.

ing the pattern set in mounting Abigail's family portraits, Patience placed her sister Sarah's likeness first. This image was followed by the profiles of Sarah's husband, Thomas Morris, and their children, Sarah S., Lewis S., Anthony S., and Powel. A second image of Thomas is mounted at lower right on the left-hand page, apparently depicting him at a later sitting. The proximity of these two families in the album expresses the marriage of two of Patience's sisters to two Morris brothers, Joseph and Thomas. Most striking in these groupings is the placement of the women at the head of each household, prioritizing familial connection over traditional gender hierarchy.[14]

The Marshall–Tyson family structure was complex, and multiple images of a single sitter helped to record various levels of interrelationship. For instance, three portraits of Sarah S. Morris document her several places within the family. First, she appears as Isaac Tyson's sister-in-law, the wife of Isaac's brother Elisha E. Tyson. Second, her sil-

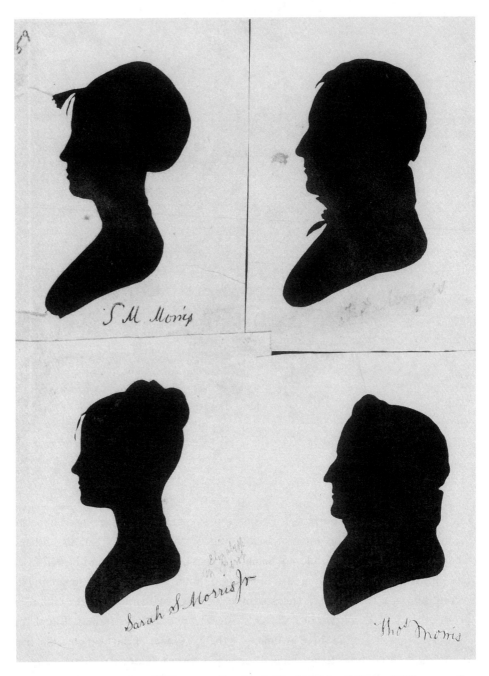

Figure 21. *This page:* Moses Williams, attrib., *Sarah Marshall Morris;* Moses Williams, attrib., *Thomas Morris;* unidentified artist at the Peale Museum, Baltimore, *Sarah S. Morris Jr.;* and unidentified artist, *Thomas Morris. Facing page:* Moses Williams, attrib., *Lewis S. Morris;* unidentified artist, *Anthony S. Morris;* and unidentified artist, *Powel Morris,* 1814–19.

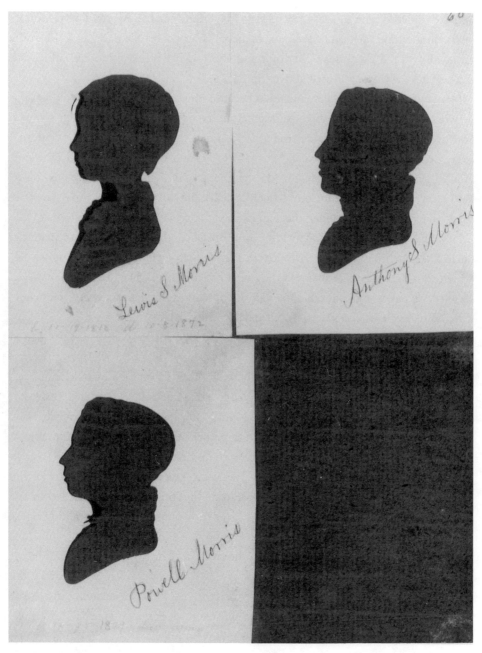

Figure 21. *Continued.*
Double page from a silhouette album assembled by Patience Marshall Tyson and Isaac Tyson. Silhouette Collection, Perot Collection, The Historical Society of Pennsylvania, Philadelphia.

houette is placed next to that of her sister, Elizabeth Marshall Morris Perot, indicating their common relation to Patience as nieces. Third, a profile of Sarah S. Morris is grouped with the likenesses of her mother, who was Patience's sister, her father, and three of her brothers, as noted above (figure 21).[15]

Many other silhouettes were included because they represent the extended kinship network of Patience Marshall, including her aunts, uncles, cousins, and their spouses. For instance, the album includes the following first cousins: the children of paternal uncle Benjamin Marshall (Hannah Marshall Haines and Benjamin Marshall); the children of paternal uncle Christopher Marshall, Jr. (Sarah Ann Marshall Collins, Elizabeth Flower Marshall Slocum, and Isaac Marshall); the son of maternal aunt Mary Parrish Collins (Zaccheus Collins); the daughters of maternal aunt Elizabeth Parrish Phile (Mary Phile Knapp and Hannah Phile Montmollin); and the children of maternal uncle Isaac Parrish (Samuel Parrish, Sarah Parrish, and Deborah Parrish Wright). Silhouettes of the spouses of many of these first cousins were placed beside them or on consecutive pages, most notably the pair documenting the marriage between maternal cousin Zaccheus and paternal cousin Sarah Ann Collins.[16]

The album was evidently not the sole creation of Patience Marshall, since it also documents the family of Isaac Tyson (1777–1864), including the silhouette portrait of his first wife, Elizabeth Thomas. Elizabeth Thomas Tyson died in 1812 and Isaac Tyson married Patience Marshall in 1814, suggesting likely dates for the album's creation. The album was probably not begun until after Isaac Tyson's second marriage commenced, though some of the portraits predate the compilation of the album. Tyson grouped portraits of his children born to his first wife—Philip Tyson, Deborah Tyson Ellis, Rachel Tyson Jackson, and Henrietta Tyson Jackson—together in the middle pages of the album. Relatives of Elizabeth Thomas Tyson included in the album are her brother Philip Thomas and sister Ann Thomas Poultney (and her husband Thomas Poultney); her first cousins Henrietta Thomas Bentley and John Chew Thomas (and his wife Mary Snowden Thomas); and her niece Elizabeth Ellicott Wethered and nephew Evan Ellicott.[17]

The sequence of silhouettes and labels evokes the vital flow of a changing and growing family. Inscribed at the bottom of the silhouette of Patience Marshall Tyson appears her first name and surname at birth, followed on the second line by her husband's family name. This addition, denoting the passage into married life, was made for many of the women portrayed in the album. Collection of the portraits over time paralleled the maturation of children: Isaac and Patience Tyson's silhouettes may have been made as early as 1814, whereas the portraits of Isaac's children probably date to the early 1820s. Henrietta Tyson, for example, was born in 1809, yet her silhouette portrays a young woman.[18]

Aside from creating a memento of a living family, silhouettes recorded likenesses for posterity. Although some of the inscriptions in the Tyson album appear to have been written during the sitters' lives, later inscriptions show the birth and death dates of the subjects, as if a descendant were working to construct a genealogy. That the Tyson album served a memorial function may be further argued from its provenance. Isaac and Patience Tyson compiled the album, and an inscription on the back suggests that it descended to Mary Ann Marshall (1789–1881), the youngest sibling of Patience. In 1881 the album was probably passed on to Mary Ann's great nephew T. Morris Perot, who executed her will. Another inscription in the album supports this suggestion: "Property of T. Morris Perot, Jr." In 1964 Charles Coleman Sellers noted that T. Morris Perot III and two other family members donated these and other silhouettes to the Historical Society of Pennsylvania.[19]

Contemporaries noted that silhouettes would preserve the memory of the deceased. A newspaper account of Peale's Museum combined the viewer's interest in the exhibits with the bustle of young girls having their profiles taken by Moses Williams and a poignant narrative about a girl mourning her mother's death. The viewer found the girl weeping over a miniature portrait of her late mother, which she was comparing with the silhouette of herself just cut by Williams. As the viewer was listening to the girl's story, her father came by and comforted her. This account links remembrance of the dead most directly with miniature portraits, a function of portraiture that Raphaelle Peale exploited in an advertisement that began, "Death Deprives us of our Friends, And then we regret having neglected an opportunity of obtaining their Likenesses." Like Raphaelle's advertisement, this tale promotes the moral that the lines of one's visage should be preserved before it is too late. The reader may infer that the little girl's silhouette will one day serve a purpose similar to her mother's more detailed miniature.[20]

Although silhouettes served this solemn purpose, the act of sitting for one was probably an entertaining counterpoint to the museum's instructive program. Catherine Fritsch recorded in her diary a playful conversation among the friends with whom she visited the museum: "In one of the rooms a man was making silhouettes. Polly coaxed me to have mine cut for her, but I couldn't think of it—with my big nose! Only Mr. Steinman and his daughter had theirs made. Here, too, were the Magic Mirrors, which afforded us much amusement—you might take your choice of a giant's face, or a dwarf's, or have seven heads!" Fritsch's juxtaposition of the physiognotrace with the

"Magic Mirrors" suggests her perception of the two installations as comparable entertainments. Whereas the mirrors distorted one's self-perception, the silhouette machine fixed an accurate portrayal on paper. Although the uncompromising accuracy of the device led Fritsch to refuse, Polly's request invokes the kind of exchange between friends that the silhouette albums document.[21]

Silhouette portraits from Peale's Museum demonstrate one meaning of a gendered cultural phenomenon in early national America. That is, although Peale designated the physiognotrace a female attraction, more men than women paid to have their silhouettes cut. Moreover, the terms of the appeal to women suggest that, even though Peale invited people of both sexes into the museum, he had unequal expectations for their engagement with the collections. Still, numerous silhouettes of women demonstrate that they enjoyed access to the museum, just as they attended other public cultural events, including the theater and circus. The most interesting story told by silhouettes, however, is in their placement into albums. Peale institutionalized, through systematic arrangement of his collections, the need to order the human world; compilers of contemporary silhouette albums similarly classified and ordered the people in their social networks. Rather than using an arrangement that focused upon the physical features and inner characters of the sitters, as Peale favored, women (and men) of that period ordered the silhouettes in a way that expressed the structure of their familial and social ties. Thus, they embraced the private sphere as their domain.

5. Subscribers to Annual Admission Tickets

IN THE EARLY national period, the social practice of associating with civic bodies was an important means of shaping one's public identity. An individual created a public persona by seeking government office, supporting economic ventures in internal improvements, joining reform societies, achieving election to learned societies, and patronizing cultural activities. In keeping with this practice, Peale offered audience members the opportunity to publicly affiliate with the museum. Beginning in 1788 audience members could purchase tickets of annual admission, and starting in 1794 the names of these subscribers were entered in a public record. Those who subscribed to a yearlong pass to Peale's Museum identified themselves, through this act, as sponsors of art and science and asserted their social equality to other subscribers. Peale promoted the museum as an example of economic, intellectual, religious, and moral excellence, and subscribers stood to gain through their association with these expressions of distinction. In turn, the accumulation of signatures served Peale's interests financially and as a communal endorsement.[1]

From shortly after he opened for business until the time of his death, Peale hoped to boost the museum's income through the sale of annual tickets. Peale first advertised tickets of annual admission in 1788 for one dollar, and the price increased to two dollars in 1796, to five dollars in 1801, six in 1802, and ten by 1819. In 1802 Peale started offering six-month tickets for half the annual ticket price. In 1823 he began to record three-, six-, and twelve-month tickets. By 1798 Peale limited admission with the annual ticket to the daytime, and by 1817 subscribers could purchase annual tickets for day or evening admission, or for both. Recent scholarship indicates that many more people attended Rembrandt Peale's Baltimore museum in the evenings than in the day, and the Philadelphia museum may have experienced a similar visiting pattern. By limiting admission with a long-term ticket to the daytime, Peale could hope to collect additional entrance fees from the same patrons attending the evening performances and experiments.[2]

Peale distributed tickets through a variety of methods. Of course annual tickets could be purchased at the museum, but this was not the only place at which they were available. In the first years that annual tickets were offered, Peale sold them by going from house to house, a form of distribution that he found "irksome" and apparently discontinued by 1790. When the members of the newly organized Board of Visitors and Directors of the Museum convened in 1792, they promised to "assist Charles Willson Peale in the disposal of cards for admittance to the Museum." In 1799 Peale attempted to broaden his distribution network by sending out groups of tickets to friendly businesses, including a color shop, a grocer, an ironmonger, a minister, an attorney, two printers, two tailors, and a hatter. Whether or not this approach was successful, it was certainly consistent with contemporary business practice. Subscriptions for publications, balls, lectures, and other amusements were often collected through agents. Peale, for instance, served as a subscription agent for lectures by a Mr. Green on astronomy and electricity, and for Alexander Wilson's *American Ornithology*.[3]

As such, a subscription was a social expression of mutual validation, not simply an economic exchange of money for services or a product. The relationship between Alexander Wilson and Peale in the publication of Wilson's volumes on ornithology provides a particularly rich demonstration of the reciprocal benefits enjoyed between an author and a subscription agent. Wilson consulted preserved specimens at Peale's Museum to draw some of the illustrations published in his study of American birds. Wilson expressed appreciation for this repository by donating bird specimens, bird nests and eggs, and minerals to the museum. By selling subscriptions through the museum, Wilson publicly associated the worth of his project with the established reputation of Peale's natural history collections. Similarly, Peale benefitted through Wilson's published acknowledgment of the museum. Wilson's book validated Peale's claims that the museum was an institution of scientific and educational value, since even such a serious and specialized student of ornithology could learn through the museum. Subscribers to books like Wilson's knew that their names would be printed in the opening pages, thereby extending the fellowship in pursuit of science to the sponsors of the project. Author, agent, and subscriber entered into a system of mutual recognition of each other's importance to the proliferation of scientific knowledge. Because this system was played out in public documents, such as newspaper advertisements and published subscription lists, each subscriber's public identity gained the attribute of scholarship.[4]

Peale attempted to increase annual ticket sales by offering his audience a variety of additional incentives. For those subscribers who purchased annual tickets in 1790, Peale granted free admission to an exhibit of his "moving pictures" (another term for his "perspective views with changeable effects"). Extended admission privileges were offered as a bonus to anyone who enrolled in Peale's course on natural history, a series of lectures he offered in the winter of 1799–1800 and again in 1800–1801. En-

Figure 22. Unidentified artist, Engraved six-month admission ticket, 1813. Massachusetts Historical Society, Boston.

graved tickets (figure 22) certified one's position as a patron and may have been a significant enough souvenir to inspire some visitors to become subscribers. Beginning in 1794, Peale promised to preserve subscribers' names in a bound volume, so that contemporary and future "Friends of Science" could be known to each other.[5]

Peale sometimes rewarded donors of artifacts and specimens with extended free admission to the museum. For instance, in 1797 Peale presented one annual ticket to Jesse Roberts for his donation of an animal curiosity, "a hog with one eye & proboscis." Benjamin Owren's gift of "a Large Saw fish" was sufficiently impressive that Peale granted him, his wife, and his five children admission to the museum for a year. The broad range of animals, minerals, and human curiosities received through this type of exchange included a monkey from Mr. Jacob Baush; a pair of parakeets from Miss Ann Dick; bones found seventy-five feet below ground from the Rush children, Julia, Samuel, and Benjamin, Jr.; an instrument (viameter) for measuring distances traveled by a vehicle on wheels from John Parry; "an Indian Bow" from Master David Gratz and a bow from Calcutta from Theodore Gratz.[6]

Although the most obvious reward for donor-subscribers was free admission, some contributors also gained professional recognition by having their names exhibited with items they donated. James Reid Lambdin, a portrait painter, received an annual ticket in 1823 "for presenting a Number of Indian Articles." Extant labels from Peale's Museum attest to the public recognition accorded to Lambdin and other donors (figure 23). Lambdin may not have anticipated that in five years he would himself become a museum keeper in Pittsburgh, but this gift publicly linked him to the institution that inspired his own collection of natural and human productions. Perhaps bridge builder Lewis Wernwag anticipated more immediate returns from his exchange of "a Model Bridge" for an annual ticket. Display of his works in Peale's Museum validated Wernwag's status as a technological innovator, and public acknowledgment of his gift to the museum added the distinction of benefactor. In turn, Peale inexpensively expanded the collections through these means, his only cost being occasionally forgone admission fees. In fact, not every donor received free admission. The next two chapters examine more fully the ways in which donations served both the museum's purpose and the donors' interests.[7]

Early national Americans developed their public identities not only through subscriptions, but also through endorsements, memberships, and offices held in civic organizations and government bodies. Peale himself actively participated in this process, and as a young man he started to shape his public persona. As an aspiring poet and painter, Peale applied to the Hominy Club, a literary society in colonial Annapolis. During the Revolution, Peale crafted his political identity as a radical Whig through his membership in the Whig Society and the Constitutional Society, his service in the Pennsylvania militia, and his role as agent for the Committee of Safety. Peale's position as officer of the Philadelphia Emigrant Society promoted his image as benevolent protector of the less fortunate. Peale's identity as a man of science was shaped in part by the announcement of his election in 1786 to the American Philosophical Society, by his subscription later that year to the building fund for its new Hall, and by his annual renewal as one of its three curators from 1788 to 1811.[8]

Peale's subscribers also participated in the cultural practice of developing their public lives and status through subscriptions, memberships, and offices held. At the start of each year, the Philadelphia newspapers announced the new and continuing officers of benevolent organizations, financial institutions, and learned societies. These announcements provide a quick sketch of the many public associations that Peale's subscribers established beyond the museum. They contributed to internal improvements, not to mention their personal financial success, as officers of the Schuylkill and Susquehanna Canal Company (Zaccheus Collins and Samuel Magaw) and the Delaware and Schuylkill Canal Company (Elias Boudinot). Political participation extended to artisans in local partisan activity (such as tinsmith Thomas Passmore, tailor

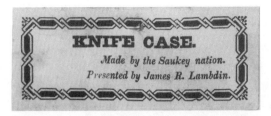

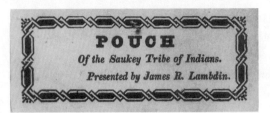

Figure 23. Labels from Peale's Museum for Native American artifacts donated by James Reid Lambdin, ca. 1823. Peabody Museum of Archaeology and Ethnology, Cambridge, Massachusetts.

William Smiley, and engraver James Thackara), as the announcements of the Democratic Republicans by ward indicate. Membership in the Society of Cincinnati reminded citizens of those who had offered distinguished service as officers in the Revolutionary army (Henry Knox, Matthew McConnell, Thomas McKean, Thomas Mifflin, Thomas Lloyd Moore, and Walter Stewart). Subscribers pronounced their ethnic loyalties by affiliating with the Hibernian Society (Edward Fox and Henry Toland), the Society of the Sons of St. George (William Young Birch), and the German Society (John Peter Gabriel Muhlenberg). They committed themselves to social reform by their work in the Philadelphia Society for Alleviating the Miseries of Public Prisons (Nicholas Collin, Samuel P. Griffitts, John McCrea, Richard Wells, and William White) and the Guardians of the Poor (Abraham Garrigues). Religious devotion was marked by a guiding role in the Society for Establishing Sunday Schools (George Meade and William White) and the Bible Society (Ashbel Green, Joseph Pilmore, and William White). Expressions of leisure and refinement were evident in the office of manager of the Dancing Assembly (George Meade, John Swanwick, and Walter Stewart). Regular listings of these affiliations in the newspapers defined an individual's economic, social, political, and cultural self, and made public these social webs of like-minded citizens.[9]

Peale ensured that his audience would regard subscription to an annual ticket as prestigious by first securing the patronage of the economic, political, and intellectual elite. The subscription book opened in 1794 with the signatures of President George Washington and Vice President John Adams, followed by the signatures of eighty-eight United States senators and representatives. The concentration of names of the politically empowered on the first pages of the book suggests that Peale exerted significant effort to ensure an auspicious beginning to this public record. Peale may have recruited support of such great magnitude through the influence of a few politically empowered Americans who had become patrons of the museum earlier. Just as the theater and circus in Philadelphia announced days on which the president was anticipated in the audience, Peale used the attendance of prominent figures to promote the museum. To the present day, the first page of names in the subscription book stands in some histories as a sign of the importance of Peale's Museum in American cultural history.[10]

Besides public affiliation with institutions, one's occupation was an important public marker of social station, and a composite profile of Peale's subscribers indicates that they belonged to the middle and elite ranks of society (appendix). Stuart Blumin's history of the American middle class divides the early national occupational structure into four levels—high nonmanual, low nonmanual, high manual, and low manual—with the second and third categories being considered the "middling sort." Comparison of Peale's subscriber base and Blumin's breakdown of contemporary Philadelphians by occupational level shows that annual ticket buyers were of significantly higher than average occupational status (table 1). Despite Peale's identification with Philadelphia's artisan culture, both unskilled laborers and skilled craftsmen were vastly underrepresented among the subscribers. Only 12 percent of Peale's subscribers worked in manual occupations, compared with Blumin's estimate of 50 percent in the urban population at large. Conversely, 62 percent of Peale's subscribers were in high nonmanual occupations, nearly three times as many as in Blumin's sample of Philadelphians (22 percent). Even after discounting from the subscriber total the eighty-eight United States senators and representatives, whose patronage did not recur in subsequent years, the percentages of nonmanual workers among Peale's subscribers remain disproportionately high.[11]

Public officials constituted the largest occupational group among museum subscribers in 1794. Their signatures probably served the museum and its audience in different ways. To Peale's audience, the patronage of notable politicians established a distinguished base for the subscription list, and ordinary citizens could join the ranks of such officials by paying the price of an annual ticket. For the museum, Peale may have hoped that endorsements by public officials would improve his chances for government subsidy. Peale first petitioned the Pennsylvania General Assembly for support in 1792, and the relative absence of state legislators from the subscription rolls may indicate a reluctance to sanction his future pleas for state funding. That four elected state

Table 1: Occupational Status of Peale's Subscribers Compared with Occupational Status of Contemporary Philadelphians for Whom Occupation Was Identified, 1794

Group	Nonmanual Status		Manual Status		Total
	High	Low	High	Low	
Philadelphians					
Number	197	244	360	89	890
%	22.1	27.4	40.5	10	100
Subscribers, All					
Number	195	80	38	0	313
%	62.3	25.6	12.1	0	100
Subscribers, Excluding U.S. Congressmen					
Number	108	79	38	0	225
%	48.0	35.1	16.9	0	100

officials who did buy annual tickets were all Philadelphians suggests their allegiance to local institutions rather than their political support.[12]

In turn, Peale validated the power of at least eleven of these federal and state politicians by adding their likenesses to the museum's portrait collection. The catalogue of portraits, which Peale published in 1795, sketched the public life of the sitters. For each portrait, Peale assigned a number, named the subject, listed titles or affiliations that distinguished the sitter, and provided anecdotes that exemplified the subject's character. The entry for the portrait of subscriber Thomas Mifflin (figure 24) is typical of the catalogue format:

> No. VIII. The Honorable Thomas Mifflin, Esq. elected Brigadier General by Congress, 1776, in the beginning of the Revolution did much service by exerting his great abilities in rousing his fellow citizens, by animated and affectionate addresses, to turn out in defence of their endangered liberties; was President of Congress when General Washington resigned his commission: elected Governor of Pennsylvania, in 1788, in which station he still continues.

Although Peale's portrait depicts Mifflin in civilian attire, the catalogue reminds the audience of his military contribution to the Revolution. In this way, the museum presented powerful visual and verbal representations of the upper echelon of American society, defining the affiliations, deeds, and character traits necessary to excel in a merit-based hierarchy.[13]

Figure 24. Charles Willson Peale, *Thomas Mifflin*, 1784. Courtesy of Eastern National Park and Monument Association, Independence National Historical Park, Philadelphia.

Early national rhetoric divided the economy into three productive sectors—commerce, manufactures, and agriculture—providing contemporary categories for grouping many of Peale's subscribers. Ideally these three sectors operated in harmony with one another, but the rhythms of war and peace between Britain and France divided Americans along partisan lines. In the most inflammatory rhetoric, the executive branch's apparent sympathies for Britain were perceived to be the political legacy of Federalist Toryism, and popular sentiment toward France was seen as evidence of the terror to which democratization would lead. Legal struggles also demonstrated that the interests of these three sectors sometimes fell into sharp conflict. Manufacturers argued the necessity of patent laws, tariffs, and even embargoes to establish domestic markets, whereas commercial interests vehemently opposed such restrictions, seeing them as destructive of trade. Although the theater and circus audiences were split over these issues during the 1790s, the composition of Peale's audience demonstrates that not all cultural institutions were similarly divided.[14]

More of Peale's subscribers were employed in commercial occupations than in the other two sectors, reflecting the centrality of commerce to the port economy of Philadelphia. Of the 313 subscribers whose occupations were identified, 74 (24 percent) worked in jobs related to commerce: 42 merchants, 3 sea captains, 9 ironmongers, 6 grocers, 6 shopkeepers, 2 bankers, and 6 scriveners, conveyancers, notaries, or brokers. Twelve of the United States congressmen were also merchants, as were several state and local officials. Commercial subscribers were among Peale's wealthiest audience members, who contributed the distinction of economic success to the member list. For subscribers on the margins of this category, especially younger ones, affiliation with such wealthy merchants as James Calbraith may have been a public sign of aspiration. Peale, too, received special benefits from his association with commercial subscribers. The museum depended upon their international trade connections to bring him artifacts from Africa, South America, the South Pacific islands, and Asia. In addition, merchant John Swanwick exhibited his collection of Italian paintings at Peale's Museum in 1787.[15]

Mechanics and manufacturers subscribed to annual tickets, although not in the same proportion as their frequency in society (see table 1). Thirty-one subscribers (10 percent) were identified as craftsmen or manufacturers. Ten were leather workers or cloth workers, nine were carpenters or furniture makers, six were metalsmiths, four were printers, stationers, or booksellers, and one was a painter, one an engraver, one a distiller, and one a biscuit baker. The group of leather and cloth workers consisted of tailors, cordwainers, an upholsterer and umbrella maker, and a hatter. The carpenters were house builders, cabinetmakers, joiners, and a Windsor chair maker. Metalsmiths worked in gold, silver, tin, and copper, and one was a watchmaker, as Peale himself once had been. Mechanic-subscribers shared with the museum an interest in converting natural productions into manufactured goods, which Peale promoted in his emphasis on "useful knowledge." Engraver James Thackara and bookseller William Young Birch independently proposed the need for an illustrated encyclopedia, which would have served as a technological compendium. Works created by silversmith Christian Wiltberger, such as a teapot (figure 25) he produced about the time of his subscription, demonstrate his command of materials and contemporary style. Not themselves members of the economic elite, craftsmen like Wiltberger created the fine, custom furnishings that decorated the homes of such wealthy Philadelphians as Peale's commercial subscribers. Whereas Wiltberger's craftsmanship allowed him to participate peripherally in Philadelphia's high culture, Frederick Graff actually achieved the social position symbolized by his museum subscription. Graff was a carpenter at the time he subscribed, but rose to renown for his instrumental role in the transformation of the Philadelphia waterworks from a steam-driven system to a gravity-fed dam system. Although Graff's patronage of the museum probably did not enable this success, the museum provided an institutional framework in which technological innovation was promoted as a form of achievement worthy of public recognition. Peale would later more fully embrace this constituency by inviting local manufacturers to exhibit their products in the museum.[16]

Peale's principal audience had mainly an urban character; only John Adlum, remembered for his contribution to American wine-grape cultivation, may be identified principally with agricultural pursuits. However, thirteen subscribers who were United States congressmen were also planters or farmers (see appendix). Many more of Peale's subscribers recognized the importance of agriculture to a strong American economy through their membership in the Philadelphia Society for the Promotion of Agriculture. Among Peale's subscribers were twenty-five members and eight honorary members of the agricultural society. These were bankers, lawyers, merchants, ministers, and public officials, and their varied professions indicated the breadth of people who believed that agricultural independence was central to sustained political independence. Among this group of subscribers, John Beale Bordley was particularly active in writing pamphlets relating to American agricultural production.[17]

Peale received considerable support from Philadelphia's clergy, an occupational bloc that validated the museum as a place of moral education. Fourteen of Peale's subscribers were clergymen, and twelve of them purchased their tickets on the same day, probably on a group visit. In addition to those fourteen, four United States representatives were also ministers. These clergymen were ordained as Episcopalians, Presby-

Figure 25. Christian Wiltberger, *Teapot,* 1790–1810. Virginia Steele Scott Gallery, The Henry E. Huntington Library, Art Collections, and Botanical Gardens, gift of Elizabeth Fleming Rhodes.

terians, Baptists, and Lutherans. Peale's minister-subscribers had participated earlier in the year on both sides of the fight over the theater. As such, this coalition of ministers for and against the theater provided an important unified endorsement of Peale's claims that the museum advanced Christian reverence for nature and promoted a moral citizenry. Among the petitioners against the theater who endorsed Peale were Thomas Fleeson, Ashbel Green, Henry Helmuth, William Marshall, Joseph Pilmore, John Blair Smith, William Smith, and William White. Ministers tolerant of the theater who subscribed to annual tickets were Nicholas Collin, Samuel Magaw, John Andrews, and John Ewing. Nicholas Collin, the minister of the Swedish Church in Philadelphia, was a particularly avid supporter of the museum. He helped Peale both through his secular interests in natural history and by his status as a voice of the church. In 1793 Collin facilitated an exchange of bird specimens between the Philadelphia Museum and the Swedish Academy of Natural Sciences. In 1800 Collin published a series of articles proclaiming the religious and moral worth of Peale's lectures on natural history. Peale also enjoyed substantial support from Philadelphia's Quakers, the religious group most consistently opposed to the theater. Quakers among Peale's subscribers included John Ashbridge, the Bringhursts, Samuel Coates, Jasper Cope, the Cowperthwaites, Richard Hopkins, Thomas C. James, and the Marshalls, but there is no evidence about their individual views on the theater issue. Also among Peale's subscribers in 1794 was Henry Hill, the wealthy gentleman who orchestrated the pro-theater campaign on behalf of the stockholders of the New Theatre on Chestnut Street.[18]

Support from the clergy, a particularly well-educated group, helped Peale gain credibility for the museum as a place of learning. During the theater debate, "Philanthropos" dichotomized education and superstition. Ministers, true to their knowledge of "science and literature," "Philanthropos" proposed, would naturally abandon their opposition to rational entertainments. In this context, the academic achievements of Peale's minister-subscribers were particularly important. Many of Peale's minister-subscribers graduated from institutions of higher education, including the University of Pennsylvania, the College of New Jersey, the University of Halle, the University of Aberdeen, and Yale College. These educated ministers were among the faculty and administration of the University of Pennsylvania, an institution with which Peale actively sought to affiliate the museum. John Andrews, an Episcopal minister, was professor of moral philosophy and vice-provost at the time he purchased his ticket in 1794. John Ewing, a Presbyterian clergyman, was professor of natural philosophy and provost of the university, and Henry Helmuth, a Lutheran, was professor of German there. William Smith, an Episcopalian, had been professor of ethics and provost at the College of Philadelphia, which merged with its rival, the University of the State of Pennsylvania, in 1791 to form the consolidated University of Pennsylvania. Samuel Magaw, also an Episcopalian, had been professor of moral philosophy and vice-provost at the College of Philadelphia, and he resigned upon the consolidation, to prevent a contest between himself and his friend Andrews for the post they had each held at the separate institutions. Just as the museum portraits validated the power of several politician-subscribers, Peale's portraiture celebrated the prominence of two minister-subscribers. Peale hung an oil painting of William White in the museum and published an engraving of Joseph Pilmore. By grouping the print of Pilmore in a series that included images of George Washington and Benjamin Franklin, Peale elevated this clergyman to the status of founding father.[19]

Medical professionals made up another educated group of Peale's subscribers. At least sixteen physicians, five medical students from the University of Pennsylvania, and one dentist purchased annual tickets in 1794. These doctor-patrons taught at the University of Pennsylvania, practiced at the Pennsylvania Hospital and the Philadelphia Dispensary, and belonged to the College of Physicians of Philadelphia. Another four doctors were among the congressmen who subscribed in 1794. A number of Peale's exhibitions supported medical interests. Because mineralogy was a branch of chemistry in the medical school curriculum, Peale's mineral collections probably gained the attention of some physicians. Other exhibits more directly engaged medical knowledge. As early as 1795, Peale advertised displays of diseased samples from humans, such as skin and horn-shaped growths, and by 1808 he accessioned "human preparations" of apparently normal human limbs, organs, and a fetus. Physician Benjamin Rush proposed to Peale a gallery of portraits of the infirm, but Peale painted just a small group of subjects with skin pigmentation disorders and epithelial growths. As medical curiosities, Peale also exhibited portraits of people who lived extraordinarily long lives. Doctor-subscriber William Martin shared Peale's interest in this phenomenon, and he maintained a section in his copy book entitled "American Longevity." These displays may have been viewed either as medical case studies or as extremely sensational exhibits, but support from medical subscribers bolstered the scientific legitimacy of the collections. In turn, Peale paid homage to the medical profession by hanging portraits of prominent physicians in the gallery. Although none of the doctors who subscribed in 1794 were recognized in this manner, Peale did exhibit portraits of Benjamin Rush, James Woodhouse, and Caspar Wistar, each of whom patronized the museum in other ways.[20]

Strikingly few men whose primary occupation could be listed as scientist were among Peale's subscribers. One explanation for this absence is that the concept of professional scientist was somewhat of an anachronism in the 1790s. Even those individuals identified chiefly with scientific pursuits worked in other occupations. Frenchman François André Michaux was a botanist, who, like other eighteenth-century practitioners of this science, financed his work through a commercial garden. David Rittenhouse, a noted astronomer and mathematician, was also director of the United States Mint, an appointed position that credited his technological and organizational abilities. Similarly, many serious practitioners of science earned their living by other means. Rittenhouse's successor at the mint, Elias Boudinot, was a United States congressman from New Jersey when he purchased his annual ticket in 1794. Besides succeeding in politics, Boudinot made a significant contribution to early American science by donating money to the College of New Jersey to establish a cabinet of natural history specimens. Zaccheus Collins made a living as a merchant, and he, too, was actively involved in the scientific community. Collins was an avid botanist who collected, preserved, and arranged plant specimens, and he held offices in the American Philosophical Society and the more exclusive Academy of Natural Sciences. Notable among the scientifically interested minister-subscribers were John Ewing, who pursued the study of astronomy and William Smith, who taught chemistry at the College of Philadelphia.[21]

Although the educated elite among Peale's subscribers included clergy, university-educated doctors, and scientists, just a handful of Philadelphia's many private instructors and boarding-school operators purchased annual tickets. In 1794, only subscribers Joseph Sharpless and Benjamin Tucker were schoolmasters, and John C. Moller was a music instructor and a member of the Philadelphia City Concert. Perhaps Peale's admission policies restricted the utility of annual tickets to such teachers. Only the person whose name appeared on the ticket could use it for admission, so a teacher could not use an annual ticket to send students to the museum. Peale later revised that policy to accommodate educators. In 1825, Peale recorded the sale of seven group tickets that read like the one made out to "School 2 pupils at one time & teacher."[22]

Peale's restriction of a ticket to a single person may also have limited the usefulness of subscriptions to innkeepers, who were closely involved in the promotion of public leisure in Philadelphia. Because inns and taverns were the center of a great deal of social and political activity in the early national period, the absence of such prominent hotel keepers as Philip Oellers is as important as the presence of subscribers George Hill, an innkeeper, and Benjamin Horn, a taverner. Hotel proprietors hosted balls, lectures, concerts, and animal exhibits, and they sold tickets for promoters of other amusements. Oellers, Peale's near neighbor to the west on Chestnut Street, was notable for his offerings of grand balls and public holiday celebrations. The notation "Not Transferable" on the annual ticket may have been devised in part to prevent innkeepers from sharing an annual ticket with their lodgers. Peale was particularly aware of the importance of "strangers" or travelers to his patron base and, probably in a moment of exaggeration, once claimed that more strangers than Philadelphians were members of his audience.[23]

In addition to public affiliations and occupations, wealth and its display marked social status among early national Americans. In the ranking of Peale's subscribers according to their taxable wealth by occupation (table 2), the United States senators were assessed the highest property values, whereas surveyors and those whose occupations were unidentified received the lowest assessments. Mechanics ranked consistently lower than people employed in commercial pursuits. Of the well-educated subscribers, attorneys and clergymen ranked in the upper half, whereas doctors were at the lower end of the scale. However, individuals within an occupational group represented a wide range of levels of wealth. For example, the wealth of the merchants among Peale's subscribers ranged from the lowest to the highest 10 percent, relative

Table 2: Ranked Average Wealth of Peale's Subscribers (*N* = 162) by Occupation, 1794

Occupation (*N*)	Average Wealth (Pounds)	Percentile
U.S. Senator (2)	4,548	90th
Elected Official, Pa. (4)	3,405	90th
Banker (2)	1,977	80th
Gentleman (7)	1,690	80th
U.S. Representative (3)	1,167	70th
Scientist (1)	1,161	70th
Elected Official, Philadelphia, City or County (5)	995	70th
Appointed Public Official, Federal, State, or Local (20)	935	70th
Merchant (28)	613	60th
Apothecary (2)	561	60th
Dentist (1)	558	60th
Attorney (6)	522	60th
Ironmonger (9)	377	60th
Clergyman (9)	294	50th
Bookseller, Stationer, or Printer (4)	200	50th
Scrivener, Conveyancer, or Broker (5)	172	50th
Distiller (1)	106	40th
Innkeeper (1)	54	30th
Carpenter or Furniture Maker (5)	51	30th
Leather or Cloth Worker (6)	49	30th
Grocer (3)	47	30th
Doctor (9)	39	20th
Painter or Printmaker (2)	38	20th
Shopkeeper (5)	30	20th
Metal Worker (6)	28	20th
Clerk (11)	26	20th
Educator (1)	4	10th
Surveyor (2)	0	Zero
Unidentified (2)	0	Zero

to that of other subscribers (appendix). Stuart Blumin proposed that, in wealth and status, the middling ranks of society were in fact closer to the lower sort than they were to the elite. However, some Philadelphians of the middling sort asserted their place as respectable citizens by means of subscription to Peale's Museum and through other public associations. Whatever their material circumstances, through the act of subscribing, Peale's audience members joined the ranks of other refined members of society who appreciated science, art, religion, history, and moral education.[24]

Figure 26. Bishop William White House, Philadelphia. Courtesy of Eastern National Park and Monument Association, Independence National Historical Park, Philadelphia.

The most significant marker of wealth was the home in which a person lived, whether that person owned or rented it. Peale's subscribers were slightly more likely than average to own their home. Whereas 29 percent (forty-seven) of Peale's subscribers for whom assessments were found owned their homes, only 19 percent of Philadelphians in 1774 could make this claim. Many of Peale's wealthiest subscribers, including United States Secretary of the Treasury Alexander Hamilton, Secretary of State Edmund Randolph, and Secretary of War Henry Knox, rented their houses, and their tax assessments suggest that they occupied spacious living quarters. George Latimer, for example, rented a dwelling in New Market Ward that received the fourth highest assessment of any property inhabited by a Peale subscriber. The grandeur of Latimer's home surely announced his high social status. Seventy-four subscribers (46 percent) rented their primary residence and another two subscribers both owned and rented property. The renters included silversmith Christian Wiltberger, engraver James Thackara, painter Matthew Pratt, clerk John Stagg, Jr., schoolmaster Joseph Sharpless, and shopkeepers Jasper Cope and Edward Bartlett, whose assessments suggest more modest living arrangements. Many of Peale's subscribers (25 percent, or forty-one of the subscribers assessed) neither owned nor rented property, and therefore must have been still living with their parents or boarding. Those whose assessments included, in addition to a primary residence, property that was undeveloped or that was rented to others, were accorded further social distinction. By this standard, William Bingham was by far the wealthiest subscriber because of the other houses, offices, stables, and lots for which he was assessed. The clarity with which one's dwelling asserted social standing may be demonstrated by comparing subscriber William White's stately brick house (figure 26) with the more modest brick houses in contemporary Philadelphia (figure 27). Such shopkeepers as Edward Bartlett and such skilled laborers as Christian Wiltberger probably occupied houses of this smaller type. The third story, the broader street frontage, and the greater depth of White's house were clear signs of his elevated social position.[25]

Slaveholding among Peale's subscribers was another mark of their wealth, although the museum membership was widely divided on the propriety of this institution. Perhaps twenty-one of the subscribers shared Peale's material interest in perpetuating slavery. The slave for whom Peale was taxed in 1794 was probably Moses Williams, who was later manumitted and worked as the silhouette cutter at the museum. Other slaveholders included gentleman John Beale Bordley, judges Benjamin Chew and Edward Shippen, banker John Nixon, scientist David Rittenhouse, merchant James Calbraith, and silversmith Christian Wiltberger. In addition to twelve subscribers whose taxable property included at least one slave, George Washington and eight southern congress-

Figure 27. John Moran, *Queen Street between Swanson and Front Streets,* Philadelphia, 1867. The Library Company of Philadelphia.

men who were also planters by occupation were slaveholders. Another twenty-six of Peale's patrons were taxed for indentured servants. On the other hand, several of Peale's subscribers actively opposed slavery through their affiliation with the Pennsylvania Society for Promoting the Abolition of Slavery (Nicholas Collin, Miers Fisher, Samuel P. Griffitts, Caleb Lowne, John McCrea, and Richard Wells). With respect to the museum, as in society at large, the issue of slavery was more than just whether or not a person could afford a slave. Peale mounted a number of exhibitions, discussed in chapter 7, that proposed the place of nonwhites within a harmonious society. That members of Peale's audience both owned slaves and worked for the abolition of this institution indicates the potential for divergent responses to these displays.[26]

Although Philadelphia was considered a "walking city," one that was traversable by foot, the ownership of horses or carriages distinguished the socially elevated from those beneath them. The term "walking city" describes not only a mode of transportation, but also an ideal in early Philadelphia that hierarchies would be obscured by the proximity of people of all ranks to one another. The discovery, then, that sixty-four of the assessed subscribers (40 percent) were able to arrive at the museum on horseback or in some type of horse-drawn conveyance conflicts with this vision (table 3). Instead of indicating unity across social rank, this finding suggests that wealthy patrons of Peale's Museum materially demonstrated their high social standing.[27]

Peale's Museum was not the only cultural institution with which the subscribers affiliated. Peale's patrons maintained memberships or affiliations with Philadelphia's institutions of learning—in particular, the American Philosophical Society, the University of Pennsylvania, and the Library Company of Philadelphia (table 4). In chapter 1, it was explained how Peale emphasized his own attachments to these institutions to promote the museum's reputation as a serious enterprise. Of Peale's subscribers, 142 (35 percent) were similarly affiliated to at least one of these three institutions. Of the fifty-three museum subscribers who were also members of the American Philosophical Society, twenty-one held offices in the society. Like Charles Willson Peale, five subscribers—William Bradford, Nicholas Collin, Zaccheus Collins, William Hembel, Jr., and David Rittenhouse—served as curators of the society. The sixty-six affiliates of the University of Pennsylvania were non-degree-earning matriculates; graduates who earned a B.A., B.M., A.M., M.D., LL.D., or D.D.; recipients of honorary degrees (A.M., LL.D., or D.D.); or officers and professors of the university. The ninety-five subscribers identified with an interest in the Library Company of Philadelphia were all shareholders, which entitled them to borrowing privileges. The Library Company

Table 3: Distribution of Riding Equipment and Horses among Peale's Subscribers, 1794, Grouped by Level of Wealth

Level of Wealth (Percentile)	Owners of Riding Equipment	Owners of Horses	Owners of Either
90th	15	16	16
80th	12	14	14
70th	9	10	11
60th	6	8	8
50th	3	6	7
40th	4	5	5
30th	1	2	2
20th	0	1	1
10th	0	0	0
Zero	0	0	0

shareholders were a socially broader group than affiliates of the other two institutions, and included a shopkeeper (William Hembel, Jr.), a printer (John Ormrod), an engraver (James Thackara), and a goldsmith (Rowland Parry).[28]

A significant portion of the subscribers asserted their place as culturally interested citizens through repeated patronage of Peale and the several institutions that he helped to establish. Sixty-six of the people who subscribed in 1794 were continued supporters of Peale in one or several ways. Twenty of these sixty-six purchased annual tickets in at least one subsequent year. The most devoted patron of Peale's projects was John Beale Bordley, earlier known as a Maryland planter and by 1794 a Philadelphia gentleman. Bordley was the key sponsor of Peale's trip in 1767 to study with Benjamin West in London, and he was a member of the museum's Board of Visitors, a donor to the museum's library, and a return subscriber to annual tickets. Among the twenty-seven members of Peale's 1792 Board of Visitors, eighteen were subscribers in 1794. Peale's project in 1795 was the formation of the Columbianum, or American Academy of the Fine Arts. Six of its thirty-two founding members were subscribers to the museum in the previous year. In addition to those six, Philip D. Price was both a subscriber to Peale's Museum and a member of the rival Columbianum that emerged in opposition to the one Peale supported. Ten years later Peale helped to found the Pennsylvania Academy of the Fine Arts, still a vital art school and gallery, and six of Peale's 1794 subscribers were also charter members of this academy. Among those six was the academy's first president, George Clymer. Twenty-nine of the subscribers from 1794 sat for privately commissioned portraits,

Table 4: Affiliations of Peale's Subscribers in 1794 with Institutions of Learning

Affiliation with:	American Philosophical Society (APS)	University of Pa. (UP)	Library Company of Philadelphia (LCP)
Only One Institution	11	28	55
APS and Another		8	10
UP and Another	8		6
LCP and Another	10	6	
All Three	24	24	24
Total	53	66	95
% of Peale's Patrons	13.2	16.5	23.7

either miniatures or oil paintings, by Peale. Peale clearly benefitted from his reliable base of patrons, but these loyal subscribers also gained through their continued association with Peale. For instance, a request to serve on the board of the museum singled out a select group of patrons as esteemed members of society. Peale also honored twenty subscribers by including their portraits among those of other important men of the Revolution, government, or science.[29]

Peale's subscribers may be grouped according to other social units, including gender, familial attachments, proximity to the museum, and neighborhood. To a great extent, the very idea of a public self was gender-specifically male, as early national women were expected to define themselves through their domestic lives. Peale's subscribers are a case in point. Of the 401 signatures recorded in 1794, only 5 names are clearly those of women (about 1 percent): Elizabeth F. Marshall, Margaret Marshall, Margaret Meredith, Abigail Parent, and Mrs. Smiley. Of these five women, all but Abigail Parent signed the book along with a male family member. In the most extreme instance, the inscription "Mrs. Meredith" follows Samuel Meredith's signature in the same handwriting, suggesting that he signed for himself and his wife. The actual number of women who held annual tickets may be expanded by noting that forty-four subscribers purchased an additional fifty-eight tickets for unnamed patrons. Even if all of the extra tickets were for women, as the ones purchased under the signature "Deglos & son espouse," clearly were for a husband and wife, the percentage of women among the group remains at a low 16 percent (63 of 459). And because those ticket holders remained anonymous, women were almost categorically excluded from the distinction of "Friends of Science" that Peale offered to his subscribers.[30]

Patterns of ticket purchases suggest that familial attachment was among the defining characteristics of Peale's audience. Benjamin Chew and his son Benjamin Chew, Jr., each purchased tickets on January 29, 1794. Likewise, John Beale Bordley and his stepson John F. Mifflin made same-day purchases of annual tickets. James Bringhurst and his nephew Joseph Bringhurst, Jr., both purchased tickets on February 5. Charles Marshall, Jr., bought his ticket in July, and his uncle's family purchased three tickets in December. This uncle, Christopher Marshall, Jr., was the apothecary partner of Charles Marshall, the father of the young man who purchased his ticket earlier in the year and who apparently worked in family business. Signatures following Christopher's in the subscription book were those of Margaret Marshall, his wife, and Elizabeth F. Marshall, his daughter by a previous marriage to the late Elizabeth Flower. In August, Zaccheus Collins, a son-in-law of Christopher Marshall, Jr., purchased an annual ticket. Peale's own kinship ties were reflected in patronage: subscriber John Stagg, Jr., and Peale were brothers-in-law. Stagg was married to Margaret DePeyster

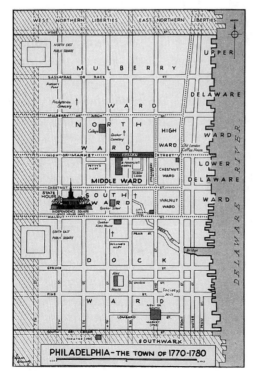

Figure 28. *Above:* John Hills, *Plan of the City of Philadelphia and Its Environs,* 1796. The Library Company of Philadelphia. *Left:* Philadelphia, 1770–80. Peale exhibited his collections in the outbuildings to his home on the southwest corner of Third and Lombard Streets. In 1794, he moved to Philosophical Hall, located on the west side of Fifth Street, just south of Chestnut. Philosophical Hall is situated on the State House yard, which encompasses the block from Fifth to Sixth Street and from Chestnut to Walnut Street. Peale expanded his display space in 1802 to the upper floor of the State House. By 1794 Mulberry Ward was divided into North and South Mulberry Wards along Race Street, and Dock Ward was divided into Dock and New Market Wards. The new Dock Ward spanned from Walnut to Spruce Street. Source for map at left: Sam Bass Warner, Jr., *The Private City: Philadelphia in Three Periods of Its Growth* (Philadelphia: University of Pennsylvania Press, 1968), p. 2. Source for ward divisions: Jefferson Moak, Philadelphia City Archives.

and Peale to Elizabeth DePeyster. The repetition of seventy-one surnames in subsequent years of the subscription book further suggests that families participated together in public leisure.[31]

Proximity to the museum may have been a secondary factor in attracting subscribers, and Peale's move in 1794 to a central part of the city facilitated access for most subscribers. In fact, Peale's relocation to Philosophical Hall from his home on Lombard Street (figure 28) halved the distance that his urban subscribers had to travel, on average, to the museum (table 5). Because settlement was densest along the Delaware River and in the central wards of the city, after 1794 Peale's Museum served a more highly concentrated pool of actual and potential patrons. Peale continued this ease of access when in 1802 he moved next door into the State House.[32]

The distribution of Peale's patrons throughout the city reflects settlement patterns of the population at large. Peale's subscribers were most heavily concentrated along the Delaware River and in the center of the city, from Walnut Street to Arch Street (figure 28). This distribution is significant because the population of each neighborhood had distinguishing characteristics. In contrast to observations of the historical walking city, Stuart Blumin demonstrated that high nonmanual workers more often lived in the core, whereas low nonmanual workers typically resided on the periphery. Peale's subscribers generally mirrored this pattern, so proximity to the museum was further indication of one's social standing.[33]

Finally, the importance of neighborhoods as early national social units extended to common participation in public culture. Thirty-five subscribers who lived next to one

Table 5: Average Number of Blocks Traveled by Subscribers to Peale's Museum at the Two Locations It Occupied in 1794

Place Ticket Was Purchased	Lombard Street	Philosophical Hall	Difference
Lombard Street			
All Subscribers	5.33	2.07	3.26
All except Congressmen	4.84	3.56	1.28
Ambiguous	6.08	4.75	1.33
Philosophical Hall			
All Subscribers	5.96	4.22	1.74
All except Congressmen	5.96	4.32	1.64
Average	5.53	2.75	2.78

another purchased tickets to Peale's Museum on the same day. Merchant John Brown (40 Pine Street), gentlemen Thomas Lloyd Moore (42 Pine Street), and former proprietor of Pennsylvania John Penn (44 Pine Street) purchased consecutive tickets on January 30, 1794. In addition to being his neighbor, Thomas Lloyd Moore also owned the house in which John Penn lived. Another eight pairs of neighbors purchased consecutive pairs of annual tickets, and sixteen more subscribers had consecutive addresses but purchased their tickets on separate days.[34]

Analysis of Peale's subscriber base reveals a complex picture of the social dynamics among early national patrons of learning and leisure. Public affiliation was a widely practiced means of asserting social equality, and Peale extended the distinction of "Friend of Science" to Philadelphians living in widely dissimilar social circumstances. Yet two broad categories of people—women and the unskilled labor force—were largely excluded. Even for those included, subscriptions and other voluntary affiliations offered perhaps no more than the illusion of community. Through such memberships, individuals on the lower margins of "respectability" maintained a sense of connectedness to the larger civic enterprise. Yet these associations did not advance their material lives. Despite their shared place in a public record, some subscribers lived in grand homes and others in spare ones, some rode through town and others walked, and a select few saw their likenesses held up as examples to the rest of the museum's audience.

6. Donors of Minerals, Natural Resources, and American Manufactures

THROUGH THE objects they presented to the museum, donors at once responded to previous visits, expressed personal and professional interests, and helped to shape future exhibits. Peale depended upon such gifts to continually expand the collections, and he encouraged this form of support through his advertising campaign. Donors gained recognition for their philanthropic gestures, as Peale regularly published brief descriptions of recent acquisitions and identified the contributor of each item. Like subscribers to annual tickets, donors participated in an exchange with Peale that benefitted themselves and the museum. Through gifts of minerals, natural resources, and American products, Peale's audience served the museum by improving the collections and aided themselves by solidifying their public identities as miners, manufacturers, scientists, teachers, and inventors. At the same time, Peale and his donors promoted the link between the study of natural history and the advancement of the nation's economic potential.

Contemporary visual representations suggest the eventual extent and arrangement of Peale's mineral collections. A floor plan drawn by George Escol Sellers, Peale's grandson, indicates that the mineral display filled seven cases in the museum (figure 29). In *The Long Room* (figure 13), Titian Ramsay Peale II and Charles Willson Peale delineated the form of these cabinets and the approximate density of the arrangement. Each case was glazed by three panels horizontally and four panels vertically. In a letter to mineral collector Stephen Elliott, Peale noted that the glass panels measured twelve by sixteen inches, providing a total display area of four feet by four feet per case. The watercolor indicates that, on each of three or four shelves per panel, Peale placed approximately four specimens, suggesting a display of almost twelve hundred minerals. The actual size of the collection was considerably larger; Peale estimated in 1819 that the mineral specimens numbered about eight thousand.[1]

Although the mineral collection grew to a significant size, its origins were humble. In 1787 Manasseh Cutler described the display of minerals and clays at the bottom of a diorama that included a tree and a number of preserved animals. The collection expanded gradually through gifts from Peale's audience. Benjamin Franklin made the

107

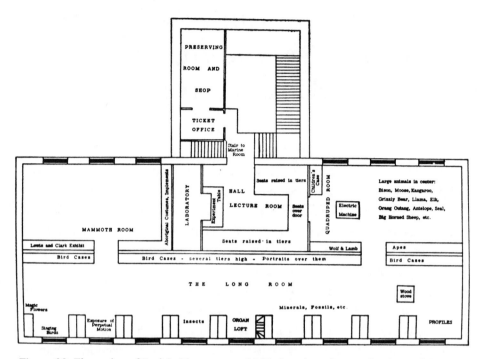

Figure 29. Floor plan of Peale's Museum, ca. 1820, based on the recollections of George Escol Sellers. American Philosophical Society, Philadelphia.

first significant donations of minerals, including specimens from Derbyshire, England, in 1788 and Scotland in 1791. Peale's first concerted effort to collect minerals for the museum followed a recommendation in 1792 by the Board of Visitors that he acquire a collection of European minerals for comparison to American specimens. Peale announced to the board his intentions for the future direction of the museum, including "a small display of the minerals and Fossils that I have collected, the collecting and arrangement of which I conceive may [be] made an important class of this Museum and be highly usefull to America." In July a committee of the board—John Beale Bordley, Caspar Wistar, and John Vaughan—endorsed the importance of an expanded mineral collection. Echoing Peale's concern with "useful knowledge," the Board of Visitors identified an economic motive for forming such a collection. Greater knowledge of American minerals would attract "landed Men . . . to attend to the Concerns of Natural History." Clearly that segment of Peale's audience would gain most from "knowledge of the useful or curious Clays, Minerals, and other Fossils that are within the Bowels of their own Lands."[2]

During the next two years, Peale publicly requested donations of mineral specimens and other natural resources in terms that expressed the economic stakes of the collections. In a notice published in the *General Advertiser* in 1793, Peale asked donors to supply a description of each mineral's identifying characteristics, where it was found, whether it was abundant or scarce, and whether or not it was easily collected. By accumulating such data, the museum would store both minerals and the information necessary to facilitate their excavation. As the board had done, Peale identified in his advertisement the economically interested audience for a mineral collection as "the land-holder." In his next plea for donations, Peale broadened his list of desired items, asking for "specimens of the various kinds of wood growing in America" and "all sorts of Fossils, Minerals, Spars, Stones, Sand, Clay, Marle and earthly substances." Peale also expanded his notion of interested parties from landowners to manufacturers who might transform the materials into saleable products, "especially in the manufacturing of Porcelain, Earthen and Stone wares, and in the various useful metals." Peale's request for marl, a naturally occurring fertilizer, may have implied a benefit to agricultural interests as well.[3]

A number of donors shared Peale's interest in the economic significance of American minerals. Mining and refining were among the earliest American industrial pursuits, and donors registered their place in the production of raw metals by giving to the museum specimens from their mines and foundries. Reiterating the terms of Peale's early requests for donations, published lists suggested the future benefits of mineralogical collections to American landholders. In 1795, for instance, Peale listed recent acquisitions in the *Aurora,* including "a piece of the root of a walnut tree impregnated with iron ore found on the land of Gen. J. Chambers in Franklin county, Pennsylvania, the walnut tree falling down, discovered a bed of ore: presented by gen. Chambers." Although this item implies that James Chambers stumbled into the iron business, his Loudon Iron Works (established circa 1790) at Franklin County was just one of several operated by generations of his family.[4]

Daniel Buckley, Peale's most generous donor of metal ores, also promoted his personal interest in numerous mines through gifts to the museum. Buckley entered the business in partnership with his brothers-in-law Thomas Brooke and Matthew Brooke, Jr., when they purchased Hopewell Furnace in Berks County, Pennsylvania, in 1800. Among Buckley's first contributions to the museum were samples of iron ore used at Hopewell, as well as ore from their mine, Jones Good Luck Mine. The entry for the latter specimen noted that the ore was used at Warwick Furnace of Chester County, Pennsylvania, and Joanna Furnace in Berks County, documenting Buckley's connection with competing furnaces. Buckley's donation of an iron specimen from

Cornwall Furnace further hints at his business relationship with other prominent producers. Iron ores from Lancaster and Chester Counties, from Baltimore, and from Zanesville, Ohio, constituted Buckley's other gifts to Peale's Museum, and suggest the extent of the donor's business contacts.[5]

Although these donors were promoting their self-interest through such gifts to the museum, their actions were also linked to contemporary concern with the need to develop American manufactures. In the 1790s economically minded men like Alexander Hamilton and Tench Coxe (both patrons of the museum) expressed the importance of developing American manufactures to the long-term security of a national economy. Only by developing these industries could the country gain economic independence from commercial fluctuations caused by European naval wars. Institutions were established to promote these goals, including, in 1787, the Pennsylvania Society for the Encouragement of American Manufactures and the Useful Arts. Proponents of the movement published their arguments in pamphlets and in letters to the newspaper editors. Encouragement of American manufacturers became a standard topic of salutes at public celebrations, and these, too, were printed in the newspapers. A toast offered at the 1809 anniversary dinner of the Tammany Society in Philadelphia is typical: "Manufactures—A new declaration of independence, and a release from our broad cloth bondage, by an honest patronage of domestic industry. 2 guns, 17 cheers—music, The Loom and the Shuttle." Patriotic music followed public toasts, and the song title "The Loom and the Shuttle" connects advancement of the textile industry with freedom from "broad cloth bondage."[6]

The American manufactures movement gained momentum after the British ship *Leopard* attacked the American frigate *Chesapeake* in 1807. The Jefferson administration responded with legislation first restricting, then completely halting, trade with Europe. During the embargo, manufacturing societies proliferated, not just in Philadelphia, but also in Baltimore, Washington City, and Charleston. While the American manufactures movement gained greater attention in the press, Peale in 1808 asked his audience to contribute examples of their products:

> [A]s the subject of domestic manufacture deservedly occupies universal attention, and the Museum already possesses many interesting articles of home made manufacture, in connections with the natural productions of our country; manufacturers are solicited to send to the proprietor SPECIMENS of their work, to be in a more important manner exhibited to the public[.]

Despite Peale's tardiness in endorsing the movement publicly, his collection of minerals was probably perceived to serve its aims. A toast presented at the Manufacturers' and Mechanics' Dinner of 1809, for example, links minerals with the larger cause: "The clays and the metals, the soil and the sinews of America—More valuable than the mines of Potosi." Following Peale's request for American manufactures, makers of ceramics, textiles, and artists' supplies proclaimed their contributions to the national cause by donating their raw materials and finished products to Peale's Museum. Simultaneously, exhibitions within the museum promoted the financial interests of individual manufacturers who responded to Peale's call for donations.[7]

Producers of ceramics donated samples of their clays and glaze materials, as well as finished goods ranging in quality from everyday stoneware and earthenware to finer queensware. In 1808, the year that he opened his pottery in partnership with typefounders Archibald Binny and James Ronaldson, Alexander Trotter contributed local clay and quartz, which made up the body of his wares, feldspar used in glazes, and English clay for comparison. Trotter was building a reputation for the production of queensware, a common import, and the accession record elevated the enterprise to "Porcelain manufactory." The elevation of queensware to porcelain indicates nationalist sentiment that American manufactures would immediately rival the finest imports. Unlike Daniel Buckley, who donated only raw materials from his iron business, Trotter also contributed examples of redware, and unfinished white ware and yellowware. The connection between Trotter's business and Peale's Museum continued beyond the enthusiasm over the embargo. Robert Griffith, a craftsman employed by Trotter, Binny, and Ronaldson's Columbian Pottery, later presented "a Cup and Saucer, and Tumbler, of queens ware" to the museum.[8]

Other local potters responded to Peale's invitation to promote their wares in the name of American economic development. Branch Green, a potter who relocated from New Jersey to Philadelphia, advertised his Germantown stoneware factory through donations to Peale's Museum. Green contributed clay and four pieces of his stoneware to the Peale collection of American manufactures. Chester County potter Thomas Vickers presented a sample of clay from Delaware, a piece of earthenware, and a stoneware "Porter Bottle." For comparative purposes Peale included in his displays examples of European pottery, including an English creamware jug and two Derbyshire vases. In this way, the display of American manufactures mirrored the mineral collection, each holding native productions up to the example of foreign counterparts.[9]

During this period Peale also acquired examples of American textiles, an industry which many believed should be the cornerstone of a national economy. In 1802 an industry proponent identified only as "Franklin" expounded, in the *Aurora. General Advertiser,* the view that cotton would provide the best opportunity for an integrated national economy, that production would be a boon to the South in particular, that new laborsaving technology would make the industry increasingly viable, and that interstate coastal trade would significantly expand. Each of these eventualities would decrease American dependence upon trade with Europe. This argument echoed the plan offered by Tench Coxe as well as the declared mission of the Pennsylvania Society for the Encouragement of Manufactures and the Useful Arts. Although Peale apparently did not display cotton, he did exhibit the wool and finished material produced at David Humphreys' woolen mill in Connecticut in 1802. Peale's published list of recent accessions described Humphreys' donation as a "specimen of superfine broad cloth, which obtained the first premium from the Domestic manufacturing society of Philadelphia—and a specimen of second quality—both made by col. Humphreys of New Haven. Specimens of wool of the Merino sheep, full blooded and mixt." The premium was probably awarded by the newly instituted Philadelphia Premium Society, which announced its first set of awards in July 1808. In order to compete for the fifty-dollar prize, the maker of "the best piece of superfine broad cloth" had to produce it from wool shorn from living sheep and had to approximate the best imports. Peale honored Humphreys by including his portrait in the gallery, but celebrated him first as a diplomat, then a poet, and finally a manufacturer. Peale's donors further advanced their interests in the textile industry by giving minerals used to dye cloth. Linen printer Thomas Bedwell contributed alum, a natural salt that facilitates the adhesion of dyes to cloth, to the museum in 1805.[10]

Silvain Godon and his partner Rubens Peale publicized their paint factory through donations to Peale's Museum. Godon and Rubens Peale produced a bright yellow paint by combining lead with chromic acid, which they derived from naturally occurring chromate of iron. Peale and Godon donated specimens of the mineral source and a sample of the finished chromate of yellow paint to the museum in 1809. Despite initial optimism about the potential profitability of the venture, Charles Willson Peale encouraged his son to sell his share in the business, since the pigment discolored when exposed to light. Rubens seems to have escaped unscathed from the failure of the business, but in 1812 Godon was in prison, apparently for debts incurred. Although display in the museum may have improved the business prospects of some donors, it was not enough to rescue this ill-fated product.[11]

Talbot Hamilton also contributed mineral specimens that related to the production of fine arts materials. Not himself a manufacturer, Hamilton's donation identified him as a benefactor to the fine arts. Hamilton's obituary indicates his dedication to the arts, and his will, witnessed by landscape painter Thomas Birch, lists the paintings and prints bequeathed to the Pennsylvania Academy of the Fine Arts. Charles Willson Peale, of course, is noted as one of the founders of the academy. Hamilton also proclaimed this interest through his donation of minerals to Peale's Museum. In 1807 Hamilton presented specimens of two minerals used to manufacture art supplies: black chalk used for drawing and red ochre, a pigment used in manufacturing paint.[12]

Whereas Peale's manufacturer-donors were interested in mastery of the land for production, a small group of contributors were interested in control over natural resources for the larger project of nation building. Most notably, Thomas Jefferson, through the gift of minerals from the Lewis and Clark expedition, asserted American dominion over the newly purchased Louisiana territory. Augustus Edward Jessup and Titian Peale later donated minerals from the Long Expedition, another scientific and military demonstration of control over the American West. The museum, in turn, validated the importance of these naturalists and explorers by including portraits of Lewis, Clark, Jessup, Titian Peale, and other members of the Long Party in the gallery. Jefferson's likeness also held a place of honor in the museum, although the portrait catalogue celebrated him primarily as a statesman. Marquis d'Yrujo, the Spanish minister plenipotentiary to the United States, asserted the extent of his nation's empire by contributing "a handsome collection of woods, shells, and minerals which was brought from the Island of Luconia one of the principal Philippine Islands." Peale advertised the new collection of 133 specimens and requested that an American donor respond by contributing samples of wood from all the trees native to this country. In terms that exemplify the nationalism inherent in such collection building, Peale asserted, "there can be no doubt but in the United States of America, there will be found a very great, rich and beautiful variety of woods, far beyond what our general ideas on this subject led us to suppose." Despite Peale's certainty on this matter, he apparently never received a large donation of American wood specimens.[13]

In addition to promoting a material interest in the mineral collections, Peale established a scientific context by continually rearranging the display according to then-current mineralogical practices. In his first systematic classification of the minerals in 1793, Peale relied on Linnaeus and on Ephraim Chambers's *Cyclopaedia: or An Universal Dictionary of Arts and Sciences.* The Linnaean system divided all minerals into four basic crystal shapes—hexagonal prism, cube, tetragonal prism, and octahedron. Chambers grouped minerals in seven categories—metals, salts, sulphurs, semimetals, stones, gems, and petrifactions—and described their physical and chemical properties, geographical and geological distribution, and technological details about processing for use. In the supplement to Chambers's encyclopedia, the editor, G. L. Scott, emphasized the chemical composition over other qualities, and classified minerals like animals, into orders, families, genera, and species. By 1804 Peale rearranged the collection according to Richard Kirwan's *Elements of Mineralogy,* which divided minerals into earths and stones, salts, inflammables, and metals, and classified them according to externally observable physical properties. Rubens Peale later reordered the collections on the basis of Parker Cleaveland's system, which grouped minerals by their internal crystal structure. Although none of these systems precluded the economic potential of minerals, only Chambers offered technological information on how to process them for use.[14]

Among Peale's scientific audience for the minerals, none was as deeply committed to the problems of classification as René-Just Haüy. Charles Willson Peale pronounced this Frenchman "the most profound mineralogist in Europe," probably in acknowledgment of Haüy's contribution to a new branch of science called crystallography. According to Haüy's theory, minerals should be grouped according to their internal crystal structure, not their outward physical qualities. Rembrandt Peale, traveling in Europe to add portraits to his father's collection, established contact with the eminent French scientist. Rembrandt encouraged Haüy to support American interest in mineralogy, and Haüy responded by donating to Peale's Museum two collections of minerals gathered primarily in Europe. The donation served to promote Haüy's new classification system insofar as each specimen was labeled according to the shape of its crystal: "mesotype pyramide" (pyramidal zeolite), "anitimoine oxyde aciculaire" (needle-shaped muriated antimony), and "amphibole dodicaidre" (dodecahedral hornblende). The museum endorsed Haüy's ideas when Rubens Peale adopted the crystallographic system after Parker Cleaveland described it for readers in English. Charles Willson Peale validated Haüy's eminence within the field by adding his portrait to the museum in 1808 (figure 30).[15]

Haüy also presented Peale with copies of his publications and related minerals to support the superiority of his new approach to mineral classification. For instance, in 1808 Haüy donated a copy of his essay "Sur l'arragonite" and examples of the minerals discussed therein. To Haüy, this article proved his theory that crystal structure was a more accurate means than chemical analysis of classifying minerals, so he believed that its place in the museum commemorated a turning point in the history of science. Haüy made his case by comparing aragonite to calcite. The chemical composition of the two minerals denoted them members of the same class, whereas their crystal structure indicated their dissimilarity. Despite Haüy's confidence that this comparison secured the primacy of his theory over others, a German chemist used the same evidence to argue that both chemical composition and crystal structure were essential to a comprehensive analysis.[16]

Peale's American donors of minerals included a number of gentleman amateurs who actively participated in Philadelphia's learned societies. Their contributions to the mu-

Figure 30. Rembrandt Peale, *Abbé René-Just Haüy*, 1808. Mr. and Mrs. Fred D. Bentley, Sr.

seum demonstrated that their accomplishments reached beyond economic success to encompass the attainment of scientific knowledge. These donors include merchants Zaccheus Collins, Reuben Haines, and Charles J. Wister; printer and bookseller Solomon W. Conrad; and attorney Mahlon Dickerson; all of whom were Philadelphians, and planter Stephen Elliott of Beaufort, South Carolina. These men belonged to the American Philosophical Society, an institution of demonstrated importance to Peale's legitimacy, and some also belonged to the Academy of Natural Sciences (which was established later). In addition to donating to the museum, thus publicly expressing their interest in mineralogy, some of these men maintained private cabinets in their homes. Like the women who compiled silhouette albums, these audience members participated in the activities of collecting, ordering, and displaying that Peale exemplified to the community. Elliott's cabinet also contained preserved birds, and having interests ranging to plant life as well, he exchanged information on these subjects and shared specimens with the Peales. A portion of the cabinet accumulated by Reuben Haines remains intact and on exhibit at the Haines homestead, Wyck, now a historic house museum in Germantown, Pennsylvania.[17]

Joseph Cloud, who was "the Melter and Refiner" of the United States Mint, expressed an interest in both science and manufactures through his affiliation with the museum. In pursuit of knowledge that served both his occupation and his interest in chemistry, Cloud was involved in improving the technology for separating metals from their ores. In September 1808 Peale paid eleven dollars for "Mr. Clouds Blowpipe made of Copper." Soon after, Peale advertised spectacular evening demonstrations of the blowpipe in which metals were combusted by the intense heat that the machine generated. Cloud experimented with the blowpipe, extracting palladium from gold ore and then comparing the properties of palladium and platinum. The museum provided a way for making such experiments public, and Cloud presented specimens of these three metals even before he published the results. Cloud also donated a mineral that caused a bit of a sensation, a piece of gold recently discovered in Cabarrus County, North Carolina.[18]

Many of Peale's mineral donors were physicians, and training for their occupation involved formal education in chemistry, a subject related to mineralogy. Among Peale's donors of minerals, John Redman Coxe, Adam Seybert, Benjamin Silliman, and James Woodhouse all studied medicine at the University of Pennsylvania. Archibald Bruce attended medical lectures at Columbia College and received a medical degree from the University of Edinburgh. At least a dozen more contributors to Peale's collection of minerals were designated "Dr." in the museum's accession record.[19]

For many of these donors, the science of mineralogy was an important part of their professional identity. Donor James Woodhouse was a prominent member of the learned community of Philadelphia, serving as the professor of chemistry in the medical school at the University of Pennsylvania from 1795 until his death in 1809. He was followed in that position by John Redman Coxe, another donor of minerals. Archibald Bruce held a joint chair in materia medica and mineralogy at the College of Physicians and Surgeons of the State of New York. Their French counterpart, René-Just Haüy, was professor of mineralogy at the Muséum d'Histoire Naturelle and later occupied the chair in mineralogy at the Sorbonne. Donations from such prestigious donors helped to certify the scholarly importance of the museum.[20]

For these academics, Peale's Museum was an avenue for publicizing their research in mineralogy. By donating recent publications and specimens about which they wrote, members of Peale's scholarly audience gained recognition for their accomplishments. Benjamin Silliman, the first professor of chemistry and natural history at Yale College, donated pieces of a famous meteorite after he had chemically analyzed it and published on the subject. First noted in the *Connecticut Herald,* news of the meteorite that fell at Weston, Connecticut, on December 14, 1807, was soon reprinted in Philadelphia newspapers. The meteorite was not limited to the esoteric inquiry of the intellectual elite. It was a curiosity that an entrepreneur was able to display in taverns of New York and then Philadelphia, charging twelve-and-a-half cents per visitor. Even in scientific discourse, Silliman felt compelled to dismiss a number of outrageous theories, the prevalence of which indicated the level of wonder inspired by this particular mineral specimen. Silliman and his colleague James L. Kingsley rejected suggestions that meteorites were stones fused by lightning, objects erupted from terrestrial or lunar volcanos, or solidified atmospheric gases. With caution they forwarded the theory posited by late president of Yale, Thomas Clap, that meteorites may be "terrestrial comets, revolving about the earth in the same manner as the solar comets revolve around the sun."[21]

Donations by chemist James Woodhouse asserted his contributions to both science and American manufactures. In 1805 Woodhouse wrote about a new source of coal found in Lehigh, Pennsylvania. In a prefatory letter to John Redman Coxe, who published the findings in *The Philadelphia Medical Museum,* Woodhouse argued the twofold significance of his research. By studying "inflammable substances" found on American soil, chemists serve the interests of both the arts and mineralogy. Woodhouse devoted the body of his research article to comparing the chemical composition of Lehigh coal with that of coal found along the James River in Virginia, and concluded with remarks about the manufacturing applications best suited to this new type of coal: "The Lehigh coal promises to be particularly useful, where a long continued heat is necessary, as in distilling, or in evaporating large quantities of water from various substances; in the melting of metals, or in subliming of salts; in generating steam to work steam engines; and in common life, for washing, cooking, &c." Woodhouse presented a copy of the article and a sample of Lehigh coal to the museum in 1805. Peale later solidified Woodhouse's prominent place in the academic community by painting his portrait posthumously for display in the museum. Upon painting *James Woodhouse* for the museum, Peale described the subject as "the first who professed and cultivated the useful knowledge of Chemistry in Philada."[22]

Through another gift of mineral specimens, Woodhouse defended his patriotic commitment to the American manufactures movement. In 1808 Woodhouse became entangled in a rhetorical battle with another Philadelphia chemist, Adam Seybert, over the economic potential of a recent mineral discovery, a zinc ore found near Philadelphia. Woodhouse published his analysis of blend or the sulphuret of zinc, which had been found at Perkiomen Creek in Montgomery County, Pennsylvania. In his article Woodhouse described the mine site and the specimens found there, assessed the chemical composition of the ore, and concluded that blend could not currently be produced for profit in the United States or in Europe. Adam Seybert published a sharp rebuke of Woodhouse's position. Invoking the politically loaded Embargo of 1807, Seybert charged that Woodhouse was discouraging American manufactures. Seybert argued that technology was presently available to transform the Perkiomen ore into two new exports, zinc and brass. Woodhouse defended both his scholarly findings and his patriotism, responding to Seybert's attack, "In every analysis I have made, public utility has been my sole object, and to that object my attention has always been cheerfully devoted, without any regard to labour or expense." Woodhouse took his case to the public by donating a specimen of Perkiomen blend to Peale's Museum.[23]

Through his donations to the museum, Adam Seybert promoted geological mapping for the advancement of science and manufactures. Geology was distinguished from the descriptive science of mineralogy by its potential to explain the origin of the earth. Secular and religious interests were served by geological hypotheses of either catastrophic or evolutionary change. For Seybert, though, geology offered its most significant contribution to the industrial future. In his published checklist of forty minerals that commonly occur in America, Seybert presented the name of each specimen in English, French, and German, the geographic and geological distribution, an external description and, in some cases, notes on applications. For example, he discussed the uses of various clays in making pipes, bricks, and earthenware; ochres in manufacturing paints; and slate in producing an increasingly popular roofing material. Geological mapping enhanced knowledge about the types of minerals that occur together in nature. In terms of manufacturing interests, more information on where minerals were plentiful and on how difficult their extraction would be hinted of the viability of different industries by region. Seybert's project therefore answered Peale's call in the 1790s for donations of minerals and descriptions of the circumstances in which they were found.[24]

While a number of Peale's donors wrote articles on mineralogy, a select few also published journals devoted to this and other scientific subjects. John Redman Coxe edited *The Philadelphia Medical Museum,* which included mineralogical essays. Coxe regularly donated copies of his journal to Peale's Museum. Benjamin Silliman founded *The American Journal of Science and Arts;* the library at the museum apparently did not contain it. Archibald Bruce distinguished himself as the first American to produce a specialized journal of science, *The American Mineralogical Journal.* Between 1810 and 1814 Bruce published four numbers of his periodical, at least three of which were owned by the museum.[25]

In addition to donors affiliated with institutions of higher learning, Peale's audience for the minerals also included boarding school teachers and public lecturers. French emigrant Silvain Godon, for instance, settled in Philadelphia after working on geological surveys of the Boston area and the District of Maine. As his counterparts in the universities were doing, Godon published his geological research in the scholarly journals. Though he was counted among the learned community, Godon never gained an academic affiliation. Instead, he taught classes on mineralogy within the looser structure of the public lecture circuit, typically an itinerant existence. Beginning in 1808, Godon offered a series of lectures and field trips, as Peale indicated in his letter informing Stephen Elliott of recent developments in Philadelphia:

> Mr. Godon is a frenchman from Paris, he has been in the Eastern States & made his observations and collections in the environs of Boston Rowd Island, New York & Jersey, and has as yet only seen a very small part of Pennsylvania, He has given a course of Lectures on Mineralogy to about 18 or 20 Pupels. Rubens has been a constant attendant, and will accompany him to explore the neighbourhood when the White covering of this season passes away.

Peale sold tickets for Godon at the museum, lending institutional support to the Frenchman's enterprise. In turn, the museum gained as Godon helped to educate Rubens Peale and donated mineral specimens to the collection.[26]

Talbot Hamilton, a boarding school teacher, contributes another important dimension to Peale's audience: a link between the museum and a female audience for natural history. A chemistry syllabus published by the Young Ladies' Academy, where

Hamilton taught, shows that young women were educated in terms recognizable in Peale's mineral displays:

> INTRODUCTORY remarks, on the effects of heat and mixture, and on the different objects of Chemistry.
>   Of Salts.
>   Of Earths.
>   Of Inflammable Bodies.
>   Of Metals.
>   Of Waters.
>   Of Airs.

The division of minerals into salts, earths, inflammables, and metals derives from Richard Kirwan's system of mineral classification, one of the systems by which Peale arranged his collections.[27]

The inclusion of science in the curriculum of women's academies demonstrates that the potential audience for natural history crossed gender lines. In fact, Peale noted the presence of women in the audience on the first night that Joseph Cloud performed experiments with his blowpipe. Outside the museum, schoolteacher Benjamin Tucker perceived sufficient interest among Philadelphia women to propose "a course of Le[c]tures on Chemestry for Ladies," and he requested assistance from Rubens Peale. Although Rubens seems to have declined the invitation, Tucker offered a course of public lectures in chemistry and targeted women as his primary audience. Tucker sustained the lectures as an annual offering from 1809 to 1813, but his advertisements shifted first to a more equal appeal to men and women, and finally to the omission of reference to gender. Still, Tucker's lectures further the suggestion that early national audiences for natural history were not composed solely of men. Although Peale's donors of minerals were mostly men, a few women also contributed to this collection.[28]

For the most part, donors of minerals, natural resources, and manufactures—especially physicians, academics, manufacturers, and collectors—stood to have their material or intellectual interests promoted through such public exhibitions. Their participation in building the collections demonstrates how audience members moved well beyond simply responding to exhibits offered to them by Peale. Whereas visitors who published responses to the museum helped to shape its meaning and value, donors helped to determine the very contents of future displays. Through their contributions to the museum, donors expressed their interests. They also helped to define the purpose of a museum in a republic and the relationship of such an institution to the community it serves. By promoting both their own businesses and the larger cause of

American manufactures, donors participated culturally in lessening a tension that pervaded economic and social life, the tension between competition and civic duty. The museum provided an institutional structure in which self-interest and philanthropy could be practiced simultaneously.

7. Donors of Artifacts
of Human Difference

BY DISPLAYING artifacts from Native American and non-Western cultures, Peale helped to define the boundaries of community. Peale exhibited these artifacts in terms of harmony, proclaiming hope that his museum would promote the peaceful co-existence of diverse peoples. Yet Peale's conception of the human world was also based on his belief that all of nature is structured hierarchically. Thus, although Peale proposed a broadly inclusive model of community, he also defined social ranking—particularly by race—as natural. Peale's audience participated in the representation and structuring of communities through their donations to the museum. Many of these donors were merchants, military officers, and explorers, people for whom the maintenance of hierarchy was a matter of significant material consequence. Race relations in the early republic were characterized by tense interactions between whites and non-whites. Growing numbers of free blacks settled in Philadelphia, meaning that the rigid boundary between slave and master was replaced by a looser set of relationships between the races. The push west brought whites increasingly into hostile contact with Native Americans, and the newspapers were filled with reports of battles, conquests, and treaties. Within this context, Peale and his audience constructed a cultural model in which white America behaved benevolently toward other races and simultaneously maintained a sense of superiority over them.

Peale first declared his interest in harmony in the domestic sphere, and he expressed visually his belief that unity and hierarchy were consistent qualities of human social structure. Peale's early family portrait, *The Peale Family Group* (figure 31), demonstrates the artist's concern with domestic harmony. In this narrative portrait, three generations of the Peale family delight in the gift of artistic knowledge passed from Charles Willson Peale to his brother St. George, the two leftmost figures. Included among the family are servant Margaret Durgin, who stands at right, and the family pet in the foreground. Peale established pictorial harmony by repeating and overlapping triangular forms throughout the canvas. The four family members at left and the two seated at center form one triangle; the four figures at right and, again, the two seated at center define a second; and the entire group forms a third, the apex of which ex-

Figure 31. Charles Willson Peale, *The Peale Family Group,* 1772–1809. Courtesy of The New-York Historical Society, New York, New York.

tends above the canvas. A fourth triangular plane recedes into space, and is defined by the sides of the tabletop, and echoed by the slant of the canvas at left and the wall that recedes into space at right. The interrelated gestures of the figures further unify the canvas, connecting them in physical contact and parallel movement. Contemporary viewer John Adams understood the overall effect, noting in the portrait "a pleasant, a happy cheerfulness in their countenances, and a familiarity in their air towards each other." Yet the unity among the figures does not imply equal status for all. Through her undirected gaze, which implies psychological distance, and by her physical distance from the Peale family, the servant Margaret Durgin demonstrates how Peale's conception of harmony ordered the socially lower on the perimeters of the social fabric; she is simultaneously among the family and removed from its inner core. Concord and social hierarchy were consistent in Peale's world view.[1]

Peale advanced his notion of domestic harmony through his writings, ordering the family according to appropriate gender roles. In a pamphlet entitled "An Essay, to Promote Domestic Happiness," published in 1812, Peale advised his readers on the proper behavior of a husband and wife. Peale counseled women to attend dutifully to their homes and their husbands, and he strongly urged them not to complain or argue. In short, Peale proposed that women should promote harmony within the family by deferring to their husbands. Peale recommended that men ought to forswear alcohol, resist borrowing money, and consult their wives in financial matters. In everyday life, Peale explained, you should "emulate the illustrious characters before you, and soon you will feel yourself superior to all mean and low companions." Peale summarized the social benefits of this model in the following terms:

> By a harmony of sentiments, industry will be promoted; good order and economy in all domestick affairs will be observed, their reputation will be in high estimation with the publick; their relations will love and esteem them; their children will recevei [*sic*] good instruction; and their parents (if living) will rejoice, and give praise to their Creator, that they have been blessed with such issue.

Peale ended his pamphlet on a note asserting that his advice was not simply socially expedient, but also reflective of Christian virtue. He closed by quoting a passage from the Book of Luke, in which even the prodigal son is welcome in the family unit.[2]

Despite Peale's public embrace of domestic harmony, disruption characterized much of Peale family life. According to art historian Phoebe Lloyd, Raphaelle Peale and his father engaged in a lifelong struggle. A source of anguish to his father, Raphaelle was known for excessive drinking and levity and for lack of application in his profession as a painter. In contemporary terms, Raphaelle's transgression was dissipation. His marriage to Patty McGlathery, an Irish Catholic, was supposedly equally troubling to the Peale patriarch. Peale's assertion of harmony veiled his more problematic assertion of control, which has been revealed only by its failure. The eighteenth-century longing for harmony must be paired with its antithesis, discord.[3]

For Peale, however, harmony, not conflict, was the natural state of being, and he promoted this belief through exhibits of living animals. In 1797 Peale argued his point by exhibiting an eagle and a chicken living together peacefully in a single space. The newspaper announcement read:

A SINGULAR ASSOCIATION.

In the inclosure, made for living animals, adjoining Peale's Museum, is a curious Cock, having a spur, growing on its head;—This fowl, since the death of its own species, has deserted its wonted cage, and regularly roosts, each night, with one of the Eagles;—This fact is astonishing—as, the Eagle is well known to be the greatest enemy to poultry.

In 1810 Rubens Peale repeated this theme by displaying a rattlesnake, a squirrel, and a bird together in a single cage. If harmony were the natural state among lower animals, then surely humans could also be expected to live in peace.[4]

In 1789 Peale exhibited an African bow in terms that simultaneously promoted interracial harmony and subordination of blacks to whites. Originally the property of Jambo, an African prince and later slave to Colonel Jacob Motte in South Carolina, the bow and arrows symbolized a benevolent master's trust in a faithful slave. Overcoming the fear of uprising, Motte fostered mutual acceptance of his and Jambo's unequal stations in life. Through his resignation to enslavement, Jambo enabled his master to grant him control over his native weapon. Master and slave lived harmoniously, though hierarchically. Peale also exhibited the bow and arrows as artifacts of the American Revolution. In this context, the African artifacts exemplified collective success through a woman's acceptance that her personal interests were less significant than her country's. During the Revolution, the British commandeered the home of Rebecca Motte, widow of Jambo's master. American troops hesitated to confront the British for fear of destroying Mrs. Motte's house. She not only granted permission to attack, but also forwarded the patriotic cause by offering Jambo's bow to shoot flaming arrows at the house. In harmony Motte and the soldiers accomplished their aims, whereas lack of cooperation by Motte would have prevented military success and the return of her house. Although the house was set aflame, the British and American soldiers combined efforts to put out the fire. Once again, harmony of purpose was valued above difference—in this case, political difference. The African bow was donated by Otho Holland Williams, whose military service in the Revolution Peale honored by including his likeness among the museum portraits.[5]

Such exhibits responded to contemporary anxiety about the possibility of slave revolts. The 1791 uprising in St. Domingue crystallized especially fear of the instability of slavery as an institution. Many refugees found sanctuary in Philadelphia, and their stories were told repeatedly to their hosts. Thanking Peale for sponsoring his passage to America, one escapee named John Thomas Carré told of his children's horrifying experience, "Death under a thousand shapes, one more terrible than another has threatened their lives. [A] year is hardly elapsed Since they have been Eyewitnesses of the murder of forty white peoples, men, women, and children barbarously butchered by their own Negroes, in my neighbourhood." In contrast to Peale's image of a passive slave prince, Carré's vision was of violent barbarians. Against Peale's insistence of racial harmony in the African bow exhibit, the presence of French-speaking refugees, personal testimonials such as Carré's, and newspaper accounts of the St. Domingue revolt proclaimed the potential for total social upheaval. Moreover, slavery was not the only institution that depended upon peaceful maintenance of hierarchy. Tension among diverse social ranks offered subtler cause for uneasiness about the stability of harmony. Despite early national rhetoric about an increasingly equal society, rich and poor lived in dramatic relief to one another.[6]

Public ritual insisted upon the stability of this order and quelled fears that violence might break out. Audience behavior at Peale's Museum, the theater, civic festivals, and other public sites served as important cultural demonstrations of social structure and harmony. By the same token, disruptions at such gatherings offered stark reminders that greater unrest was possible. Peale expected civil behavior from his visitors, and he characterized those who violated decorum as "Rude and uncultivated." Philadelphia's theaters established a hierarchical arrangement of audiences, yet occasional violence among audience members illustrated potential ruptures in that order. Fourth of July celebrations, with their simultaneous significations of rebellion and liberty, were particularly loaded public enactments of harmony. Announcements of music to be performed, transparencies to be illuminated, and fireworks to be displayed on Independence Day in 1791 carried the warning that "it will be impossible to carry the plan forward without order being preserved." When chaos erupted, pamphleteers, adopting the rhetorical vocabulary of the Revolution, blamed the outbreak on aristocratic imposition upon the people. A report two years later, in the same newspaper, applauded a peaceful gathering in Fayetteville, North Carolina: "The harmony which was predominent through the day, the expression of pleasure, planted on every countenance, for the happy return of the anniversary of an event ever sacred to the freedom and liberty of America; bespoke their gratitude for those whose blood defended their rights and invested them with the enjoyment of the privileges of a free and happy people." Even those at the bottom of the social structure, this item implies, were better off in a free society than under a monarch.[7]

Peale believed that through cultural representation within his exhibitions, he could promote social harmony. In one celebrated episode in the museum's history, Peale claimed that his orderly world in miniature resulted in a peaceful accommodation among enemy Native Americans. Late in 1796 during a series of treaty negotiations in Philadelphia, a number of tribal delegates visited Peale's Museum on the same day. Overcoming their initial hostility for one another, the delegates embarked on a dialogue that concluded with truces among traditional foes. Peale asserted his museum's role in subduing their violent tendencies: "Now, for the first time, finding themselves in peace, surrounded by a scene calculated to inspire the most perfect harmony, the first suggestion was,—that as men of the same species they were not enemies by nature, but ought forever to bury the hatchet of war." At least one contemporary believed that other viewers would similarly benefit from the exemplification of harmony at the museum: "So pleasing an assemblage in one view, must forcibly tend to lead the mind to serious reflections, and confirm sentiments of *good will, love* and *charity* to each fellow being." That this commendation appeared in the Federalist *Gazette of the*

United States demonstrates that Peale's vision of racial harmony was one concept that attracted audience members across party lines.[8]

Ironically, the possibility of peace was brought about by the American army's military conquest of Native Americans. Peale's donors of Native American artifacts included the military officers who directed the campaign in the Northwest Territory in the early 1790s. Most notable was General Anthony Wayne's contribution of three calumets, or peace pipes. By emphasizing Wayne's diplomatic skills rather than his military prowess, the exhibit obscured the means by which harmony was achieved. Wayne led American troops against the Miamis, the Shawnees, and other nations in present-day Ohio, and this campaign culminated in victory and the Treaty at Greenville in August 1795. Secretary of War Timothy Pickering's instructions to Anthony Wayne on the eve of treaty negotiations make clear the material stakes of that accord: "The final cession and relinquishment by the Indians of the entire body of land lying eastward and southward of the general boundary . . . from the mouth of the Cuyahoga to the mouth of the Great Miami . . . are to be an indispensible condition of peace." Thus, both the exhibition of Wayne's peace pipes and Peale's claim that his harmonious exhibition produced peaceful settlements obscured two important considerations. First, the peace pipes and the presence of Native American chiefs in Philadelphia followed a bloody demonstration of American power. Second, the accommodation among the races signaled the gradual replacement of Native American with American control of the land. Although both races might have welcomed a harmonious coexistence, this peace clearly benefitted one race at the expense of the other.[9]

Peale expanded his display of harmony among races by adding, in 1797, an exhibition of ten wax figures representing native peoples of the Americas, the South Pacific, Siberia, China, and Africa. Two of the figures were portraits, depicting Red Pole and Blue Jacket, who were principals in the battles against Anthony Wayne, parties to the Treaty at Greenville, and representatives of the Shawnees at Philadelphia in December 1796. Blue Jacket was a particularly apt choice for Peale's display, since he was once a formidable adversary of the American military in the Northwest Territory who eventually urged the Shawnee nation to negotiate peace. Although Peale implied that Native Americans had to be persuaded to abandon violent solutions to their differences with other peoples—whether they were whites or Native Americans of other nations—a speech attributed to Blue Jacket offers an opposing perspective on who instigated war and for what reasons. In anticipation of conflict with the American army under Josiah Harmar, also a donor of Native Americana to the museum, Blue Jacket is said to have addressed his followers in 1790 with these words: "We as a people have made no war, but as a people we are determined to meet the approaches of an enemy, who come not to check the insolence of individuals, but as a premeditated design to root us out of our land." Blue Jacket maintained alliances with other Native American nations and with the British to oppose by force any American aggression, but finally conceded defeat in 1795. The terms of his resolution with Anthony Wayne, as discussed above, necessitated exactly what Blue Jacket had feared, "the final cession and relinquishment . . . of land." Blue Jacket's conversion was less an embrace of harmony than a pragmatic acknowledgment that he lacked sufficient support to fend off Wayne and that the annuity offered to him by the American government was the best he could achieve under the circumstances.[10]

A gift from Thomas Jefferson of objects gathered during the Lewis and Clark Expedition was the next major addition to Peale's exhibition of Native American artifacts. The centerpiece of the new display was a wax model of Meriwether Lewis wearing the buckskin costume given to him by the Shoshone chief Cameahwait. Suspicious that Lewis was leading him into an ambush by the enemy Blackfeet, Cameahwait reportedly insisted that the American wear the clothes of the Shoshones. If the Blackfeet attacked, Lewis's death would stem from his own duplicity. A contemporary watercolor by Charles Saint-Mémin depicts Lewis dressed in the legendary outfit (figure 32). Through Lewis's regal bearing, conveyed by his posture, stance, and the attitude of his head, Saint-Mémin asserts his subject's superiority to the absent Shoshone chief. In contrast to Saint-Mémin's presentation of Lewis, Peale portrayed him holding a calumet in his left hand and placing his right hand over his heart. By replacing the weapons favored by Saint-Mémin with signs of conciliation, Peale's representation of Lewis invited hope for friendship between whites and Native Americans. Peale expressed this message also in text; a label accompanied the wax figure and was purported to quote Lewis's words: "Brother, I accept your dress.—It is the object of my heart to promote amongst you, our neighbors, peace and good will—that you may bury the hatchet deep in the ground never to be taken up again—and that henceforward you may smoke the Calmut of Peace and live in perpetual harmony, not only with each other, but with the white men, your brothers, who will teach you many useful arts." In this exhibition, too, Peale developed a hierarchy between the white man and the Native American. Lewis is the ambassador of "peace and good will," and it is the Shoshone who has to be convinced to "bury the hatchet." Whites are basically peaceful, Peale implied; Native Americans are violent. Moreover, Lewis promised that "the white men . . . will teach you many useful arts," assuming the superiority of his own civilization. Interestingly, this exhibit embodied the ideal of harmony by placing a white man in Native American dress.[11]

Figure 32. Charles B. J. F. Saint-Mémin, *Captain Meriwether Lewis*, 1807. Courtesy of The New-York Historical Society, New York, New York.

In addition to synthesizing harmony and hierarchy, this exhibit tested the boundaries of race, an important consideration for defining community in early national America. Lewis was dressed in Native American costume, indicating his ability to move from one civilization to another. The wax figure of Blue Jacket even more profoundly blurred the line between the races, since he was by birth white. Born Marmaduke Van Swerangen, Blue Jacket was captured by the Shawnees, who adopted him. Both examples demonstrate the potential for a white man to successfully enter Native American life. But the exhibits left unanswered the converse question: Could a Native American productively enter American society?[12]

Peale further examined fluidity of natural boundaries, including those separating humans from other species. In 1799 Peale exhibited the "Ourang Outang, or Wild Man of the Woods." The woodcut used to promote the exhibit visually advanced the ambiguity of species (figure 33). In this print, Peale depicted the orangutan within the conventions of genteel portraiture. The full-length figure of the ape stands upright with one hand hanging at his side and the other extended and grasping a pole, not unlike a gentleman holding a walking stick. Furthering the parallel between this subject and human portrait-sitters, Peale directed the orangutan's intelligent gaze back at the viewer. For Peale the blurred line between humans and apes could be explained in terms of race. In discussing the stuffed orangutan in the museum, Peale asked the people in his audience, "How like an old Negro?" In other words, the boundary across species was mediated by differences within the human species. Blacks stood a step closer than whites to the apes in Peale's view of natural hierarchy.[13]

Exhibits of albinism and changes in skin pigmentation offered a view of racial difference that perhaps was unsettling to Peale's audience: that the boundary between the races may not be fixed and that the prevailing social order may not be stable. By including albino animals and, later, a painting of an albino woman (figure 14) in the museum, Peale followed the example of Thomas Jefferson, who discussed albinism in the context of the institution of slavery. In his *Notes on the State of Virginia*, Jefferson described albinism as "an anomaly of nature, taking place sometimes in the race of negroes brought from Africa, who, though black themselves, have in rare instances, white children, called Albinos." Despite the seeming inversion of racial categories, these white children of black parents were still identifiable with their race of origin: "They are of a pallid cadaverous white, untinged with red, without any coloured spots or seams; their hair of the same kind of white, short, coarse, and curled as is that of the negro; all of them well formed, strong, healthy, perfect in their senses, except that of sight, and born of parents who had no mixture of white blood." Jefferson seemed comforted by the fact that albinos were rare, that they remained racially distinct, and that their children were typically dark skinned: "The middle one [of three Albino sisters] is now alive in health, and has issue, as the eldest had, by a black man, which issue was black." Significantly, Jefferson included his account of the albino in his chapter "Productions Mineral, Vegetable, and Animal," an enumeration of the natural resources of the state. In this way Jefferson linked slaves to other natural commodities. Descriptions of albinos' strength and of their ability to bear normal offspring asserted that this "anomaly" is a curious accident of nature, not a pattern that will eventually undermine racial distinction and the economic structures dependent upon it.[14]

Dr. John Redman Coxe treated the potentially emotionally charged topic of albinism in the rational language of medical observation. Coxe studied whether physi-

PEALE's MUSEUM.

OURANG OUTANG, or WILD' MAN OF THE WOODS.

THIS Curious Animal, so nearly approaching to the human species as to occasion some Philosophers to doubt whether it was not allied to mankind, is now in this useful repository; which is constantly encreasing by the accession of uncommon subjects from all parts of the globe—It consists at present of

QUADRUPEDS—more than 100 of AMPHIBIOUS animals, upwards of 150 of BIRDS—near 700.

INSECTS—many thousands.

FISHES—a number of—and a great variety of shells;

MINERALS & FOSSILS—1000 specimens of PICTURES, and 11 figures of

WAX-WORK,

Representing the persons of various savage nations, all in their proper habits, and surrounded by their implements of war, husbandry, &c.

Also, a powerful ELECTRICAL MACHINE with a medical apparatus. Admittance as usual one quarter of a dollar each time.

Figure 33. Unidentified artist, *Ourang Outang, or Wild Man of the Woods* (Peale's Museum advertisement), *Claypoole's American Daily Advertiser,* April 13, 1799. The Library Company of Philadelphia.

cal surroundings of the pregnant mother had an impact, whether the lack of pigmentation was determined at conception or later, whether men or women were more susceptible, and whether other animals were prone to albinism. Coxe examined an albino man whose father was "of a brown complexion" and whose siblings included one with "sandy hair" and two with "brown hair." Whereas Jefferson discussed only African-American albinos, Coxe's subject was clearly white. Coxe further expanded the parameters of this phenomenon by noting, "In the animal creation man is not alone subject to this change of structure.—In Mr. Peale's museum, are the opossum—mouse—rat—muskrat—flying and ground-squirrel, with white hair and red eyes; and a white black-bird, and a white yellow-bird, with black eyes." In this expanded realm, the uncommon white skin color does not threaten racial hierarchy. Instead, it is an occurrence that happens not only to whites and blacks, but also to humans and lower animals. As it does not threaten the boundary between man and other mammals, it does not subvert the hierarchy between the races.[15]

Peale's most extensive commentary on deviations of skin color in humans followed his painting in 1791, *James,* "a person born a Negro, or a very dark Mullatoe, who afterwards became white." In fact, the color of James's skin had not fully transformed, and remained in a patterned limbo between white and black. Although Peale's painting of James is now lost, a mid-eighteenth-century painting, *Portrait of Mary Sabina,* demonstrates earlier interest in this subject (figure 34). Like Peale's subject James, the inscription to the painting of Mary Sabina indicates that she was a slave. An image of this child was also engraved for inclusion in French naturalist Georges Buffon's *L'histoire de l'homme* (1749). As a slave, James fit the model of racial ambiguity with which Jefferson was concerned. The fact that James's father was white—and perhaps even the planter who owned him—added the dimension of miscegenation to the anxiety over race, and implicated the upholders of slavery as the potential source of their own downfall. Like Jefferson's account of albinism, Peale described James in terms that distinguished him from whites:

James is about fifty years old, his hair is black, with a few white spots, short and much curled (more like a mulatoe's than a negro's); the white spots on his head, and two white spots of hair on his chin, give him an odd appearance; He gave me the following account of the changes:—a portion of the black becomes of a reddish brown colour by degrees, and remains so about six months, when it changes further and becomes white—upon this change the white parts are very tender, and are soon burnt by the sun, even to their becoming sore for a time: and afterwards the white, which is now nearly the whole of his skin, is more tender and more susceptible of injury from the sun, than it used to be in the black spots. He added, that the changes of colour, from black to white, have been much more rapid of late than for-

Figure 34. Unidentified artist, *Portrait of Mary Sabina*, 1740–45. Colonial Williamsburg Foundation, Williamsburg, Virginia.

merly. His skin is of a clear wholesome white, fair, and what would be called a better skin than any of the number of white people who were present at different times when I saw him.

Also consistent with Jefferson's record of this phenomenon, Peale reported that all of James's known children were "all black as negroes commonly are." The repetition in newspapers and periodicals of Peale's description of this racial transformation attests to the resonance of this topic for early national Americans.[16]

Despite the clinical presentation of such exhibits, contemporary audience response to Peale's later portrait of an albino woman demonstrated the emotional impact of challenges to racial boundaries. In 1818 Rubens Peale added to the museum a portrait by Charles Willson Peale of Miss Harvey, an albino woman who was then touring the United States. The sketch of a seated woman at the center of *The Long Room* (figure 14) preserves an approximate representation of the lost painting, *Miss Harvey, The Albiness*. In the words of German traveler Ludwig Gall, the painting "displays an ideal of feminine beauty. I cannot recall having seen such a beautiful woman in real life. Her hair reaches to the floor." Gall also observed a related exhibition of a living albino boy, and in describing the youth, the terms of his account shift from awe to terror: "Among Dr. Peale's living oddities is a boy, the son of an albino who died here, called, oddly enough, a white Negro. The boy's appearance is striking. His teeth are of the most beautiful ivory, his skin as delicate and white as the petals of a lily, his long, silky hair as white as alabaster. But the dull, fire-red eyes are repulsive—eyes that distinguish this person from others. Daylight blinds these eyes; they see only in moonlight and twilight." If Gall could not quite pronounce the boy evil on the basis of the "eyes that distinguish this person from others," he showed no such reservations in his judgment of Miss Harvey: "But what is beauty without a soul, for which you search the fire-red eyes in vain?" Whereas Peale couched such exhibits in the benevolent terms of harmony, his audience readily translated the rhetoric for their own purposes. A woman "without a soul" was clearly beyond the limits of civilization.[17]

Peale further examined hierarchical relationships among humans by exhibiting artifacts of deformity and infirmity. As in the displays of various races, Peale's presentation of the productions of physically handicapped persons simultaneously included them in a broad definition of community and identified their unequal place in the social order. Martha Ann Honeywell and Sarah Rogers were itinerant artists, the first born without hands and the second with disabled hands and feet. Accession records included descriptions of both women's disabilities and working methods, as well as descriptions of a work of cut paper made and presented by Honeywell, a drawing done by Rogers and donated by William Hamilton of Woodlands, and three paintings by Rogers, at least one of which was also donated by her. A silhouette portrait cut by Honeywell for a customer in Philadelphia demonstrates the type of object included in Peale's display (figure 35). In 1807, a broadside advertising a visit by Martha Ann Honeywell to Philadelphia characterized her performance in terms that were consistent with Peale's ideal of harmony (words that were handwritten in the original are italic below):

THE

Wonder of the World.

TO BE SEEN at *John Hays in state street*

oppisite the Collige

A YOUNG LADY, born without hands, and with only three toes, on one foot; who is not so much a subject of wonder and admiration for her great ingenuity and elegance in embroidering artificial flowers fit for framing, and in cutting with rich variety and taste, gentlemen's watch papers, as for the peculiar felicity of her disposition and her entertaining style of conversation, diffusing gaiety all around her; indeed, her cheerful and sportively engaging aspect at once dispels those painful sensations which the deprivation of her limbs excites in the sympathising breast of her visitors, which give place to the most felicitous impressions, resulting in an admiration of the unparalleled good sense and cheerful resignation of this young Lady to her peculiar lot, which she has rendered by her persevering industry, spirit and wisdom, a happiness to herself, and a very instructive and consolatory example to the world generally, and to her own sex particularly.

Large flowers, &c. for sale by the young Lady, at the above place.

Admittance, 25 cents—Children, half price.

Despite Honeywell's physical limitations, she was hard-working, self-supportive, and resigned to her station in life. Although her gentle manner inspired "felicitous impressions" and "admiration" from her viewers, she was still presented as a spectacle, a "wonder of the world." The exhibition of Honeywell as a performer and the display of her artistic production at Peale's Museum had the double effect of promoting acceptance of the handicapped and continuing to hold them out as spectacles.[18]

Peale also mounted sensational exhibitions of bodily abnormalities caused by injury. In 1795, for instance, Peale announced the addition of a painting of John Gallaway and a horn-shaped growth amputated from his chest, and he graphically described the gruesome accident that caused the growth. As a sailor, Gallaway "was at the siege of Carthegena; when by an accident, four cartridges took fire, which burned him; especially about the breast in a terrible manner; this burn was, for many years a bad sore, however at last it had nearly healed up, when again his breast was unfortunately hurt, by being jamed between a boat and a ship, which bruised his breast sorely." A horn grew out of the scar tissue. Gallaway's particular affliction may suggest additional cultural meanings for the painting and the horn. Perhaps the fact that his injury stemmed from a burn resonated with memories of destructive and deadly fires and fear of fu-

Figure 35. Martha Ann Honeywell, *John Snyder, Jr.*, 1808–15. The Library Company of Philadelphia.

ture conflagration. The city of Philadelphia passed laws during this period against building frame houses, an act designed to prevent the rapid spread of fire. Reports of urban devastation by fire throughout the life of Peale's Museum demonstrate that this issue remained an important concern. The pathos that the Savannah fire generated in Philadelphia was indicated by the stream of 559 people who paid to see Peale's Museum on the day that receipts were to be donated to the devastated city. Peale not only helped the Savannah community to rebuild after it had been struck, but also participated in developing strategies for reducing the risk of fires and promoted technology for extinguishing them. In advertising his improved fireplaces, Peale claimed that one benefit of his design was that the flame could be put out quickly and completely. When the city of Annapolis wanted to purchase a fire engine in Philadelphia, Peale helped city officials price the models offered by Philip Mason and Patrick Lyon and finally acted as an intermediary between the Maryland city and Lyon in the commission.[19]

Whereas Peale's exhibits confronted fears about deformity and injury, the greatest early national concern with an individual's body was its protection from illness and death. Injury to mothers and infants at childbirth was commonplace, as was death of the newborn. Such perils were particularly familiar to the Peale family. Peale's second wife, Elizabeth DePeyster, and the child she was carrying, died in childbirth in 1804. Also terrifying were the overwhelming yellow fever epidemics that hit Philadelphia each autumn, starting in 1793. Those who could afford to leave town retreated to the country air until the rainy season began in late October or early November. From the standpoint of the museum entrepreneur, Peale was aware that this annual exodus greatly reduced numbers of museum visitors. From 1793 to 1796 Peale stopped advertising during the fever months, but in September 1797 he claimed that the museum *"stands in an airy and healthy situation, and free from the epidemic that at present afflicts the city. It may, therefore, be frequented with the greatest safety."* Published notices in broadsides and in the newspapers listed the numbers of burials by church and demonstrated that no one was exempt. Quakers and a number of Protestant clergymen blamed the spread of the disease on the prevalence of vice in the city. Moral weakness led to physical weakness, and yellow fever was a particular sign of divine retribution. Although Peale did not subscribe to religious explanations of disease, he did link good health with moral behavior. Indeed, Peale proposed that the reward for hard work and abstinence from alcohol was the extension of human life expectancy to the age of two hundred.[20]

Peale's portraits of John Strangeways Hutton, Yarrow Mamout (figure 36), Benjamin Franklin, Timothy Matlack, and perhaps even his late self-portraits exemplified the human potential for long life. Moreover, this reward was available to people of varying social status. Whereas Peale, Matlack, and Franklin belonged to the intellectual and political elite, Hutton and Mamout were considerably lower in social rank. Hutton was a white laborer, who worked as a sailor and later as a skilled craftsman. In both occupations, Hutton was a model citizen, and his reward was longevity. In Peale's words, "He was ever a quiet, temperate, and hard-working man; and is now a good humoured, hearty old man; he can see, hear, and walk about, and has a good appetite, with no complaints whatever, except from the mere weakness of old age." His single transgression was a night of drunkenness, which resulted in his narrow escape from death and his capture by enemy Spanish forces. The narrative of Yarrow Mamout's life was similarly one of spiritual resignation to his station as a slave, and later a free black. His portrait conveys the quiet passivity of a man who did not resist his place in life. For both of these working men, moral living and acceptance of one's social circumstances resulted in extraordinarily long lives. Hutton was allegedly 108 years old at the time of this portrait, and Mamout, 134. Accounts of longevity recurred in the Philadelphia newspapers, with one description claiming to document the life of a 175-year-old African-American man. If the individual reward for a moral life

Figure 36. Charles Willson Peale, *Yarrow Mamout,* 1819. The Historical Society of Pennsylvania, Philadelphia.

was longevity, the social reward was high collective productivity and an orderly citizenry.[21]

Peale's exhibits and writings not only proposed that long life accompanied socially acceptable behavior, but also supported the other side of this view—that a hastened death resulted from criminal, and perhaps even immoral, behavior. In one such exhibit, Peale displayed the trigger finger with which Mr. Bruliman shot and killed Robert Scull. Having left his trade of silversmithing, Bruliman became an officer in the colonial British army. Upon being caught at counterfeiting, he was discharged from his commission. Desperate because of his inability to earn a living, he committed a murder, expecting to end his own life as well through the punishment of hanging. The finger therefore stood as an emblem to Bruliman's forsaken manual skill as a silversmith and to its misapplication in creating counterfeit money and in killing another person. The exhibit also suggested that severe consequences may follow less heinous violations of the social code. When Rubens Peale recorded the finger in the accessions book in 1810, he cited his father's catalogue entry from 1790, when it first entered the collection, which recounted the story with a slant on the moral it held for the more innocent. Bruliman set out "to shoot the first person he should meet." That person "was a pretty young Girl, whose beauty disarmed him." Next, Bruliman encountered Dr. Cadwalader, who politely greeted the triggerman, and the killer "was so struck with his gentlemanly manner and pleasing address, that he forebore to execute his desperate resolution." Bruliman continued on his search for a victim, and settled on a man playing billiards in a public house: "The Sack of one of the Players happening to strike his Hat, the wretched man, eager for an opportunity of accomplishing his desire to leave the world, instantly shot Mr. Scull one of the company, who died of the wound—This little story offers a striking proof, that amiableness and Politeness of manners are not only pleasing, but useful, in our common with the world." Beauty and gentlemanly deportment enabled two potential victims to escape unharmed, whereas the relative coarseness of men playing a morally suspect game made them vulnerable to Bruliman's depravity. Such exhibitions of humanity promoted community standards of proper behavior.[22]

Members of Peale's audience joined in the definition of physical, social, moral, and religious human order through their donations to the museum. With the gift of a tree branch, one patron invoked Christianity as the religious justification by which Euro-Americans asserted their ascendancy over Native Americans. The museum accession book bears the following record (strikeout text is in the original): "A branch of the *Siba Frandosa* from a tree of that name, under ~~which~~ the shade of which, Christopher Columbus first caused the Christian God to be publickly invoked in the New World. It is in the Island of Cuba, and a Lamp has been kept constantly burning under it for the last two hundred Years—The Tree is yet in vigor. Presented by Dr. Pendergrast." This specimen manifested the heroic accomplishment of Columbus and celebrated the Western impulse for voyage and discovery. Like Peale's displays of peace pipes, the branch proclaimed nonviolent interaction between Europeans and Native Americans. Just as Peale's engraved admission ticket (figure 8) and painting *Noah and His Ark* (figure 12) used light as symbols of knowledge, civilization, and Christianity, the lamp in the narrative of the tree signified the positive legacy of European entry into the Americas. Peale endorsed the spirit of discovery by including images of Christopher Columbus, Amerigo Vespucci, Ferdinand Magellan, and Hernando Cortez among the museum portraits.[23]

In turn, explorers collected or donated many of the Native American artifacts displayed at Peale's Museum, and the museum provided an institutional context for celebrating military and scientific expeditions that facilitated westward expansion. The first large group of Native American artifacts shown at Peale's Museum was collected by Lewis and Clark and donated by Thomas Jefferson. Many of the objects were carefully labeled with the nation or tribe of their origin: for example, "Catsop," "Pallotepallers," "Seioux, or Sow, Darcota Nation," "Crow's," "Saux," "Ioway's,"

"Raneird's or Foxes," "Winnebagou's or Puount's," "Sacks," "Otoe's," "Blackfoot," "Enesher, Skillute, Pishquitpahs," "Yankton," "Teton," and "Sharone's." Some artifacts were accompanied by less specific information about origin, whereas others were said to come from a well-known chief, such as the Nez Perce leader Neeshneparkkeook.[24]

The terms in which Peale recorded the artifacts from the Lewis and Clark "voyage and Journey of Discovery" suggest that both the expedition and the exhibition valued dominion over land and Native Americans, as well as the advancement of knowledge. As historian James P. Ronda phrased it, "The knowledge was not to be gathered by the explorers for its own sake, however, but in the service of government and commerce." In Peale's accession records, the place names where Lewis and Clark collected Native American artifacts expressed white control over the vast region. For instance, Peale listed objects collected near "Lewis's River," identifying the West with one of the American explorers responsible for helping to "settle" it. Similarly, locating native people on the "Plains of Columbia" negated their prior claim to the land. Two silver medals of George III of England and a Spanish dollar, all collected from Native Americans, indicated precedents for settlers in these regions, despite the Pallotepallers' claim to have "never previously seen white-men."[25]

Peale's installation of Native American artifacts, including those gathered on the Lewis and Clark Expedition, furthered the theme of harmony by including numerous calumets and other ceremonial devices that symbolized peace and understanding. Examples of peace pipes, ornamented with eagle feathers, horse hair, carvings, and porcupine quill work, are extant at Harvard University's Peabody Museum of Archaeology and Ethnology (figure 37). Peale also recorded other objects consistent with this theme, such as "Wampums, of various discriptions, indicating, Peace, War, choice of either, Hostilities commencing, and a disposition for them to cease &c from different nations." Documenting Native American weaponry, Lewis and Clark donated a bow and arrows "from different ~~nations~~ Tribes of Saux." Although signification of the potential for peaceful coexistence between Native and Euro-Americans predominated, one item demonstrated that if hostility occurred, white men would prevail: "Amulets—taken from the Shields of the Blackfoot Indians who attacked Capn. Lewis and were killed by himself and party on the 27th of July 1806. near the Rocky Mountain."[26]

Accession records relating to foodways and clothing provided familiar categories by which visitors could compare their lives with those of Native Americans. Peale recorded donations of roots and bread made from them, and he described the process by which the roots were converted. In one instance, the record demonstrated the nutritional value of these natural productions, relating the donation to the larger concern with the

Figure 37. Calumet collected during the Lewis and Clark Expedition and donated to Peale's Museum. Peabody Museum of Archaeology and Ethnology, Cambridge, Massachusetts.

economic potential of the West: "This article for several weeks constituted the principal part of the food of Lewis and party." One donation of roots "by Neeshneparkeook, the great chief of the Pollotepallers as an emblem of the poverty of his nation which he discribed in a very pathetic manner," projected an image of Native Americans as worthy of sympathy and perhaps even charity, rather than enmity and fear. Such images invited whites to assume the paternal role of caretaker of a less fortunate race. Beaded, fringed, and painted garments, tobacco pouches, and moccasins helped to evoke images of these native peoples, and allowed museum visitors to find shared practices or measure the degree of difference between themselves and Native Americans. Perhaps particularly menacing were the "Legings, ornamented with the hair of Scalps taken by the Indian who wore it, and marked with stripes shewing the number he had ~~taken~~ scalped. of the Sow Nation." On the other hand, the following entry offered a category of authority similar to one of American society: "A Dress made of Crow or Raven Skins, worn by the Police Officers of the Saux, Nation."[27]

Subsequent expeditions added Native American artifacts and natural history specimens to the museum, linking these categories together as parallel enterprises. For instance, Titian Peale collected objects during his trips to Florida from 1817 to 1818 and to the West between 1819 and 1821. The early trip was financed privately by William Maclure, and he and Titian were joined by Philadelphia naturalists Thomas Say and George Ord. From this adventure, Titian contributed to his father's museum the contents of an Indian burial mound, which he and his colleagues excavated on the St. John's River. A year later Titian Peale embarked on the Long Expedition, which traveled up the Missouri River. Principal among Titian's donations to the museum were drawings and preserved natural specimens of quadrupeds, birds, reptiles, and fish, as well as seeds and an anatomical preparation. The younger Peale also donated materials used by Native Americans of the region: pumice from Council Bluffs, currently part of Nebraska, and pipestone from the Great Sioux River. Charles Willson Peale later added to the museum paintings that he had executed from drawings by Samuel Seymour, the staff artist for the Long Expedition. One showed a village of the Kanza peoples and another the interior of a Kanza lodge. The third was a landscape depicting the falls of the Ohio River, and the final painting showed the expedition party. Just as Peale placed preserved animals in habitat settings to reproduce their living conditions for viewers, with these paintings he enabled visitors to envision Native Americans in their environment.[28]

Peale celebrated American exploration by exhibiting portraits of the military officers and the naturalists of the Lewis and Clark, Pike, and Long Expeditions. These include the bust portraits of Lewis and Clark, and the later wax figure of Meriwether Lewis in the native dress given to him by the Shoshone chief Cameahwait. From the Long Expedition, Peale added portraits of Major Long, William Baldwin, Augustus Edward Jessup, Thomas Say, and Titian Peale. Explorer Zebulon Pike was also painted in military uniform for museum visitors. Displaying these portraits along with the images of Columbus, Vespucci, and Magellan, and Cortez, which Peale added in 1816, validated both European and American exploration and control in the New World.[29]

Explorers were not alone in identifying their material interests with land occupied by native peoples; Peale received numerous donations from ship captains, military officers, and merchants. Through their gifts to the museum, these military and commercial figures demonstrated the breadth of their enterprises. Weaponry and clothing were the types of artifacts most frequently presented to the museum. Bows with poisoned arrows from South America and Africa were among the most deadly objects. Examples of feather caps and mantles from Hawaii and armor from Persia and India were among the most exotic. In 1792 Peale publicized the donation by George Wash-

Figure 38. Rembrandt Peale, *Man in a Feathered Helmet,* 1805–13. Bishop Museum, Honolulu, Hawaii.

ington of a feather cloak and hat from Tahiti, and Rembrandt Peale later painted a man wearing a similar costume (figure 38). Bark clothing from Africa, the South Pacific, and the Northwest Coast were recurring items contributed. "A pair of Chinese Lady's Shoes, made to fit the wife of a native of that country, who supplied the ship Samson with necessaries when at China" at once attested to the custom of foot binding and recalled amicable trade relations with the East. Hookahs or hubble-bubbles were fairly common donations, and one accession in particular reiterated social hierarchies that were recognizable to Philadelphians: "Two Hubble Bubbles, one handsomely ornamented, such as is used by the Middle Class of People. and the other is such as the Lower Class of Gento'es smoake. presented by Mr. Tiffin." An Algerian pocketbook indicated commercial contact with a people once hostile to Americans, just as medals of Edward Preble and oil paintings of Stephen Decatur and Joel Barlow celebrated American military and diplomatic efforts to free American captives and negotiate peace with Algiers and later Tripoli. In short, these collections of non-Western artifacts articulated the same themes that were projected in the Native American collections—difference as exotic, parallels to American social norms within objects reflecting obvious difference, and peace through cooperation or force—but on a world scale.[30]

Embodied within Peale's representation of humanity was the assumption that a consensus was possible that benefitted all races, classes, genders, and people of various physical capacities. Yet this harmonious vision depended upon resignation to unequal social and material circumstances. Resistance to one's station was perceived to be a disruptive response to natural order. Slaves who resisted their master's authority, Native Americans who fought displacement from their land, and the lower sort who disrupted public gatherings were particularly guilty. More subtly, these exhibits invited people of all social levels to behave in a morally upstanding, economically productive manner, lest they remove themselves from the orderly existence of community life. Many of the patrons who added to the collections stood to benefit from such a model of peaceful, though unequal, coexistence among the various peoples of the earth. However, not all of Peale's audience members accepted this vision of the world. A number of Peale's subscribers belonged to anti-slavery societies; perhaps they found in exhibits of racial ambiguity a sign of hope rather than fear. Similarly, one contemporary visitor, Emanuel Howitt, perceived in Peale's exhibits of Native American artifacts not a model of harmony but a history of racial injustice. Critiquing first the quality of Peale's exhibition, Howitt wrote:

> A well-executed specimen of the figures, costumes, and martial equipage of these people, would probably become, in a short time, an object of uncommon interest to the curious: but it might not alone remain an object of that interest to the philosopher;—it would stand a monument of national odium: for, if the present system of oppression and extermination continue,—these people, who are fast delining and contracting their boundaries,—will shortly be known only in the record of Christian violence, towards those whom they please to term savages, and the knowledge of their personal appearance, their arts and ingenuity, be derived only from these repositories of a nation whom they hospitably received, and by whom they have been repaid by bloody injustice, war, and expulsion from the land of their ancestors.[31]

Epilogue

PEALE'S REPRESENTATION of the world was clearly structured, and he intended his audience to extend the economic, social, moral, intellectual, and religious lessons of the museum to their daily lives. He selected the categories of exhibits and he chose the systems by which displays were arranged. His "world in miniature" situated humans at the top of the natural order. Humanity, too, was ordered. Peale provided exemplars of military, political, and intellectual authority, as well as images of the range of human races, the sick and the well, and the moral and criminal. In gridlike, systematic arrangements of animals and artifacts, hierarchical relationships were made to appear natural. But was a visit to the museum a completely controlled, even controlling, experience?

In *The Artist in His Museum* (figure 1), Peale commanded significant control of vision. By adding a large curtain to his composition and lifting it for viewers to enter the space represented, Peale announced his ability to reveal the secrets of the natural and artificial worlds. The taxidermy kit at bottom left and the painter's palette and brushes at center right further asserted his central role in constructing this orderly world. Peale invited the viewer into the museum, but he clearly maintained an authoritative stance over this domain.[1]

Within certain exhibits Peale employed actual curtains to extend control of vision to his audience, but these encounters were in the end similarly structured. For instance, when Peale displayed *Rachel Weeping* (figure 39), he attached a curtain to the picture and a poem to the curtain. The verse, published in *The Freeman's Journal*, read:

> Draw not the curtain, if a tear
> Just trembling in a parent's eye
> Can fill your gentle soul with fear
> Or arouse your tender heart to sigh.
>
> A child lies dead before your eyes
> And seems no more than molded clay,
> While the affected mother cries,
> And constant mourns from day to day.

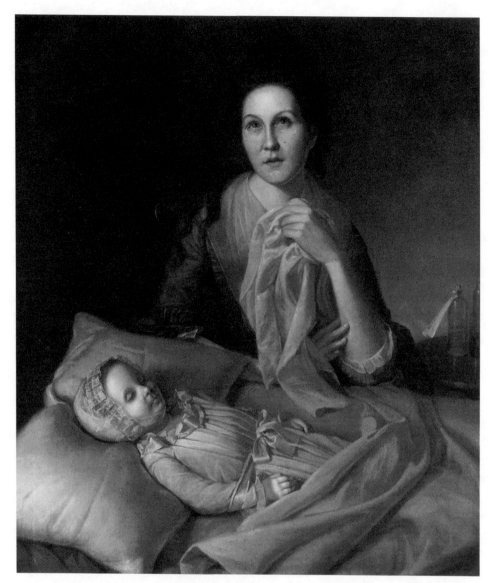

Figure 39. Charles Willson Peale, *Rachel Weeping*, 1772–76. Philadelphia Museum of Art: Given by the Barra Foundation, Inc.

Visitors had the option to leave the curtain in place or to remove it, and thereby individually controlled their engagement with the picture. Yet Peale still governed the terms of the experience. The curtain set the experience up as a special type of event, and it established a level of decorum. Anyone who pulled back the curtain intruded upon a mother's private moment of grief, and could not help but sympathize with the subject.[2]

Peale similarly draped objects that exemplified physical abnormality, which resulted in exhibits that offered the same dynamic of perceived audience control within a structured display. In 1795, Peale hung the hideous portrait showing John Gallaway's bare, scarred, horned chest behind a curtain. As the curtain in front of *Rachel Weeping* protected the mother's privacy, this curtain also upheld a standard of decency by protecting viewers from nudity and deformity. But with the curtain Peale also conditioned viewers to expect a shocking display if they dared to look, and he engaged them in a suspenseful moment of self-preparation. Peale also veiled the deformity of a cow, announcing the exhibit in the same advertisement as the portrait of Gallaway: "The Cow with 5 legs, 6 feet and two tails, which was kept at the Museum for some years alive, is also preserved; but as such objects are not agreeable to the sight of every one, that limb is covered with a curtain." Within this draped display, Peale constructed a scene sure to provide a titillating shock, and at the same time he normalized the animal for those who chose to avoid the shock.[3]

In an engraved gift acknowledgment (figure 40), Peale used a curtain to symbolically include donors in the act of revealing nature for the enlightenment of others. An allegorical figure pulls back a curtain to expose a natural environment inhabited by animals native to land, water, and air. The inscription, "Of grains are Mountains form'd," indicates that from the individual gifts of audience members Peale's Museum is collectively built. Peale orchestrates this communal effort, and he accepts responsibility for preserving all donations and applying them to the service of "public utility." This image, then, is emblematic of the museum as a system of mutual benefits that profited both Peale and his active audience members.[4]

The museum's various constituencies worked within the structures Peale created to promote their own economic, social, and intellectual interests. For instance, as museum keeper, Peale collected, preserved, and exhibited objects. He advertised in the newspapers, requesting specific categories of desired items. Audience members responded by donating artifacts and natural history specimens that reflected their own concerns. Peale then installed the contributions in his displays, labeled them with the names of the donors, and advertised the new acquisitions in the newspaper. For Peale, these relationships inexpensively expanded the collections. For donors, such gifts afforded them public recognition as cultural benefactors. In addition to this distinction, donors also promoted their business ventures, scholarly accomplishments, and attitudes about the proper parameters of community. In each of these ways, the museum's audience capitalized on the structured environment crafted by Peale.

Of grains are Mountains form'd.

To advance the interest of the Museum, or Repository of Nature and Art, is indirectly conducing to the public benefit; permit me therefore, to join my assurances of obligation for any assistance you may render the institution by

And since it is from the science, zeal and liberality of individuals that we must be indebted for the developement of Nature's boundless stores, as well as the ingenuity of art; it shall be my endeavour so to dispose of them as may insure their preservation and public utility.

Sir, with respect,

Museum, Philadelphia,   180

Figure 40. James Akin after Charles Willson Peale, Gift acknowledgment from Peale's Museum, 1801–4. American Philosophical Society, Philadelphia.

Audience members who participated in other forms of patronage similarly served both Peale's and their own interests. Travel writers contributed to Peale's fame, even when they criticized him, and they found the museum to be one of the many cultural sites that attracted readers to this popular genre of books. Purchasers of silhouette portraits and annual tickets similarly benefitted themselves and Peale. The sensation that the physiognotrace caused at the museum attracted thousands of paying customers, who enjoyed the modest cost, the accurate though simple likenesses of themselves, and the amusement of sitting for their portraits. In addition to the opportunity for personal financial gain, Peale perceived in the product a chance for scientific inquiry into physiognomic character. Members of Peale's audience shared his interest in ordering the paper portraits they collected, but kinship and not head type was the characteristic that determined the syntax of the albums they produced.

Subscriptions to annual tickets also contributed to the financial success of the museum. Peale gained prestige for the institution as he collected the signatures of the nation's most powerful politicians, wealthiest merchants, and most esteemed intellectuals. The elite, in turn, had their elevated place confirmed in the institutional structure of the museum and through the process of public affiliation with one another. Patrons from the middling sort also gained through their purchases of annual tickets. They achieved easy access to the museum and the privilege of publicly associating as "Friends of Science." Despite the apparent leveling of elite and middling in the act of subscribing, the double row of portraits on display in the museum demonstrated the persistence of an elevated realm. Though identified by their achievements, rather than by birthright, this select group of portrait-sitters—some of whom were also supporters of the museum—constituted the height of the republican social structure.

In its various dimensions, Peale's Museum demonstrates the potency of public culture in the early republic. The impulse toward order in the museum is suggestive of a broader need to establish economic, social, and political structures within a country recently independent of monarchical rule and colonial status. The museum contributed to the formulation of responses to a number of pressing questions: Who would control the nation's economic resources and what forms of production would predominate? How would the society balance the impulses toward individual and community gain? Who would share in what tasks and in what privileges? Who would command the stations of authority and upon what grounds would they govern? Peale's verbal and visual statements resonated variously with the elite and the populace, men and women, white and black, Democratic Republican and Federalist, Quakers and people of other denominations, and infirm and well. The composition of Peale's audience suggests that, despite the inclusive rhetoric, early republican cultural institutions ironically contributed to the continuation of social inequality. Significantly, the gender and socioeconomic profile of Peale's audience was disproportionately male and high in status. Similarly, the absence of African-Americans from the museum echoed their marginal place in the social and economic order of the early republic. The hierarchical world that Peale crafted for exhibition best served men who belonged to the middle and higher ranks of society. For these patrons, the ideals embodied in the museum displays—nature as a resource, technology as a means of utilizing that resource, morality and order as tools for developing a productive society, and harmony and hierarchy as natural—all bolstered their elevated place in the community.

Appendix: Subscribers to Peale's Museum in 1794, Grouped by Occupation and Ranked by Wealth

Subscriber and Occupation[a]	Secondary Occupation[b]	Taxable Wealth (Pounds)	Percentile[c]	Per-Head Tax[d]	Source[e]
U.S. Senators (Total = 20)					
Morris, Robert: Pa.	Merchant	8,765	90th		2e; 5; 6
Izard, Ralph: S.C.	Planter	330	60th		2e; 5; 6
Bradford, William: R.I.	Doctor, Lawyer				6
Bradley, Stephen R.: Vt.	Lawyer, Judge				5; 6
Brown, John: Ky.	Lawyer				5; 6
Burr, Aaron: N.Y.	Lawyer				5; 6
Butler, Pierce: S.C.	Planter				5; 6
Cabot, George: Mass.	Merchant				5; 6
Edwards, John: Ky.	Planter				5; 6
Frelinghuysen, Frederick: N.J.	Lawyer				5; 6
Gunn, James: Ga.	Lawyer				6
Jackson, James: Ga.	Lawyer				5; 6
King, Rufus: N.Y.	Lawyer				5; 6
Langdon, John: N.H.	Merchant				5; 6
Livermore, Samuel: N.H.	Lawyer, Judge				5; 6
Martin, Alexander: N.C.	Merchant				5; 6
Mitchell, Stephen M.: Conn.	Lawyer, Judge				5; 6
Monroe, James: Va.	Lawyer, Planter				5; 6
Rutherfurd, John: N.J.	Lawyer				6
Vining, John: Del.	Lawyer				6
Average or Overall ($N = 2$)		4,548	90th		
Pa. State Officials (Total = 4)					
Bingham, William: State Senator	Banker	9,703	90th		1c; 2b; 4b; 5
Mifflin, Thomas: Governor		2,032	90th		1c; 2e; 5
Swanwick, John: State Representative	Merchant	1,572	80th		1c; 2f; 4a
Latimer, George: Speaker, House of Representatives		313	60th		1c; 2f; 4a
Average or Overall ($N = 4$)		3,405	90th		
Bankers (Total = 2)					
Nixon, John: President, Bank of North America		2,174	90th		1c; 2f; 5
Wells, Richard: Cashier, Bank of North America		1,780	80th		1c; 2h
Average or Overall ($N = 2$)		1,977	80th		

(continued)

Subscriber and Occupation[a]	Secondary Occupation[b]	Taxable Wealth (Pounds)	Percentile[c]	Per-Head Tax[d]	Source[e]
Gentlemen (Total = 9)					
Hill, Henry		3,650	90th		1c; 2f
Moore, Thomas Lloyd		2,276	90th		1c; 2f
Bordley, John Beale		2,116	90th		1c; 2f; 5
Turner, William		2,031	90th		1c
Mackenzie, William		1,258	80th	30s	1c; 2f; 5
Penn, John		505	70th		1c; 2f; 5
Heath, Charles P.		0	Zero	15s	2h, 1795, 1797
Ball, Blackall William					1e
Caldwell, Andrew					1a
Average or Overall (*N* = 7)		1,690	80th		
U.S. Representatives (Total = 68)					
Fitzsimons, Thomas: Pa.	Merchant	2,445	90th		2e; 5; 6
Muhlenberg, Frederick A.: Pa.; Speaker of the House	Minister	1,056	70th		2i; 5; 6; 9a
Griffin, Samuel: Va.	Lawyer	0	Zero		2b; 6
Armstrong, James: Pa.	Doctor				6
Bailey, Theodorus: N.Y.	Lawyer				6
Blount, Thomas: N.C.	Merchant				5; 6
Boudinot, Elias: N.J.	Lawyer				5; 6
Bourne, Benjamin: R.I.	Lawyer				5; 6
Bourne, Shearjashub: Mass.	Lawyer				6
Cadwallader, Lambert: N.J.	Merchant				5; 6; 7a
Carnes, Thomas P.: Ga.	Lawyer				6
Christie, Gabriel: Md.	Unknown				6
Coffin, Peleg, Jr.: Mass.	Unknown				6
Coit, Joshua: Conn.	Lawyer				6
Coles, Isaac: Va.	Unknown				6
Dayton, Jonathan: N.J.	Lawyer				5; 6
Dearborn, Henry: Mass.	Doctor				5; 6
Dent, George: Md.	Unknown				6
Forrest, Uriah: Md.	Unknown				6
Foster, Dwight: Mass.	Lawyer				6
Foster, Theodore: R.I.	Lawyer				5; 6
Gilbert, Ezekiel: N.Y.	Lawyer				6
Giles, William B.: Va.	Lawyer				5; 6
Gillespie, James: N.C.	Unknown				6
Gilman, Nicholas: N.H.	Clerk				5; 6
Glen, Henry: N.Y.	Unknown				6
Gordon, James: N.Y.	Trader with Indians				6

(*continued*)

Subscriber and Occupation[a]	Secondary Occupation[b]	Taxable Wealth (Pounds)	Percentile[c]	Per-Head Tax[d]	Source[e]
Gregg, Andrew: Pa.	Farmer				5; 6
Harrison, Carter B.: Va.	Unknown				6
Hartley, Thomas: Pa.	Lawyer				5; 6
Heath, John: Va.	Lawyer				6
Hiester, Daniel: Pa.	Farmer				5; 6
Hindman, William: Md.	Lawyer				5; 6
Holten, Samuel: Mass.	Doctor				5; 6
Hunter, John: S.C.	Planter				6
Learned, Amasa: Conn.	Minister, Land Speculator				6
Lee, Richard Bland: Va.	Unknown				5; 6
Lyman, William: Mass.	Unknown				6
Macon, Nathaniel: N.C.	Planter				5; 6
Madison, James, Jr.: Va.					5; 6
Malbone, Francis: R.I.	Merchant				6
Montgomery, William: Pa.	Judge				6
Muhlehnberg, John Peter Gabriel: Pa.	Minister				5; 6; 9a
Nicholas, John: Va.	Lawyer				5; 6
Niles, Nathaniel: Vt.	Preacher, Inventor				5; 6
Page, John: Va.	Unknown				5; 6
Parker, Josiah: Va.	Planter				5; 6
Pickens, Andrew: S.C.	Planter, Merchant				5; 6
Preston, Francis: Va.	Lawyer				6
Rutherford, Robert: Va.	Unknown				6
Scott, Thomas: Pa.	Lawyer				6
Sherburne, John Samuel: N.H.	Lawyer				6
Smilie, John: Pa.	Unknown				6
Smith, Israel: Vt.	Lawyer				5; 6
Smith, Jeremiah: N.H.	Lawyer				5; 6
Smith, Samuel: Md.	Merchant				5; 6
Sprigg, Thomas: Md.	Unknown				6
Tracy, Uriah: Conn.	Lawyer				5; 6
Trumbull, Jonathan: Conn.	Unknown				5; 6
Van Alen, John E.: N.Y.	Farmer, Surveyor				6
Van Cortlandt, Philip: N.Y.	Farmer				5; 6
Van Gaasbeck, Peter: N.Y.	Merchant				6
Venable, Abraham B.: Va.	Lawyer				6
Wadsworth, Jeremiah: Conn.	Merchant				5; 6
Walker, Francis: Va.	Unknown				6

(continued)

Subscriber and Occupation[a]	Secondary Occupation[b]	Taxable Wealth (Pounds)	Percentile[c]	Per-Head Tax[d]	Source[e]
Watts, John: N.Y.	Studied Law				6
Williams, Benjamin: N.C.	Planter				6
Winn, Richard: S.C.	Merchant				5; 6
Average or Overall (*N* = 3)		1,167	70th		
Scientists (Total = 3)					
Lerebower, Alexandre					11c, p. 206
Michaux, André: Botanist					5
Rittenhouse, David: Instrument Maker; Astronomer; Mathematician; Director of U.S. Mint; and State Treasurer of Pa.		1,161	80th		1c; 2i; 5; 10a
Average or Overall (*N* = 1)		1,161	70th		
Elected Officials of the City and County of Philadelphia (Total = 5)					
Lewis, Mordecai: Common Councilman	Merchant	2,302	90th		1c; 2b
Barclay, John: Alderman	Banker: President of Bank of Pa.	1,573	80th		1c; 2f
Baker, John: Alderman; County Treasurer		882	70th		1c; 2g
Chew, Benjamin, Jr.: Common Councilman	Attorney	219	60th		1c; 2b
McCrea, John: Common Councilman	Unknown	0	10th	30s	1c; 2j
Average or Overall (*N* = 5)		995	70th		
Appointed Public Officials (Total = 25)					
Chew, Benjamin: Judge, High Court of Errors and Appeals, Pa.		3,643	90th		1c; 2b; 5
Stewart, Walter: Inspector of the Revenue and Surveyor of the Port		3,245	90th		1c; 2f
Fox, Edward: Vendue Master		2,188	90th		1c; 2l
Delany, Sharp: Collector, Port of Philadelphia		2,078	90th		1c; 2b
Shippen, Edward: Justice, State Supreme Court, Pa.		1,728	80th		1c; 2b; 5

(continued)

Subscriber and Occupation[a]	Secondary Occupation[b]	Taxable Wealth (Pounds)	Percentile[c]	Per-Head Tax[d]	Source[e]
Peters, Richard: Judge, U.S. District Court, Pa.		1,214	80th		1c; 2j; 5
Randolph, Edmund: Secretary of State		645	70th		1c; 2h; 5
Allibone, William: Superintendent of Piers and Lighthouse, Philadelphia		629	70th		1c; 2f
Hamilton, Alexander: Secretary of Treasury		542	70th		1c; 2j; 5
Knox, Henry: Secretary of War		425	60th		1c; 2e; 5
McKean, Thomas: Chief Justice of Pa.		417	60th		1c; 2f; 5
Ingersoll, Jared: Attorney General, Pa.		405	60th		1c; 2e; 5
Meredith, Samuel: U.S. Treasurer		330	60th		1c; 2e; 5
Dallas, A. J.: Pa. Secretary of the Commonwealth		325	60th		1c; 2i; 5
Coxe, Tench: Commissioner of Revenue		324	60th		1c; 2j; 5
Smith, Jonathan Bayard: Register General of Pa.; Philadelphia Alderman	Merchant	248	60th		1c; 2i; 5
Wolcott, Oliver: Comptroller of Revenue		124	50th		1c; 2b; 5
Moylan, Stephen: Commissioner of Loans		100	50th		1c; 2b; 5
Boys, Nathaniel: Philadelphia Commissioner for Lighting and Paving the Streets		50	30th		1c; 2f
Nicholas, Lewis: Brigadier General, Debtors Department		50	30th		1c; 2b
Bradford, William: U.S. Attorney General					1c; 5
Breece, Charles: Constable					1i
Burrall, Charles: Assistant Postmaster General					1b
Irvine, James: Retired Major-General, Pa. militia					1h; 5
Trist, H. B.: Collector, Port of New Orleans, as of 1802					7a
Average or Overall (*N* = 20)		935	70th		

(continued)

Subscriber and Occupation[a]	Secondary Occupation[b]	Taxable Wealth (Pounds)	Percentile[c]	Per-Head Tax[d]	Source[e]
Merchants (Total = 42)					
Calbraith, James		2,770	90th		1c; 2a, 1795
Coates, Samuel		2,269	90th		1c; 2l; 5
Mulowny, John ("Captain")		1,722	80th		1c; 2f
Meade, George		1,711	80th		1c; 2b; 5
Clymer, George		1,693	80th		1c; 2j; 5
Fries, John		1,368	80th		1c; 2e
McConnell, Matthew		1,201	80th		1c; 2j
Miller, John, Jr.		837	70th		1c; 2f
Boehm, Daniel		745	70th		1c; 2i
Collins, Zaccheus		745	70th		1c; 2i
Thomas, Luke		610	70th		1c; 2e
Miller, Alexander I.[?] [or J.?]		556	70th		1c; 2f
Pennock, George		191	60th		1c; 2h
Clement, Jacob		150	60th		1c; 2d, 1795
Blanchard, John D.		128	50th		1c; 2e
Roberts, Michael		127	50th		1c; 2e
Sutcliff, Joshua		105	50th		1f; 2f, 1796
Brown, John		100	50th		1c; 2f
Fricke, Augustus		55	40th		1c, suppl.; 2e
Hewes, Josiah		35	30th	30s	2e
McCormick, David		30	20th	30s	1c; 2e
Holmes, Hugh		8	20th	30s	1c; 2a, 1795
Mussi, Joseph		4	20th	30s	1c; 2e
Drinker, Joseph D.		0	10th	30s	1c; 2a, 1795
Morris, Richard Hill		0	10th	30s	2j, 1794, 1796
Jones, Isaac C.		0	10th	20s	1d; 2e
Higbee, Joseph		0	Zero	15s	1e; 2f
Beck, Henry		0	Zero	$1.00	1h; 2i, 1796
Beauchamp, William					1g
Bridges, Robert, Jr.					10c
Caldwell, James					10c
Correy, Robert: Wine Merchant					1c
Field, Joseph					1i
Garrigues, Abraham					1h
Henderson, Robert					1c
McCallmont, George					1h
Massey, William					1e
Rees, David					1c
Simson, John					1d; 1g
Stein, Philip					1c

(*continued*)

Subscriber and Occupation[a]	Secondary Occupation[b]	Taxable Wealth (Pounds)	Percentile[c]	Per-Head Tax[d]	Source[e]
Stewardson, Thomas					1g
Williams, Jonathan					5
Average or Overall (*N* = 28)		613	60th		
Apothecaries (Total = 3)					
Marshall, Christopher, Jr.		1,122	70th		1c; 2e
Marshall, Charles, Jr.		0	Zero	$1.00	1c; 2j, 1796
Thomson, Jesse					1h
Average or Overall (*N* = 2)		561	60th		
Dentists (Total = 1)					
Gardette, James		558	70th		1c; 2j
Average or Overall (*N* = 1)		558	60th		
Attorneys (Total = 8)					
Mifflin, John Fishbourne		1,955	80th		1c; 2f
Fisher, Miers		1,013	70th		1c; 2b
Caldwell, John		85	50th		1c; 2b
Barton, William		58	40th		1e; 2h
Hallowell, John		21	20th	30s	1c
Tod, William H.		0	10th	25s	1c; 2b
Leaming, Thomas, Jr.					1e
Magaw, Algernon Sydney					7a
Average or Overall (*N* = 6)		522	60th		
Ironmongers (Total = 9)					
Wistar, Richard		1,530	80th		1c; 2j
Bringhurst, James		1,200	80th		1c; 2b
Lowne, Caleb		203	60th		1c; 2h
Hopkins, Richard		131	50th		1c; 2c, 1795
Carrell, John		121	50th		1c; 2a, 1795
Dilworth, Samuel		77	40th		1c; 2b
Poultney, John		70	40th		1c; 2e
Lane, William I.		63	40th		1e; 2b
Bringhurst, Joseph, Jr.		0	Zero	15s	2f
Average or Overall (*N* = 9)		377	60th		
Clergymen (Total = 14)					
White, William: Episcopal; Bishop of Pa.		1,846	80th		1c; 2j; 5; 9a

(*continued*)

Subscriber and Occupation[a]	Secondary Occupation[b]	Taxable Wealth (Pounds)	Percentile[c]	Per-Head Tax[d]	Source[e]
Marshall, William: Associate Church		450	60th		1c; 2f; 9a
Ewing, John: Presbyterian	Educator	101	50th		1e; 2b; 5; 7a; 9a
Fleeson, Thomas: Baptist		78	40th		1c; 2e
Magaw, Samuel: Episcopal	Educator	78	40th		1c; 2f; 7a; 9a
Helmuth, Henry: Lutheran	Educator	52	40th		1c; 2e; 5; 7a; 9a
Andrews, John: Episcopal	Educator	26	20th		1c; 2h; 5; 7a; 9a
Green, Ashbel: Presbyterian		16	20th		1c; 2g; 5; 9a
Abercrombie, James: Episcopal		0	Zero		1c; 2f; 9a
Collin, Nicholas: Gloria Dei (or Swedish) Church					1c; 9a
Pilmore, Joseph: Episcopal					5; 9a
Smith, John Blair: Presbyterian					1c; 5; 9a
Smith, William: Episcopal	Educator				5; 7a; 9a
Waddell, Henry L.: Episcopal					7a
Average or Overall (*N* = 9)		294	60th		
Printers and Booksellers (Total = 4)					
Wilson, William: Stationer		750	70th		1c; 2c, 1795
Ormrod, John: Bookseller; Stationer; Printer		51	30th		1c; 2a, 1795
Mountford, Timothy: Printer		0	Zero	15s	1c, suppl.; 2i
Birch, William Young: Stationer		0	Zero	10s	1h; 2j
Average or Overall (*N* = 4)		200	50th		
Scriveners, Conveyancers, and Brokers (Total = 6)					
Shoemaker, Abraham: Scrivener and Conveyancer		458	70th		1c; 2b
Lohra, Peter: Notary Public		224	60th		1c; 2l
Biddle, Clement: Notary Public; Scrivener; Broker; Soldier; Merchant		127	50th		1c; 2b; 5
Boggs, Joseph: Conveyancer and Broker		50	30th		1c; 2l
Biddle, William M.: Broker		0	10th	20s	1h; 2h

(continued)

Subscriber and Occupation[a]	Secondary Occupation[b]	Taxable Wealth (Pounds)	Percentile[c]	Per-Head Tax[d]	Source[e]
Biddle, Thomas: Broker					7a
Average or Overall (*N* = 5)		172	50th		
Distillers (Total = 1)					
Wood, William		106	50th		1c; 2h
Average or Overall (*N* = 1)		106	40th		
Innkeepers (Total = 2)					
Hill, George		54	40th		1c; 2g
Horn, Benjamin: Tavern Keeper					1c
Average or Overall (*N* = 1)		54	30th		
Woodworkers (Total = 9)					
Allwine, Lawrance: Windsor Chair Maker		100	50th		1c; 2d, 1795
Hains, Adam: Cabinetmaker; Joiner		50	30th		1c; 2g
Sink, Laurence: Cabinetmaker; Joiner		50	30th		1c; 2f
Dyer, William: House Carpenter		30	30th		1h; 2i, 1796
Webb, Joseph: Carpenter		25	20th		2f
Barry, Henry: Cabinetmaker					1c, suppl.
Cowperthwait, Thomas: Carpenter					1h
French, William: House Carpenter					1e
Graff, Frederick: Carpenter					10a
Average or Overall (*N* = 5)		51	30th		
Leather and Cloth Workers (Total = 10)					
Barker, John: Tailor		75	40th		1c; 2i
Smiley, William: Tailor		75	40th		1c; 2d, 1795
Hall, John: Tailor and Stay Maker		51	30th		1c; 2b
Benge, Samuel: Upholsterer and Umbrella Maker		50	30th		1c; 2e
Linton, William: Tailor		30	20th		1c; 2d, 1795
Guyere, Charles: Shoemaker		15	20th		1e; 2i
Carr, Thomas: Leather Breeches Maker					1c

(*continued*)

Subscriber and Occupation[a]	Secondary Occupation[b]	Taxable Wealth (Pounds)	Percentile[c]	Per-Head Tax[d]	Source[e]
Heston, Levi: Currier					1c
Robinson, Samuel: Hatter					1c
Vincent, John: Cordwainer					1c
Average or Overall (*N* = 6)		49	30th		
Grocers (Total = 6)					
Toland, Henry		112	50th		1c; 2h
McInnes, Duncan		30	20th		1c; 2j
Hertzog, Joseph		0	10th	22s 6p	1d; 2g
Cowperthwaite, Samuel					1c
Cumming, George					1c
Williamson, Daniel					1i
Average or Overall (*N* = 3)		47	30th		
Doctors (Total = 16)					
Porter, John: Physician		150	60th		1c; 2f
Griffitts, Samuel Powel: M.D.		105	50th		1c; 2j; 7b
Glentworth, Plunkett F.: M.D.		70	40th		1c; 2i; 7b
James, Thomas C.: M.D.		30	30th	30s	1c; 2a, 1795; 7b
Cumming, John: M.D.		0	20th	30s	1c; 2l
Le Breton, Stephen: Physician		0	10th	30s	1c; 2e
Gallaher, James: M.D.		0	10th	20s	1c; 1h; 2h, 1795
Price, Philip P.: M.D.		0	Zero	20s	1c; 2e
Grassi, C.F.A.: M.D. (of Bordeaux, France)		0	Zero	10s	2i; 8
Balfour, George: Surgeon					10b, v. 19, p. 114; v. 21, p. 120
Barnwell, William: M.D.					8
Conover, Samuel: M.D.					1h; 7b
Cutbush, Edward: M.D.					1e; 7b
Martin, William: M.D.					7b
Perkins, Elijah: M.D.					1c; 7b
Smith, Thomas: M.D.					Peale's 1803 subscriber list
Average or Overall (*N* = 9)		39	20th		

(continued)

Subscriber and Occupation[a]	Secondary Occupation[b]	Taxable Wealth (Pounds)	Percentile[c]	Per-Head Tax[d]	Source[e]
Painters and Printmakers (Total = 2)					
Thackara, James: Engraver		50	30th		1c; 2f
Pratt, Matthew: Limner		25	20th		1c; 2f; 5
Average or Overall (*N* = 2)		38	20th		
Shopkeepers (Total = 6)					
Bartlett, Edward		50	30th		1c; 2g
Cope, Jasper		75	40th		1c, suppl.; 2h
Clinton, John: Dealer in Shoes and Queensware		25	20th		1e; 2a, 1796
Hembel, William, Jr.		0	10th	20s	1c; 2k
Stokes, William F.		0	Zero	20s	1c; 2e
Treichel, E. Lewis					1c
Average or Overall (*N* = 5)		30	20th		
Metal Workers (Total = 6)					
Parry, Rowland: Goldsmith		80	50th		1e; 2e
Wiltberger, Christian: Silversmith		65	40th		1c; 2a, 1795; 9b
Brasier, Amable: Watchmaker		25	20th		1c; 2h
Passmore, Thomas: Tin Plate Worker		0	10th	25s	1c; 2e
Harbeson, Benjamin, Jr.: Copper and Tin Manufacturer		0	10th	20s	1c; 2e
Condon, Samuel: Smith		0	Zero	10s	2k, 1795; 3
Average or Overall (*N* = 6)		28	20th		
Clerks (Total = 12)					
Stagg, John, Jr.: U.S. War Department		60	40th		1c; 2g
Harper, Thomas		53	40th		1c; 2f
Jones, Edward H.: Office of the U.S. Treasury, Secretary		50	30th		1c; 2f
Mifflin, Benjamin: U.S. War Department		50	30th		1c; 2f
Betterton, Benjamin: U.S. War Department		38	30th		1c; 2i
Lewis, Samuel: U.S. War Department	Geographer	30	20th		1c; 1d; 2i

(*continued*)

Subscriber and Occupation[a]	Secondary Occupation[b]	Taxable Wealth (Pounds)	Percentile[c]	Per-Head Tax[d]	Source[e]
Hughes, George: Bank of the U.S.		0	10th	30s	1c; 2e
Ashbridge, John		0	10th	22s 6p	2g
Graydon, Andrew: U.S. Treasury Department		0	10th	20s	1c; 2h
Lambert, William		0	10th	20s	2e
Ely, Joseph		0	Zero	17s 6p	2g
Smyth, John: Department of State					1c
Average or Overall (*N* = 11)		26	20th		
Educators (Total = 3)					
Sharpless, Joseph: Schoolmaster		4	20th	4s	1c
Moller, John C.: Music Instructor					10b, v. 30, pp. 41, 314; 10b, v. 31, p. 62
Tucker, Benjamin: Schoolmaster					1h
Average or Overall (*N* = 1)		4	10th		
Surveyors (Total = 2)					
King, Nicholas		0	10th	20s	2i
Moore, Joshua		0	Zero	20s	2i
Average or Overall (*N* = 2)		0	Zero		
Medical Students, University of Pa. (Total = 5)					
Ball, Thomas					7b; 7c
Cabell, George					7b; 7c; 12a
Everett, Charles					7b
Hahn, John					7b
Shultz, Benjamin					7b
Diplomats (Total = 3)					
Jaudenes, Joseph de: Commissary General and Envoy to U.S. from Spain					1c
Santayana, Joseph de: Secretary of the Spanish Legation					1c

(continued)

Subscriber and Occupation[a]	Secondary Occupation[b]	Taxable Wealth (Pounds)	Percentile[c]	Per-Head Tax[d]	Source[e]
Viar, Joseph Ignatts: Consul General of Spain					1c
Sea Captains (Total = 3)					
Brown, William D.					1c
Curwen, George					1g
Hunn, John					1c
U.S. Executive Officers (Total = 2)					
Washington, George: President; General; Planter					5
Adams, John: Vice President	Lawyer				5
Agriculturalists (Total = 1)					
Adlum, John: Viticulturist; Surveyor					5; 11a
Bakers (Total = 1)					
Baker, Nathan: Biscuit Baker					1e
Occupation Not Listed (Total = 7)					
Deglos and his wife		0	Zero	10s	2i
DeVillers, Auguste		0	Zero	10s	2i
Marshall, Eliza[beth] F.: Daughter of Christopher Marshall, Jr.					12c, p. 35
Marshall, Margaret: Wife of Christopher Marshall, Jr.					12b, p. 393
Meredith, Margaret: Wife of Samuel Meredith					5
Parent, Abigail: Wife[?] of Peter Parent, a French printer					1c
Smiley, Mrs.: Wife of William Smiley					subscriber list
Average or Overall (*N* = 2)		0	Zero		

[a]Subscribers are listed by their primary occupations in 1794.
[b]"Unknown" implies that a secondary occupation was probable but not identified, whereas no listing implies no secondary occupation.
[c]Overall percentile for each occupational group was determined as described in note 24 to chapter 5.
[d]In shillings and pence, or in dollars.
[e]Numbers in this column denote the sources of the occupational information; full citations are listed at the end of the appendix. Suppl. = supplement.

Subscribers Not Definitively Identified (Total = 34)

Abel, John N.   Perhaps John Able, laborer, 15 Sassafras Alley (1c); or John Able, tanner, Brown Street, Northern Liberties (1c).

Bliss, Thomas.   Perhaps Captain Thomas Theodore Bliss, who was captured by Indians on May 20, 1776 (10b, v. 59, p. 329).

Chandler, William S[?].   A William Penn Chandler was an M.D. (1e; 1f).

Clement, James.   Perhaps James Clemens, clerk (1c).

Clemmens, Christian.   A grocer and a hostler were listed under this name (1c).

Cliffton, William, Jr.   There was William Clifton, shopkeeper, and William Clifton, blacksmith. Neither was listed as junior (1c).

Davis, David.   Perhaps the man who was listed in Blockley Township by this name, no occupation specified, was the same person (3).

Davis, James.   An ironmonger and a joiner were listed under this name (1c).

Dowers, John, Jr.   Perhaps the sail maker, but he was not listed as junior (1h).

Forman, Ezekiel.   On October 14, 1745, Ezekiel Forman of East Jersey indentured James Mahan his servant (10b, v. 30, p. 431). On November 14, 1775, Peale painted a miniature of a Mr. Forman, whom Miller identifies as Ezekiel Forman, a planter and Maryland legislator (11a; 11b, pp. 154 and 157–58). A planter named Ezekiel Forman in New Jersey was a Loyalist who enlisted in the British army and served from 1776–8; he lived in Pennsylvania after the war (*Proceedings of the New Jersey Historical Society*, v. 11, n.s., July 1926, p. 294).

Hamilton, William.   William R. Hamilton, printer (1c); William Hamilton, tailor (1c); William Hamilton of Woodlands (11a). William Hamilton signed the subscription book before Timothy Mountford, a printer, which suggests "printer" as the most likely identity. The signature of William Hamilton of Woodlands appears on a report to the president of the American Philosophical Society, William Roxburgh, December 26, 1793 (American Philosophical Society Archives), and does not match this one.

Harris, William.   John Harris, a member of the Constitutional Convention of 1776, had a son, William, who was a surveyor (10b, v. 30, p. 439). A William Harris was granted a pension as a disabled soldier of the Revolution (10b, v. 42, p. 259). A William Harris represented Chester County in the Pennsylvania Legislature in 1779 (11b, p. 337).

Howell, Samuel E.   Perhaps the iron seller of Samuel Howell & Co.; perhaps Samuel Howell, Sr., merchant (1c).

Hunter, James.   There were three men listed by this name: a merchant, a stocking weaver, and a tallow chandler (1c).

Jarvis, Charles.   A gentleman and a mariner were listed by this name (1h).

Kelly, George B.   George Kelly, blacksmith, assumed the indenture on Mary Wide in September, 1746 (10b, v. 32, p. 354). A George Kelly was paid by Nicholas Biddle as one of his "seamen" in 1776 (10b, v. 74, p. 376).

List, [?], Jr.[?].   A Nathaniel List was a cabinetmaker; Lewis List was a laborer (1c).

Moody, John.   A John Moody was sheriff in Newcastle County, Delaware. He settled with his wife in Southwark, Philadelphia County. His occupation there is unknown (10b, v. 4, p. 238).

Moon, Samuel, Jr.   A Samuel Moon was a Windsor chair maker, but he was not designated junior (1h).

Murray, James S.   A James Murray was listed as a clerk, but his middle initial was not specified (3).

Parry, Evan.   In 1794 there was a listing for Parry & Roberts, lumber merchants (1c).

Phillips, Samuel.   Perhaps a member of the merchant house Phillips, Crammond, & Co. (1c).

Poydras, J.   A Julien Poydras (d. 1824) was a native of Louisiana, and is known to have been a philanthropist; see James Grant Wilson and John Fiske, eds., *Appleton's Cyclopaedia of American Biography* (New York: D. Appleton and Co., 1888), v. 5, p. 100.

Reab, [?].   Perhaps Nicholas Reab, a cordwainer who was taxed in South Mulberry Ward (2i).

Ross, John.   There was John Ross, state representative from Chester County in the Pennsylvania House of Representatives (4a). There were also John Ross (1729–1800), merchant, 22 Pine Street (1c; 11b, p. 385); and John Ross, painter and glazier, 140 North Third Street (1c).

Smith, Richard P.   A Richard Pitt Smith was a merchant (1f); a Richard Penn Smith was a correspondent of Rembrandt Peale; a Richard Peters Smith was a member of the American Philosophical Society (8).

Smyth, Frederick.   A Frederic Smith was a chemist and apothecary; another Frederic Smith was a carter (1c).

Stevenson, William, Jr.   There is a William Stevenson, house carpenter, but he was not listed as junior (1e).

Taylor, George, Jr.   There was a George Taylor, Chief Clerk in the Department of State, but he was not designated junior (1c). There were also listings for Taylor & Bunting, grocers; and Taylor & Gaskell, merchants (1c).

Walker, Thomas Cradock.   An Episcopalian minister Thomas Cradock (1742–70) had a son, Thomas, and also a daughter, Ann, who married Charles Walker. Perhaps Ann and Charles Walker named one of their children after his uncle and grandfather (9a).

Watson, William, Jr.   In 1794 there was a William Watson, sea captain, but he was not listed as junior (1c). In 1796 there was a coach maker by this name, but he was not a junior either (1e).

Williams, James.   There was James Williams, no occupation specified; and James Williams, mariner (1e).

Wilson, George.   There were three laborers and a merchant listed as George Wilson (1c).

Wright, Jna.   In 1800 there were two Jonathan Wrights, one a mariner and the other a carpenter (3).

Subscribers for Whom Occupations Were Not Identified and Tax Assessments Were Unavailable (Total = 47)

Biddle, George
Comber, W. T.
Deas, Robert
Dewall, Grafton
Dickford, John
Dilling, Thomas
Dupasquier, P[?] P[?]
Dykscore[?], Powell C.
Ferris[?], Peter
Field, George W.
Flower, Ann[?].
Garlick, Samuel
Graff, Charles
Hargis, Abraham
Hargis, John M.
Immel, Jacob
Kennedy[?], Michael
Masfield [Warfield?], Thomas
Mathieu, Ler[?]. Fis[?].
Mifflin, Thomas, Jr.
Morris, Paul
Murray, Archibald[?]
Norris, Jesse
Pierce, Robert

Pork[?], Peter
Possils[?], Frances[?]
Procter, Levi
Rampler[?], Jas.
Reinholdt, Daniel
Reinholdt, Frederick
Reinholdt, Henry
Rinker, James
Rinker, Jona.
St. George, Henry
Selden, William B.
Shewell, Joseph
Shinckle, William
Simson, George
Smith, John
Spiro[?], James
Spyker, Jonathan
Stille, Benjamin
Stille, Gustavus
Tirel[?], Celestin
Tirel[?], Joseph
Walsh, Nicholas
Williams, William B.

SOURCES FOR APPENDIX

1. Philadelphia City Directories
    a. Biddle, Clement. *The Philadelphia Directory* (Philadelphia: James & Johnson, 1791).
    b. Hardie, James. *The Philadelphia Directory and Register* (Philadelphia: printed for the author by T. Dobson, 1793).
    c. Hardie, James. *The Philadelphia Directory and Register*, 2d ed. (Philadelphia: Jacob Johnson & Co., 1794).
    d. Hogan, Edmund. *The Prospect of Philadelphia, and Check on the Next Directory* (Philadelphia: Francis and Robert Bailey, 1795).
    e. Stephens, Thomas. *Stephens's Philadelphia Directory for 1796* (Philadelphia: W. Woodward, 1796).
    f. Stafford, Cornelius W. *The Philadelphia Directory for 1797* (Philadelphia: William W. Woodward, 1797).
    g. Stafford, Cornelius W. *The Philadelphia Directory for 1798* (Philadelphia: William W. Woodward, 1798).
    h. Stafford, Cornelius W. *The Philadelphia Directory for 1800* (Philadelphia: William W. Woodward, 1800).
    i. Robinson, James. *The Philadelphia Directory for 1804* (Philadelphia: John H. Oswald, 1804).
2. Philadelphia County Tax Assessment Ledgers, ms., Philadelphia City Archives. (Ledgers from 1794 were used unless otherwise noted.)
    a. Chestnut Ward
    b. Dock Ward
    c. High Street Ward
    d. Lower Delaware Ward
    e. Middle Ward
    f. New Market Ward
    g. North Mulberry Ward
    h. North Ward
    i. South Mulberry Ward
    j. South Ward
    k. Upper Delaware Ward
    l. Walnut Ward
3. Enumeration of Taxable Citizens in Philadelphia County, 1800, Historical Society of Pennsylvania.
4. Pennsylvania General Assembly
    a. House of Representatives, *Journal of the House of Representatives of the Commonwealth of Pennsylvania* (Philadelphia: Francis Bailey, [1794]).
    b. Senate. *Journal of the Senate of the Commonwealth of Pennsylvania* (Philadelphia: Zachariah Poulson, Jr., [1794]).
5. *Dictionary of American Biography*, 10 vols. plus supplements, edited by Allen Johnson and Dumas Malone (New York: Charles Scribner's Sons, 1928–36; reprint, New York: Charles Scribner's Sons, 1964).

6. Jacob, Kathryn Allamong, and Bruce A. Ragsdale, eds. *Biographical Directory of the United States Congress, 1774–1989* (Washington, D.C.: U.S. Government Printing Office, 1989).

7. University of Pennsylvania

   a. Society of the Alumni. *Biographical Catalogue of the Matriculates of the College; Together with Lists of the Members of the College Faculty and the Trustees, Officers, and Recipients of Honorary Degrees, 1749–1893* (Philadelphia: printed for the Society, 1894).

   b. Society of the Alumni of the Medical Department. *Catalogue of the Alumni of the Medical Department of the University of Pennsylvania, 1765–1877* (Philadelphia: Collins, 1877).

   c. *Alumni Master File,* microfilm, University of Pennsylvania Archives and Record Center, Philadelphia.

8. American Philosophical Society. Member Card File (Philadelphia: American Philosophical Society).

9. Occupational Biographies

   a. Sprague, William B. *Annals of the American Pulpit . . .,* 9 vols. (New York: Robert Carter and Brothers, 1857–69).

   b. Ward, Barbara McLean, and Gerald W. R. Ward. *Silver in American Life: Selections from the Mabel Brady Garvan and Other Collections at Yale University* (New Haven, Conn.: Yale University Press, 1979).

10. Pennsylvania History

    a. Simpson, Henry. *The Lives of Eminent Philadelphians, Now Deceased. Collected from Original and Authentic Sources* (Philadelphia: William Brotherhead, 1859).

    b. *The Pennsylvania Magazine of History and Biography.*

    c. Garvan, Anthony N. B., ed. *The Mutual Assurance Company Papers,* v. 1. *The Architectural Surveys 1784–1794* (Philadelphia: Mutual Assurance Company, 1976).

11. Peale Sources

    a. Sellers, Charles Coleman. *Portaits and Miniatures by Charles Willson Peale. Transactions of the American Philosophical Society,* n.s., v. 42, pt. 1 (Philadelphia: American Philosophical Society, June 1952).

    b. Miller, Lillian B., Sidney Hart, and Toby A. Appel, eds. *Charles Willson Peale: Artist in Revolutionary America, 1735–1791,* v. 1 (1983) in *The Selected Papers of Charles Willson Peale and His Family,* 3 vols. (New Haven, Conn., and London: Yale University Press, 1983–91).

    c. Miller, Lillian B., Sidney Hart, and David C. Ward, eds. *Charles Willson Peale: The Artist as Museum Keeper, 1791–1810,* v. 2 (1988) in *The Selected Papers of Charles Willson Peale and His Family,* 3 vols. (New Haven, Conn., and London: Yale University Press, 1983–91).

12. Genealogical Sources

    a. Brown, Alexander. *The Cabells and Their Kin: A Memorial Volume of History, Biography, and Genealogy* (Boston and New York: Houghton, Mifflin and Co., 1895).

    b. Hinshaw, William Wade, and Thomas Worth Marshall, comps. *Encyclopedia of American Quaker Genealogy,* 7 vols. (1938; reprint, Ann Arbor, Mich.: Edwards Brothers, Inc., 1969–77).

    c. Marshall, Charles, Jr., comp. *Descendants of Christopher Marshall of Dublin, Ireland and Pennsylvania and His Wife Sarah Thomson,* ms. ([Philadelphia]: Genealogical Society of Pennsylvania, n.d.).

Notes

Full details for the abbreviated citations in these notes
are given in the bibliography.

Introduction

1. For Peale's use of the concept "a world in miniature," see Charles Willson Peale to the American Philosophical Society, March 7, 1797, in L. B. Miller, 1980, IIA/21B12; *Aurora. General Advertiser,* January 27, 1800; and Charles Willson Peale, *Autobiography,* typescript, in L. B. Miller, 1980, IIC, p. 272. Nicholas Collin, a supporter of the museum, also invoked this concept in his "Remarks on the utility of Mr. Peale's proposed Lectures in the Museum," 6 parts, *Poulson's American Daily Advertiser,* pt. 2, December 18, 1800. Peale was interested in this concept strictly as a characterization of the collections and display. The phrase "a world in miniature" also echoes sociologist Howard Becker's conception of art as collectively created within "art worlds." These worlds, in Becker's view, consist of the individuals and institutions that produce, disseminate, and consume cultural products. This is an important theoretical consideration for this study, since this book argues that the museum developed through community action (Becker, 1982).

2. Scholarly interest in audience participation in cultural activity spans the boundaries of disciplines. For discussion of audiences in the history of art, see David Freedberg, *The Power of Images: Studies in the History and Theory of Response* (Chicago and London: University of Chicago Press, 1989) and Stefan Germer, "In Search of a Beholder: On the Relation between Art, Audiences, and Social Spheres in Post-Thermidor France," *The Art Bulletin,* v. 75, no. 1, March 1992, pp. 19–35. For discussion of audiences in the history of science, see Steven Shapin, "The Audience for Science in Eighteenth Century Edinburgh," *History of Science,* v. 12, pt. 2, no. 16, June 1974, pp. 95–121. Particularly appropriate to the present study is Shapin's observation, "But it is the concept of *power* residing with the audience for science which is crucial to the exercise. Without an empirical demonstration of the nature of the audience's power over a scientific enterprise, attention to the local audience again becomes meaningless" (p. 96). Also, see G. S. Rousseau, "Science Books and Their Readers in the Eighteenth Century," in Isabel Rivers, ed., *Books and Their Readers in Eighteenth-Century England* (Leicester, England: Leicester University Press and New York: St. Martin's Press, 1982), pp. 197–255. For discussion of audiences in literary and popular culture, see Fish, 1980; Radway, 1984; and C. N. Davidson, 1986.

3. *Pennsylvania Packet,* July 7, 1786, in Miller, Hart, and Appel, 1983, p. 448.

4. For discussions of the audience members depicted in this canvas, see C. C. Sellers, 1952, p. 161; Stein, 1981, pp. 157 and 163, reprinted in Miller and Ward, 1991, pp. 193 and 196–197; and Rigal, 1989, pp. 136–140.

5. For Peale's plea for government support, see *Poulson's American Daily Advertiser,* December 18, 1810. For "unwise" and "learned," see Charles Willson Peale to Philippe Rose Roume, December 25, 1803, in L. B. Miller, 1980, IIA/29C7.

6. For announcement of illumination, see *Aurora. General Advertiser,* February 25, 1797. For announcement of lectures, see *Aurora. General Advertiser,* November 21, 1799.

7. Charles Willson Peale, "Introduction to a Course of Lectures on Natural History Delivered in the University of Pennsylvania, November 16, 1799," in Miller, Hart, and Ward, 1988, p. 266. For Bache's goals for the newspaper, see *General Advertiser,* October 1, 1790. Patriotic songs: For "The Plough Boy" and "America, Commerce and Freedom," see *Aurora. General Advertiser,* July 8, 1802; and for "The Loom and the Shuttle," see *Aurora. General Advertiser,* May 15, 1809. Whereas the triad of agriculture, commerce, and manufactures defined the conventional division of economic pursuits, it was not the only one. Peale also characterized the relevance of the collections to diverse constituents in these terms: "Here may at all times be open the most instructive school for the naturalist, botanist, mineralogist, chemist, anatomist,

171

artist, mechanist, manufacturer, agriculturalist, antiquarian and lover of the fine arts . . .," *Poulson's Amer-ican Daily Advertiser,* December 18, 1810.

8. For first-offered lectures, see *Aurora. General Advertiser,* October 8, 1799. For "Gentleman and lady" admitted for one fee, see *Aurora. General Advertiser,* November 28, 1799. For a "Gentleman" may "in-troduce a lady," see *Poulson's American Daily Advertiser,* November 14, 1800.

9. For an account with pro-French bias, *General Advertiser,* April 12, 1794.

10. Rigal, 1989, pp. 136–40.

11. Kerber, 1986, pp. 189–231. Peale similarly included women among the potential audience for his polygraph, but adopted a patronizing tone in his promotion: "Ladies (if your fathers can spare the expence of 50 or 60 dollars,) urge your husbands to purchase and use the Polygraph; but let none come to 'rob me of my precious time,' through curiosity" *(Aurora. General Advertiser,* October 6, 1803).

12. Charles Willson Peale to George Washington, May 16, 1787, in Miller, Hart, and Appel, 1983, pp. 477–78. Charles Willson Peale to Edmond-Charles Genêt, May 1793, in Miller, Hart, and Ward, 1988, pp. 48–49. Genêt declined the invitation. Charles Willson Peale to Joseph Priestley, June 26, 1794, in Miller, Hart, and Ward, 1988, pp. 96–97. Thomas Jefferson's letter was printed in part in *Poulson's American Daily Advertiser,* December 6, 1804. Charles Willson Peale to Benjamin Henry Latrobe, May 13, 1805, in Miller, Hart, and Ward, 1988, pp. 833–34; Latrobe's letters appeared in *Aurora. General Advertiser,* June 14, 1805. Other entrepreneurs similarly exploited famous members of their audiences. The circus issued ad-vance notice that George and Martha Washington and, later, "Citizen Genêt" would attend particular per-formances *(General Advertiser,* April 20, 1793, and May 28, 1793).

13. For constraints as museum's strength, see *Philadelphia in 1824 . . .,* pp. 101–2. I thank Tony Lewis for sharing this account with me.

14. For Peale's account of the benefit and gratitude to participants, see *Aurora. General Advertiser,* Jan-uary 6, 1797. The owner of a live elephant exhibit similarly offered a benefit for "the sufferers by fire at Sa-vanna" in *Aurora. General Advertiser,* December 16, 1796. For other examples of this convention, see the circus benefits to provide firewood for "indigent families" *(General Advertiser,* July 16, 1793); circus ben-efit to aid refugees from the slave uprising in St. Domingue *(General Advertiser,* July 22, 1793); and the theater benefit for the relief of sailors held captive in Algiers *(General Advertiser,* March 24, 1794).

15. For the "lower sort," see B. G. Smith, 1990.

Chapter 1: Contemporary Institutions of Education and Entertainment and Their Audiences

1. My models for understanding the importance of space to cultural analysis derive from S. G. Davis, 1988, pp. 23–48, and B. G. Smith, 1990, pp. 7–39. The first address of Peale's Museum was 62 Lombard Street, on the southwest corner of Third and Lombard Streets (Hardie, 1793). Although the picture by Rubens Peale was probably painted sometime in 1859 or 1860, many years after he lived there and after the building was destroyed by fire in 1813, the work was based on a contemporary oil sketch now in the col-lection of the American Philosophical Society. The deed to Peale's house and lot on Third and Lombard Street records its purchase from John McCalla, November 20, 1780, in L. B. Miller, 1980, IIA (Add.)/3C7–D4. The deed lists the size of the lot as thirty-six feet along Lombard Street and seventy-seven feet along Third Street. For identification of the outbuildings in the painting attributed to Rubens Peale, see C. C. Sellers, 1969a, p. 197 and fig. 45, and C. C. Sellers, 1980a, p. 22. Peale's neighbors included Charles Smith, coach maker, 60 Lombard Street; John Geyer, baker, 57 Lombard Street; Stephen Bardin, grocer, 184 South Third Street; and Samuel Cuthbert, mast maker, 194 South Third Street, per Hardie, 1793, and per Hogan, 1975, which lists residents by street rather than by alphabetical order. St. Peter's Church, the Episcopal church where Peale was buried, defined more specifically public space on the Third Street block north of Lombard to Pine Street.

2. For discussions of *The Accident in Lombard-Street,* see C. C. Sellers, 1969a, pp. 223 and 224, and Richardson, 1964, p. 178. Beyond demonstrating the context in which the museum first operated, *The Ac-cident in Lombard-Street* establishes two important themes that recur in Peale's exhibits. First, the print pre-sents a moral. In the museum, Peale presented objects as examples of larger truths. For instance, a portrait was more than a likeness; it was a celebration of civic virtue or some other value. Similarly, a preserved an-

imal was meant to transcend its position as a specimen to convey lessons about the economy among all species. Second, the relationship between the girl and the sweeps depends upon viewers' expectations about the subjects' unequal social standings, which in turn depend upon attitudes about socioeconomic rank and about race. The final chapter of this book evaluates Peale's representations of hierarchies among human beings.

3. For Peale's announcement of the museum in its new location, see *General Advertiser,* September 19, 1794. After Peale relocated to Philosophical Hall, his former museum space was sometimes used by itinerant entertainers. See the notice for the animal exhibition of Co-Co and Gibonne, *General Advertiser,* July 31, 1794, and the phantasmagoria, *General Advertiser,* February 2, 1804. Peale also rented the house and outbuildings to Secundo Bossio, who first operated an inn there, and later a livery stable (Hogan, 1795, p. 127; and Stafford, 1798). James Peale was living in his brother's former house by 1801 (Stafford, 1801). The exhibition buildings were destroyed by fire in January of 1813; see *Poulson's American Daily Advertiser,* February 1, 1813. For the University of Pennsylvania in Philosophical Hall from 1789 to 1794, see the chronology in Meyerson and Winegrad, 1978, p. 240. The College of Physicians met in Philosophical Hall from 1791 to 1845, according to the *Transactions of the College of Physicians of Philadelphia,* 3d series, v. 30, 1908, p. 227. I thank Jean Carr at the College of Physicians for this information. For the location of the Library Company of Philadelphia, see Hogan, 1795, p. 131.

4. The *View of Several Public Buildings, in Philadelphia* was published in the *Columbian Magazine,* v. 4, January 1790, opposite p. 25. Descriptive text accompanied the print on page 25. For discussions of this work, see Crompton, 1960, p. 393, fig. 12, and Miller, Hart, and Ward, 1988, p. 94, fig. 12. Crompton attributes the print to James Trenchard, and Miller, Hart, and Ward, 1988, p. 94, attribute the print to James Thackara and John Vallance, probably after Charles Willson Peale.

5. Peale had lobbied annually to the state legislature for public subsidy to increase his collections and to secure permanence for his museum. After years of rejected appeals for monetary assistance, the state of Pennsylvania finally granted Peale use of the upper floor of the State House. Rubens Peale, who assumed the role of manager in 1810, consolidated the exhibitions in the State House in 1811 and the museum remained there until after his father's death in 1827. For a proposed resolution permitting Peale the use of the State House, see *Aurora. General Advertiser,* March 11, 1802, and for its passage, see *Gazette of the United States,* April 8, 1802. For Peale's move into the State House, see *Aurora. General Advertiser,* June 29, 1802. More complete divisions of exhibits in the State House and Philosophical Hall and the admission fees are given in Charles Willson Peale, "Guide to the Philadelphia Museum" (Philadelphia: Museum Press, April 1805), in Miller, Hart, and Ward, 1988, pp. 759–66. For the arrangements transferring control of the museum from Charles to Rubens Peale in 1810, see Miller, Hart, and Ward, 1988, pp. 1245–46. For the consolidation of the exhibits in the State House, see *Poulson's American Daily Advertiser,* August 5, 1811. For the political significance of the State House, see Riley, 1953, pp. 20–25.

6. For the address of Ricketts's Circus and Oellers's Hotel, see Hogan, 1795, p. 141, and for the New Theatre, see Hogan, 1795, p. 139. Peale's residential neighbors at Philosophical Hall included Timothy Pickering, Secretary of State, 155 Chestnut Street (Hogan, 1795, p. 139); Samuel Meredith, Treasurer of the United States, 171 Chestnut Street (Hogan, 1795, p. 139); Mr. Bond, Chargé d'Affaires from Britain, Chestnut Street (Hogan, 1795, p. 139); Jared Ingersoll, attorney at law, 181 Chestnut Street (Hogan, 1795, p. 139); Michael Kepley, John Blakely, and Thomas M. Smith, all attorneys at law on Chestnut Street within one block of Philosophical Hall (Hogan, 1795, p. 141); Joseph Ball, merchant, 153 Chestnut Street (Hogan, 1795, p. 139); David Simmons, coach maker, South Fifth Street (Hogan, 1795, p. 133); and Charles Bellinger and Adam Powles, bakers, 20 South Fifth Street (Hogan, 1795, p. 133).

7. This argument is based on the assumption that language used repeatedly to promote values to a society is culturally loaded and reveals deeply held assumptions. This line of argument benefits from Raymond Williams, *Keywords: A Vocabulary of Culture and Society* (New York: University of Oxford Press, 1976).

8. Peale expressed his commitment to useful knowledge repeatedly, as in his wish to collect, arrange, and preserve all "things useful and curious"; in his desire to make the museum "subservient to the interests of useful science"; and in his aspiration to "render his MUSEUM an object of still more extensive utility to his Fellow-Citizens" (*General Advertiser,* January 18, 1792; August 22, 1794; and *Aurora. General Advertiser,* March 31, 1796).

9. For Franklin's proposal leading to the establishment of the American Philosophical Society, see Franklin, 1982, pp. 197–200. For Peale's election to the American Philosophical Society, see the list of members in the American Philosophical Society, *Year Book 1985.* For Peale's fellow curators, see the *Penn-*

sylvania Packet, January 18, 1788; *General Advertiser,* January 12, 1791; January 9, 1792; January 8, 1793; January 13, 1794; *Aurora. General Advertiser,* January 9, 1795; January 21, 1796; January 13, 1797; January 8, 1799; January 6, 1800; January 6, 1801; January 5, 1802; January 10, 1803; January 13, 1804; January 7, 1805; January 7, 1806; January 3, 1807; January 2, 1808; January 7, 1809; and *Philadelphia Gazette,* January 19, 1798. Peale's first museum advertisement appeared in the *Pennsylvania Packet,* July 25, 1786 (Miller, Hart, and Ward, 1983, p. 448). On curators as librarians, see M. D. Smith, 1976, pp. 19–20. I thank Roy Goodman for providing this citation. On DuSimitière, see Potts, 1889; Huth, 1954; Sifton, 1960; and Orosz, 1985, pp. 8–18.

10. For a series entitled "Public Schools," see *Aurora. General Advertiser,* August 1, 1796; August 6, 1796; August 11, 1796; August 22, 1796; and September 5, 1796. For "A Comparative View . . .," see *General Advertiser,* June 7, 1791. For a similar argument, in which specialized study is promoted for farmers, merchants, and other occupational aspirants in place of the classical education, see "Remarks on the Prevalent Mode of Education," *General Advertiser,* December 8, 1791. Despite the rhetoric of greater inclusiveness in education, recent scholars have argued that early public education reinforced existing hierarchies among the genders and social ranks (C. N. Davidson, 1986, pp. 62–64; Kerber, 1986, pp. 189–231).

11. For moral significance of useful knowledge, see "On the Folly of Engaging in Trifling Studies," reprinted from the *Columbian Magazine* in *General Advertiser,* August 14, 1792.

12. See Peale's advertisement, *General Advertiser,* March 11, 1793. The letter from Burgiss Allison to Benjamin Rush, July 2, 1792, was published in the *Universal Asylum,* and reprinted in the *General Advertiser,* October 10, 1792. Allison donated mineral specimens to Peale in 1808 and 1810 *(Memoranda of the Philadelphia Museum,* July 27, 1808, p. 30, and April 14, [1810], p. 50).

13. See C. N. Davidson, 1986, pp. 66 and 70; Peale: *General Advertiser,* March 11, 1793. The asterisk in the quotation directs the reader to a footnote in the advertisement: "*Several persons are now employed in the collecting and preserving for its enrichment, in this and other countries."

14. For Peale's advertisement, see *General Advertiser,* August 22, 1794. The year 1794 is significant to the theater's history in Philadelphia, because in that year its proscription was unsuccessfully proposed (Pennsylvania, General Assembly, "An Act for the Prevention of Vice and Immorality, and of Unlawful Gaming, and to Restrain Disorderly Sports and Dissipation," *Acts of the General Assembly . . .* (Philadelphia: Hall and Sellers, 1794), pp. 546–52). For the circus notices, see *General Advertiser,* October 27, 1792, and *Aurora. General Advertiser,* November 5, 1796.

15. See United States Continental Congress, *Journal of the Proceedings of the Congress, Held at Philadelphia, September 5, 1774,* 1774, p. 72. For exhortation against frivolous reading, see *General Advertiser,* August 14, 1792.

16. For proscription of theater, see Pennsylvania General Assembly, "An Act for the Suppression of Vice and Immorality," *Laws Enacted in the Second Sitting of the Third General Assembly . . .* ([Philadelphia: John Dunlap, 1779]), pp. 190–93; and Pennsylvania General Assembly, "An Act for the Prevention of Vice and Immorality, and of Unlawful Gaming; and to Restrain Disorderly Sports and Dissipation," *Laws Enacted in the Third Sitting of the Tenth General Assembly . . .* (Philadelphia: Thomas Bradford, [1786]), pp. 157–65. For Hallam's place in the debates over the theater, see Geib, 1971, pp. 324–39, and "Lewis Hallam," in *DAB,* v. 4, pp. 148–49. The Quaker factor in the legislature is important to understanding the Philadelphia controversy, but this debate was also waged contemporaneously in Boston in the same terms. As Perez Morton reported on the wishes expressed in a town meeting at Boston, "They consider the right to relax from the toils of industry and the fatigues of business, by a resort to any rational and innocent amusement, as consituting no inconsiderable part of the happiness of civil society, and one of the essential blessings confirmed by Men, by a free Constitution of Government." See *General Advertiser,* November 23, 1791. For legalization of the theater, see Pennsylvania General Assembly, "An Act to Repeal so Much of an Act of General Assembly of this Commonwealth, as Prohibits Dramatic Entertainments within the City of Philadelphia and the Neighbourhood Thereof," *Laws of the Thirteenth General Assembly . . .* (Philadelphia: Thomas Bradford, [1789]), pp. 14–15.

17. For language used to justify reinstatement of the theater, see Pennsylvania General Assembly, "An Act to Repeal . . .," 1789. The censors were to be the President of the Supreme Executive Council, the Chief Justice of the Supreme Court, and the President of the Court of Common Pleas.

18. For the letter from "Blacklegs," see *General Advertiser,* January 13, 1794.

19. For Ricketts's new location, see *Aurora. General Advertiser,* October 15, 1795; Ricketts's audience,

General Advertiser, October 7, 1794; Bush Hill Gardens audience, *Aurora. General Advertiser,* June 24, 1797; and Peale's advertisement, *Aurora. General Advertiser,* December 23, 1807.

20. Society of Friends, "An Affectionate Caution, Addressed to the Members of Our Religious Society, in this City, 1st mo. 1793" [Philadelphia, 1793]; and Society of Friends, "Philadelphia, 6th of 12th mo. 1793. A Committee of Friends this Day Attended Each House of the Legislature of this State, with the Following Address and Petition . . ." [Philadelphia, 1793]. On the dates of the yellow fever in Philadelphia, Scharf and Westcott, 1884, v. 1, p. 217.

21. For petition from clergy, see *General Advertiser,* December 27, 1793. A longer version appeared in pamphlet form, "The Address and Petition of a Number of the Clergy of Various Denominations . . ." (Philadelphia: William Young, 1793). By denomination, the ministers who signed this petition were Episcopalians Joseph Pilmore, William Smith, Joseph Turner, and William White; Presbyterians Robert Annan, Ashbel Green, and John Blair Smith; Baptists Thomas Fleeson, William Rogers, and Thomas Ustick; Methodists John Dickens and Freeborn Garretson; Lutherans Henry Helmuth and Frederick Schmidt; Moravian John Meder; and Associate (Reformed Presbyterian) William Marshall. Annan, Dickens, Fleeson, Green, Helmuth, Marshall, Meder, John Blair Smith, Schmidt, Turner, and Ustick were identified through Hardie, 1794; Garretson through B. C. Smith, 1985, pp. 164–65; Pilmore, William Smith, and White through Sprague, 1859, v. 5, pp. 266–70, pp. 158–63, and pp. 280–92, respectively; and Rogers through Wilson and Fiske, 1888, v. 5, p. 310. See also, Peale, *Pennsylvania Packet,* February 28, 1787.

22. Peale, *Aurora. General Advertiser,* January 27, 1800. In Pennsylvania General Assembly, House of Representatives, *Journal of the Fourth House* . . . [convened 1793, published 1794], anti-theater petitions were recorded from Quakers (p. 16); Philadelphia clergymen (p. 44); deputies of the Third Presbyterian, Baptist, Episcopal, and Scots Presbyterian churches (p. 56); Delaware County citizens (p. 67); 1,318 members of the German Lutheran and Reformed Presbyterian churches and 205 people of various denominations from the Northern Liberties (pp. 84–85); Southwark inhabitants (p. 91); and Franklin County inhabitants (p. 96). Also recorded in Pennsylvania General Assembly, House of Representatives, *Journal of the Fourth House* . . . [convened 1793, published 1794] were petitions in favor of a law against vice, without specific notation of a position on the theater, from Westmoreland County (p. 85), Bucks County (p. 121), Washington County (p. 147), the Reformed Congregation of Marsh Creek and others (p. 182), York County (p. 196), and Chester County (p. 199). For the letter from "Mentor," which is dated February 18, 1789, see *General Advertiser,* December 28, 1793; and from "A Citizen," *General Advertiser,* January 25, 1794.

23. For the size of the stock issue, see Wolcott, 1971, p. 209; and for the theater subscribers' protest, see Henry Hill, Chairman, "The Petition and remonstrance of a considerable number of citizens of Philadelphia, and its neighborhood, subscribers to the New Theatre, by their committee appointed for this purpose," *General Advertiser,* January 1, 1794. Statements in favor of the theater recorded in Pennsylvania General Assembly, House of Representatives, *Journal of the Fourth House* . . . [convened 1793, published 1794] included a petition from theater subscribers "from Philadelphia and its neighborhood" (p. 56); a petition signed by 720 Philadelphians (p. 143); a petition (or perhaps several) from an unspecified number of Philadelphians (p. 147); and "a memorial from Thomas Wignell and Alexander Reinagle, proprietors of the new theatre in the city of Philadelphia" (p. 334).

24. See "Philanthropos," *General Advertiser,* December 31, 1793; "Sallad, Chairman," *General Advertiser,* January 10, 1794; and C. D. Johnson, 1975, pp. 575–84.

25. See "Patty Puzzle," *The Theatrical Censor. By a Citizen,* no. 5, [December 1805], p. 46.

26. For admission fees to the circus, see *General Advertiser,* May 1, 1793 (stated in dollar units), and May 9, 1793 (stated in pound units); and to the theater, see *General Advertiser,* February 14, 1791. For comments from a Moravian visitor, see Fritsch, 1912, p. 360. For financial means of working people, see B. G. Smith, 1990, pp. 92–125; and C. N. Davidson, 1986, p. 25.

27. For controversy over the proposed half-price admission, see the "Card, to Messrs. Hallam and Henry," *General Advertiser,* February 11, 1791; and "A Real Friend to the Drama," *General Advertiser,* February 12, 1791. Responses from the gallery on opening night at the New Theatre appear in *General Advertiser,* February 5, 1793. For comment that servants must leave, see *Aurora. General Advertiser,* May 1, 1795.

28. For contemporary observation of violence at the theater, see "A Frequenter of the Theatre," *General Advertiser,* October 25, 1794.

29. See Charles Willson Peale to Rembrandt Peale, October 28, 1809, in L. B. Miller, 1980, IIA/48A11

and typescript, IIA/48B5; Orosz, 1990, pp. 81 and 83; and Charles Willson Peale, *Autobiography,* typescript, in L. B. Miller, 1980, IIC, p. 217.

30. John Bennet, "Advice to a Young Lady," *General Advertiser,* May 8, 1792; and John Bennet, "Advice to a Young Lady . . . On visiting, tea-parties, &c.," *General Advertiser,* May 16, 1792.

31. For advertisement of fireworks display, see *General Advertiser,* October 22, 1794; for benefit performance, see *Aurora. General Advertiser,* June 19, 1795.

32. For lyceum announcement, see *Aurora. General Advertiser,* January 4, 1797; for the ram chase, see *Aurora. General Advertiser,* May 23, 1798; and for the *Danaë* exhibit, see *Aurora. General Advertiser,* September 23, 1806. This advertisement did not acknowledge that separate viewing times implied a gender division: "As the room is not sufficiently spacious to accommodate large companies, Monday will be appropriated for the accommodation of Ladies exclusively." Foster, 1954, p. 258.

33. For Rannie's "Notice to the Coloured People," see *Aurora. General Advertiser,* June 10, 1802, and for the postponement of the special performance, see *Aurora. General Advertiser,* June 12, 1802. For exclusion from the Washington Museum, see *New-York Evening Post,* January 7, 1824. I thank David C. Ward for sharing this last citation. For the presence of Native Americans and Anthony Wayne at the circus, see *Aurora. General Advertiser,* February 25, 1796. For attendance of Native Americans at Peale's Museum, see *Philadelphia Gazette,* December 6, 1796, in Miller, Hart, and Ward, 1988, pp. 160 and 163. For Choctaw chiefs at the Old Theatre, see *Aurora. General Advertiser,* December 31, 1803. For "Z.," see *Aurora. General Advertiser,* November 4, 1795. For a report that George and Martha Washington were expected at the circus, see *General Advertiser,* April 20, 1793; and for a report that George Washington was anticipated in the audience of the theater, see *General Advertiser,* May 7, 1794.

34. For the Othello billing, see *Aurora. General Advertiser,* July 27, 1803. Lindfors, 1983, pp. 9–14. For Ricketts as an Indian chief, see two separate notices in *Aurora. General Advertiser,* December 31, 1795. For a performance by Native Americans, see *Aurora. General Advertiser,* January 2, 1796; and for the success of the event, see *Aurora. General Advertiser,* January 4, 1796. For the Jane McCrea act at the circus, see *Aurora. General Advertiser,* January 23, 1799. Several years later, a waxworks display in Baltimore included an installation called *The Murder of Miss M'Rea, American and Baltimore Daily Advertiser,* July 3, 1815. For the popularization of this theme, see Edgerton, 1965. For the visit to the Tammany Society, see *Aurora. General Advertiser,* March 3, 1802. McClung and McClung, 1958, pp. 145–146, characterize the society:

> The original Society, called the Sons of King Tammany, had been started in Philadelphia in 1772, and was the outgrowth of a seventeenth-century fishing club. It was named after the celebrated Delaware Indian Chief Tamenend, who had welcomed William Penn upon his arrival to America, and had endeared himself to the settlers by allowing them to fish along the banks of the Schuylkill, which was then in Indian territory. In its beginnings Tammany was primarily a cultural, fraternal, and patriotic organization. In accordance with its Indian tradition, the members adopted various pseudo-Indian rites, costumes, and ceremonials.

35. See Newman, 1991; and Newman, 1992. For discussion of a celebration of French independence, see *General Advertiser,* July 19, 1792; for Jefferson's inauguration, *Aurora. General Advertiser,* February 27, 1801; for the Louisiana Purchase Jubilee, see *Aurora. General Advertiser,* February 1, 1804.

36. For the centrality of the French-British tension to American politics in this period, see R. G. Miller, 1976, pp. 91–125. Bache's arrest, see *Aurora. General Advertiser,* June 27, 1798. Peale's other major newspaper for advertising the museum in the late 1790s was *Claypoole's American Daily Advertiser.* For observations of pro-British behavior at the theater, see *Aurora. General Advertiser,* April 21 and 27, 1798. For the Democratic Republican "New Circus," see *Aurora. General Advertiser,* May 12, 1798; for the "Federal Summer Circus," see *Aurora. General Advertiser,* May 14, 1798. For Peale's illumination of the museum for the Louisiana Purchase celebration, see Miller, Hart, and Ward, 1988, pp. 670 and 672; for the 1808 Fourth of July illumination, see Miller, Hart, and Ward, 1988, p. 1096. For portraits of Hamilton, Jay, Pickering, Jefferson, and Paine, see Charles Willson Peale, "An Historical Catalogue of Peales' Collection of Paintings" (Philadelphia: Richard Folwell, 1795), nos. 58, 3, 61, 56, and [45], respectively. Jay was particularly despised by Democratic Republicans for his role as negotiator of the controversial treaty with Britain bearing his name (R. G. Miller, 1976, pp. 70–90). Pickering, as Adams's Secretary of War, was nearly as

suspect to Philadelphia's Democratic Republicans. For example, see the charge by "Cato" stating that Pickering is an "agent of the British interests," in the *Aurora. General Advertiser,* July 12, 1797.

Chapter 2: Peale's Public Presentation of the Museum

1. The *Pennsylvania Packet* (1771–90) was continued under the titles *Dunlap's American Daily Advertiser* (1791–93), *Dunlap and Claypoole's American Daily Advertiser* (1793–95), *Claypoole's American Daily Advertiser* (1796–1800), and *Poulson's American Daily Advertiser* (1800–1839). The *General Advertiser* (1790–94) became the *Aurora. General Advertiser* (1794–1824). For further discussion, see C. S. Brigham, 1947, v. 2, pp. 891, 896, 903, 916, 942, and 947; and Pennsylvania Historical Survey, 1944, pp. 10 and 152–56. For Peale's plea for donations, see *General Advertiser,* February 24, 1794. For a discussion of the mail, see Kielbowicz, 1989; and John, 1989. Travel accounts are the topic of chapter 3; donors and the objects they gave to the museum are analyzed in chapters 6 and 7.

2. Examples of political bias in the newspapers include letters complaining of anti-French sentiment in the *Gazette of the United States,* published in the *General Advertiser,* May 5, 1794; May 8, 1794; and May 19, 1794. Orientation on the Pennsylvania Constitution issue may be established in part in *Aurora. General Advertiser,* October 4, 1806, and May 7, 1807.

3. For the announcement of Peale's register, see *General Advertiser,* August 22, 1794; for discussion of snakes, see *Aurora. General Advertiser,* August 27, 1795; of birds, see *Aurora. General Advertiser,* July 7, 1800; of stoves, see *Aurora. General Advertiser,* January 26, 1796, and May 26, 1796; of bridge, see *Aurora. General Advertiser,* September 27, 1796; and of polygraph, see *Aurora. General Advertiser,* October 6, 1803.

4. For Peale's design, see Charles Willson Peale, "My Design in Forming This Museum," broadside, 1792, in Miller, Hart, and Ward, 1988, pp. 12 and 14. For Peale's request for support from the Pennsylvania legislature, see *Aurora. General Advertiser,* December 30, 1795. For Peale's threat to leave Philadelphia, see *Aurora. General Advertiser,* January 27, 1800. For Peale's statement upon opening his new galleries in the State House, see *Aurora. General Advertiser,* June 29, 1802.

5. For Peale's advertisement of George Washington's pheasant, see *Pennsylvania Packet,* March 1, 1787; moor hen, *General Advertiser,* March 26, 1794; pelican, *Aurora. General Advertiser,* May 27, 1796; Swedish birds, *Claypoole's American Daily Advertiser,* October 20, 1796; orangutan, *Claypoole's American Daily Advertiser,* April 13, 1799; anteater, *Claypoole's American Daily Advertiser,* October 24, 1799; porcupine, *Claypoole's American Daily Advertiser,* April 16, 1800; sea devil (giant ray), *Poulson's American Daily Advertiser,* April 9 and 10, 1801; two-headed snake, *Aurora. General Advertiser,* August 8, 1805; lion, *Aurora. General Advertiser,* January 14, 1809; and turtle, *Poulson's American Daily Advertiser,* June 17, 1815. For advertisement of the mastodon exhibit, see *Aurora. General Advertiser,* December 24, 1801. For advertisements about display of the stove, see *Aurora. General Advertiser,* January 26, 1796; bridge, *Aurora. General Advertiser,* September 23, 1796; physiognotrace, *Aurora. General Advertiser,* December 28, 1802; and gas lights, *Relf's American Daily Advertiser,* April 17, 1816. For notices about the portraits by Rembrandt Peale, see *Poulson's American Daily Advertiser,* November 17, 1808, and *Aurora. General Advertiser,* March 2, 1811. For announcement of wax figures, see *Aurora. General Advertiser,* August 14, 1797; armor, *Poulson's American Daily Advertiser,* July 3, 1805; and Lewis and Clark objects, *Poulson's American Daily Advertiser,* March 1, 1810.

6. Job 12.7–8 reads, "But ask the beasts, and they will teach you;/the birds of the air, and they will tell you;/or the plants of the earth, and they will teach you;/and the fish of the sea will declare to you." This passage was identified through Nicholas Collin, "Remarks on the utility of Mr. Peale's proposed Lectures in the Museum," 6 parts, *Poulson's American Daily Advertiser,* no. 1, December 17, 1800.

7. See Cutler, 1888, v. 1, p. 261. The full text reads:

At the opposite end [from a portrait of George Washington], under a small gallery, his natural curiosities were arranged in a most romantic and amusing manner. There was a mound of earth, considerably raised and covered with green turf, from which a number of trees ascended and branched out in different directions. On the declivity of this mound was a small thicket, and just below an artificial pond; on the other side a number of large and small rocks of different kinds, collected from different parts of the world, and represented the rude state in which they are generally found. At the foot of the mound were holes dug and the earth thrown up, to show the different kinds of clay, ochre, coal, marl, etc., which he had collected from different parts; also, various ores and minerals. Around the pond was a beach, on which was exhibited an assortment of shells of different kinds, turtles, frogs, toads, lizards, water-snakes, etc. In the pond was a collection of fish with their skins stuffed, water-fowls, such as the different species of geese, ducks, cranes, herons, etc.; all having the appearance of life, for their skins were admirably preserved. On the mound were those birds which commonly walk on the ground, as the partridge, quail, heath-hen, etc.; also, different kinds of wild animals—bear, deer, leopard, tiger, wild-cat, fox, raccoon, rabbit, squirrel, etc. In the thickets and among the rocks, land-snakes, rattle-snakes of an enormous size, black, glass, striped, and a number of other snakes. The boughs of the trees were loaded with birds, some of almost every species in America, and many exotics. In short, it is not in my power to give any particular account of the numerous species of fossils and animals, but only their general arrangement.

See also C[laude] M. F[uess], "Manasseh Cutler," in *DAB,* v. 3, pp. 12–14. On Peale's debt to the emblematic tradition, see Stein, in Miller and Ward, 1991, pp. 169–82.

8. Interpretations of *The Exhumation of the Mastodon* include A. A. Davidson, 1969, pp. 620–29; L. B. Miller, 1981, reprinted in Miller and Ward, 1991, pp. 145–65; Stein, in Miller and Ward, 1991, pp. 193–96; Wolf, 1982, pp. 123 and 125–26; and Rigal, 1989, pp. 45–185. Collective action is an issue explored by both Wolf and Rigal. I have also developed the discussion of collective versus individual production in relation to two other texts. Howard Becker's formulation, "Art Worlds and Collective Activity," has been an important theoretical model in conceiving the study of Peale's Museum as a cultural production, rather than the expression of one man's ideas (Becker, 1982, pp. 1–39). Also useful was Sam Bass Warner's discussion of "privatism" as the basis upon which individual enterprise and national prosperity were promoted as consistent in early America (Warner, 1968, pp. 3–21).

9. The identification of all figures, here and in subsequent paragraphs, derives from C. C. Sellers, 1952, p. 75.

10. See *General Advertiser,* January 18, 1792; *General Advertiser,* February 24, 1794; and *Aurora. General Advertiser,* November 11, 1795. For Peale's published lists of donors and donations, see Appendix II in D. R. Brigham, 1992, pt. 2, pp. 358–429.

11. For an example of Wilson's use of Peale's mounts, see Richardson et al., 1983, pp. 114–115.

12. Peale's self-consciousness as a manager may be discerned in his statement that "a number [of] men required the Eye of the Employer" (Miller, Hart, and Ward, 1988, p. 363). Peale's roles as mediator between the day laborers and the leisurely viewers is also an important concern in Laura Rigal's analysis (Rigal, 1989, pp. 66–87). For Peale's negotiation for the skeleton, Charles Willson Peale, see *Diary,* June 5–July 2, 1801, in Miller, Hart, and Ward, 1988, pp. 313–36. For the loan of tents, see Charles Willson Peale to Andrew Ellicott, July 12, 1801, in Miller, Hart, and Ward, 1988, pp. 342–44. For the loan of cash from the American Philosophical Society, see Charles Willson Peale to Robert Patterson, July 24, 1801, in Miller, Hart, and Ward, 1988, pp. 346–47. For the loan of a pump to facilitate water removal, see Charles Willson Peale to Thomas Jefferson, July 24, 1801, and Jefferson to Peale, July 29, 1801, in Miller, Hart, and Ward, 1988, pp. 348–49. For the excavation, see Charles Willson Peale, *Diary,* July 29–September 25, 1801, in Miller, Hart, and Ward, 1988, pp. 350–71. See also "The Artist and His Labor(er)s," in Rigal, 1989, pp. 95–102.

13. See C. C. Sellers, 1952, p. 75.

14. On the subject of the full-scale drawing, see Charles Willson Peale, *Diary,* June 24, 1801, in Miller, Hart, and Ward, 1988, p. 330. For reports of the discovery, *Philadelphia Gazette,* September 17, 1800, and *Gazette of the United States,* September 17, 1800. Peale commented on his pause in his drawing: "if they though[t] my offer worth excepting to let me save myself the trouble of making the drawings . . .," Charles Willson Peale, *Diary,* June 24, 1801, in Miller, Hart, and Ward, 1988, p. 331. For a report on the 1783 commission for drawings of mastodon bones, see Miller, Hart, and Appel, 1983, p. 445.

15. I thank Holly Trostle Brigham for suggesting the comparison to Raphael's *School of Athens.* For more on the interpretation of heavenly inspiration, see David Steinberg, "Charles Willson Peale: The Portraitist as Divine," in Miller and Ward, 1991, pp. 131–43.

16. For Peale's report on soil shifting, see Charles Willson Peale, *Diary,* August 8, 1801, in Miller, Hart, and Ward, 1988, p. 359; and August 16, 1801, pp. 360–61. For Peale's discussion of the rain, see Charles Willson Peale, *Diary,* August 4, 1801, in Miller, Hart, and Ward, 1988, p. 356; August 31, 1801, p. 362;

and September 1, 1801, p. 363. For discussions of the mammoth in relation to the biblical flood, see Janson, 1971, p. 199; Blane, 1824, p. 23; and Duncan, 1823, v. 1, p. 196. The interpretation of the water and storm as flood metaphors benefits from a discussion with Owen Hannaway.

17. Interpretations of *Noah and His Ark* include Stein, in Miller and Ward, 1991, p. 196; and Dillenberger, 1984, p. 130. For Peale's comment on Catton's painting, see Charles Willson Peale to George Bomford, May 1, 1819, in Miller, Hart, Ward, and Emerick, 1991, p. 716; also see C. C. Sellers, 1969b, pp. 44–45. For the quotation from Cutler, see Cutler, 1888, v. 1, p. 262.

18. For reference to the perspective machine and identification of busts, see Poesch, 1960. For information on the busts, hummingbirds, and mineral specimen from Giant's Causeway, see C. C. Sellers, 1980a, p. 121. For the landscapes, see Poesch, 1957. For *The Albiness,* see Miller, Hart, Ward, and Emerick, 1991, p. 587 n. 4. For information on the organ, see Miller, Hart, and Ward, 1988, p. 1050.

19. Interpretations of *The Artist and His Museum* include Stein, in Miller and Ward, 1991, pp. 167–218; Rigal, 1989, pp. 135–65; and Kulik, 1989, p. 3. Roger Stein's essay is the most thorough treatment of *The Artist in His Museum.* Both Stein's and Rigal's arguments have influenced substantially the course of my discussion on this painting.

20. For advertisement of Duane's memorial, see *Poulson's American Daily Advertiser,* December 18, 1810; defense by "Liberal Justice," *Poulson's American Daily Advertiser,* December 29, 1810.

21. For the memorial addressed "To the Select and Common Councils of the City of Philadelphia," see *Relf's Philadelphia Gazette and Daily Advertiser,* August 2, 1816; *United States Gazette,* August 3, 1816; and *Poulson's American Daily Advertiser,* August 5, 1816. For arguments in favor of higher rent, see "Communication. The Corporation and Peale's Museum. Let Justice Be Done," *Poulson's American Daily Advertiser,* August 5, 1816; and "A Friend to Propriety" to Mr. Poulson, *Poulson's American Daily Advertiser,* August 9, 1816. For the museum as a business, see E. to Mr. Poulson, *Poulson's American Daily Advertiser,* August 12, 1816. For Peale's success in having the rent reduced to twelve hundred dollars per year, see Charles Willson Peale to Raphaelle Peale, March 1, 1818, in Miller, Hart, Ward, and Emerick, 1991, p. 580. For John Neagle having painted several versions of a portrait of Lyon, *Patrick Lyon at the Forge,* 1825–29, see Torchia, 1989, pp. 103–40. For the contention that public and private were not precisely demarcated, see Hart and Ward, 1988, p. 405, reprinted in Miller and Ward, 1991, p. 225.

22. For Peale's requests for state financing, see *Aurora. General Advertiser,* December 30, 1795; and *Aurora. General Advertiser,* January 27, 1800. For Peale's memorial to the city government, see *Poulson's American Daily Advertiser,* December 27, 1810. For commentary by "Liberal Justice," see *Poulson's American Daily Advertiser,* December 29, 1810. For Peale's memorial to the city government, see *Relf's Philadelphia Gazette and Daily Advertiser,* August 2, 1816.

Chapter 3: *Written Responses to Peale's Museum*

1. For comment on Peale's Museum in Philadelphia directories, see Hardie, 1794, pp. 231–32; and Stephens, 1796, pt. 2, p. 67.

2. For Philadelphia guidebook, see Mease, 1811, p. 312. The quote is from the subtitle to Mease's book. *Philadelphia in 1824 . . . ,* p. 103; I thank Tony Lewis for sharing this source with me. [Mease], 1835, p. 110.

3. See Bernard, 1887, p. 200. I thank Elizabeth O'Leary and David Steinberg for sharing this item with me. Also see Duncan, 1823, v. 1, p. 195.

4. For aristocratic commentators, see H[enry] M[orse] S[tephens], "Sir Augustus John Foster," *The Dictionary of National Biography,* 21 vols., plus supplements (London: Oxford University Press, 1963–64), v. 7, p. 492; and Foster, 1980, p. 257. Karl Bernhard is grouped here on the basis of his title as Duke of Saxe-Weimar-Eisenach; N[orman] M[oore], "Charles Waterton," *The Dictionary of National Biography,* 1964–65, v. 20, pp. 906–8. For reformers as commentators, see R[ichard] G[arnett], "Frances Darusmont [Wright]," *The Dictionary of National Biography,* 1963–64, v. 5, pp. 520–22; and G[eorge] F[isher] R[ussell] B[arker], "James Silk Buckingham," *The Dictionary of National Biography,* 1963–64, v. 3, pp. 202–3. On emigration: James Flint's subtitle to his book promises to discuss "the Prospects of Emigrants" (Flint, 1822). Frederic Trautmann, in the introduction to the Gall travels, writes that Gall first saw "America as the promised land," but published his thoughts "primarily as a warning to Germans who would undertake

emigration to America lightly" (pp. 35 and 36; and Gall, 1981, pp. 41 and 43); I thank Roy Goodman for directing me to this account. Howitt's subtitle indicates that his book will be "Descriptive of the Present Situation and Sufferings of Emigrants."

5. See "A Lover of Nature" to the *Pennsylvania Packet*, March 27, 1790, in Miller, Hart, and Appel, 1983, p. 583; "A Lover of Nature" to the *General Advertiser*, March 27, 1794; "Liberal Justice" to Mr. Poulson, *Poulson's American Daily Advertiser*, December 29, 1810; "Philadelphus" to Mr. Poulson, *Poulson's American Daily Advertiser*, August 8, 1816; "A Citizen" to Mr. Poulson, *Poulson's American Daily Advertiser*, August 12, 1816; "Let Justice Be Done," *Poulson's American Daily Advertiser*, August 5 and 13, 1816; and "A Friend to Propriety" to Mr. Poulson, *Poulson's American Daily Advertiser*, August 7, 9, and 14, 1816.

6. For proposed donation of politically opposed newspaper to the museum, see *Gazette of the United States*, May 14, 1800. For controversy over Sharp Delany's political bias, see John Harrison to the people, *Aurora. General Advertiser*, April 25, 1796; and "Longinus" to Mr. Bache, *Aurora. General Advertiser*, April 29, 1796.

7. The Alien and Sedition Acts were the Naturalization Act, June 18, 1798; the Alien Friends Act, June 25, 1798; the Alien Enemies Act, July 6, 1798; and the Act for the Punishment of Certain Crimes, July 14, 1798. See Linda K. Kerber, "Alien and Sedition Laws," in *Dictionary of American History*, 7 vols. (New York: Charles Scribner's Sons, 1976), v. 1, pp. 86–87. For anecdote of visitor's account of the museum, see anonymous author to Mr. Bache, *Aurora. General Advertiser*, May 29, 1798.

8. For an account of Matthew Lyon's speech in the United States House of Representatives, see *Aurora. General Advertiser*, June 6, 1797. See also "A Lyon!!!," *Porcupine's Gazette*, June 6, 1797, and "A Lyon," *Aurora. General Advertiser*, June 9, 1797. I am grateful to Simon Newman for directing me to the account in *Porcupine's Gazette*. For Roger Griswold insults Matthew Lyon's military record, and for Lyon spits in his face, see *Aurora. General Advertiser*, January 31, 1798. Griswold beats Lyon with a "stout hickory club"; Lyon defends himself with fireplace "tongs." The men are separated and Lyon hits Griswold with a "cane"; see *Aurora. General Advertiser*, February 16, 1798. For "Proposals For publishing a rare work, entitled a New Mode of Legislation; Or, The Way to govern a Free People," see *Aurora. General Advertiser* (from the *New York Diary*), February 26, 1798.

9. For discussions of the political significance of the State House, see Melish, 1812, v. 1, p. 152; and [Wright], 1821, p. 80.

10. For Peale's scholarly audience, see Schofield, 1989. On the importance of Peale's mastodon to Cuvier's classification of the species, see Miller, Hart, and Ward, 1988, p. 144 n. 4 and pp. 1190–91 n. 1.

11. See J[oseph] J[ackson], "James Mease," *DAB*, v. 6, p. 486. Among Mease's writings were *A Geological Account of the United States* . . . (Philadelphia: Birch and Small, 1807); "An Inaugural Dissertation on the Disease Produced by the Bite of a Mad Dog, or Other Rabid Animal," M.D. diss. (Philadelphia: Thomas Dobson, 1792); "An Address on the Progress of Agriculture, with Hints for Its Improvement in the United States . . ." ([Philadelphia]: n.p., 1817); and *Archives of Useful Knowledge* . . ., edited by James Mease, 3 vols., July 1810–April 1813 (Philadelphia: D. Hogan).

12. Discussions of Peale's reliance on Linnaean order include C. C. Sellers, 1980a, p. 162; Stein, in Miller and Ward, 1991, pp. 186–90; and Kulik, 1989, p. 4. For contemporary observations on taxonomy at the museum, see Cutler, 1888, v. 1, p. 261; Hardie, 1794, pp. 230–31; Mease, 1811, pp. 311, 312, and 313; and *Philadelphia in 1824* . . ., p. 102. For the systems of Kirwan and Cleaveland, see Greene and Burke, 1978, pp. 14 and 37. For comments on the arrangement of the insect collection, see Mease, 1835, p. 110.

13. For contemporary classification of the museum, see Hardie, 1794, pp. 228–32; and Mease, 1811, table of contents.

14. See Hardie, 1794, p. 230.

15. For comment on artistic merit, see Cutler, 1888, v. 1, p. 260; Flint, 1822, p. 32; Howitt, [1820], p. 61; and [Blane], 1969, pp. 22–23.

16. For comment on historical significance, see Belknap, 1913, p. 493; Cutler, 1888, v. 1, p. 260; Howitt, 1820, p. 61; and Blane, 1969, p. 23.

17. For comment on the wax models, see Cutler, 1888, v. 1, pp. 259–60. For Washington's reported astonishment regarding the *Staircase Group*, see C. C. Sellers, 1969a, p. 272.

18. For comment on Native American exhibit, see Howitt, 1820, pp. 60 and 61.

19. See C. C. Sellers, 1969a, p. 347, for the Comte de Volney quote. Peale reported the quote in 1795 in slightly different words: "This is the temple of God!—Here is nothing but Truth and Reason!", *Aurora. General Advertiser*, December 30, 1795. See also Nicholas Collin, "Remarks on the utility of Mr. Peale's

proposed Lectures in the Museum," 6 parts, *Poulson's American Daily Advertiser*, pt. 2, December 18, 1800. For praise of the religious content of the labels, see Fritsch, 1912, pp. 359–60; I am grateful to Elizabeth Johns for bringing this account to my attention. For the comparison to Noah's Ark, see Cutler, 1888, v. 1, p. 262; and "A Clergyman," *Claypoole's American Daily Advertiser*, December 5, 1799.

20. See Nicholas Collin, "Remarks on the utility of Mr. Peale's proposed Lectures in the Museum," 6 parts, *Poulson's American Daily Advertiser*, December 17, 18, 19, 20, 23, and 24, 1800. Collin takes a more secular view of the importance of the study of nature in "An Essay on Those Inquiries in Natural Philosophy, Which at Present Are Most Beneficial to the United States of North America," reprinted in Whitfield J. Bell, Jr., "Nicholas Collin's Appeal to American Scientists," *The William and Mary Quarterly*, 3d series, v. 13, no. 4, October 1956, pp. 519–50. Collin credits Peale's Museum as one of a number of institutions serving this function, p. 547.

21. See Nicholas Collin, "Remarks on the utility of Mr. Peale's proposed Lectures in the Museum," *Poulson's American Daily Advertiser*, pt. 4, December 20, 1800, and pt. 5, December 23, 1800.

22. See *Philadelphia in 1824 . . .*, pp. 101–2.

23. See "A Dialogue on Mr. Peale's Museum," *General Advertiser*, September 8, 1792.

24. For "A Lover of Nature," see *Pennsylvania Packet*, March 27, 1790, in Miller, Hart, and Appel, 1983, p. 583; and *General Advertiser*, March 27, 1794. For Nicholas Collin's essay in support of the museum, see "Remarks on the utility of Mr. Peale's proposed Lectures in the Museum," *Poulson's American Daily Advertiser*, pt. 5, December 23, 1800. For the significance of the mineral collection, see Howitt, 1820, p. 61.

25. For mastodon discovery, see Miller, Hart, and Ward, 1988, pp. 350–76. For the official account, see Rembrandt Peale, "An Historical Disquisition on the Mammoth . . ." (London: C. Mercier, 1803), reprinted in Miller, Hart, and Ward, 1988, pp. 543–81. For other reports on the dig, see Mease, 1811, p. 313; *Philadelphia in 1824 . . .*, p. 102; and Waterton, 1825, pp. 301–2.

26. For exaggerations of the mastodon's dimensions, see Janson, 1971, p. 199; and Howitt, 1820, p. 59. For Bernhard quote, see Bernhard, 1828, v. 1, p. 140. For Hall quote, see Hall, 1818, p. 279. For Duncan quote, see Duncan, 1823, v. 1, p. 195. For a woman's reaction, see Deborah Logan to Albanus Logan, January 10, 1802, Robert R. Logan Collection, Historical Society of Pennsylvania. I thank Susan B. Heller for sharing her transcript of Logan's letter with me.

27. For contemporary comment on the mastodon exhibit, see *Aurora. General Advertiser*, January 9, 1802; Sutcliff, 1811, p. 29; and Duncan, 1823, v. 1, pp. 196–97. For Cuvier's classification of the mastodon, see Miller, Hart, and Ward, 1988, pp. 311–313.

28. See Charles Willson Peale, "Skeleton of the Mammoth . . .," broadside, 1801–2, reproduced in Miller, Hart, and Ward, 1988, p. 378; Rembrandt Peale, "An Historical Disquisition on the Mammoth . . .," in Miller, Hart, and Ward, 1988, pp. 577–78, quote from p. 578; Sutcliff, 1811, p. 29; Ker, 1816, pp. 322–23; Arfwedson, 1969, v. 1, p. 273; and Hall, 1818, p. 279.

29. See [Blane], 1969, p. 23; and Duncan, 1823, v. 1, pp. 195–96 and 198. Peale's advertisement for the "Behemoth Or Mammoth," appeared in *Aurora. General Advertisement*, May 5, 1802. See Rembrandt Peale, "An Historical Disquisition on the Mammoth . . .," in Miller, Hart, and Ward, 1988, p. 577.

30. Charles Willson Peale, "Guide to the Philadelphia Museum" (Philadelphia: Museum Press, April 1805), in Miller, Hart, and Ward, 1988, pp. 759–66. See Richard Beale Davis, in Foster, 1980, pp. xvii–xviii. Although Davis acknowledges Foster's use of other sources, he does not grant that even supposedly empirical observations depend upon conventions: "one has only to read his original on-the-spot notes to see how really spontaneous and genuine those interests were" (p. xviii).

Chapter 4: The Audience for Silhouettes Cut by Moses Williams

1. See Charles Willson Peale to Thomas Jefferson, January 10, 1803, in Miller, Hart, and Ward, 1988, pp. 480–82. See Charles Willson Peale to John Isaac Hawkins, December 17, 1805, in Miller, Hart, and Ward, 1988, p. 916. See C. C. Sellers, 1948, pp. 6–8. See *Profile Book*, January 22, 1803, American Philosophical Society, in L. B. Miller, 1980, XIA/2E10–2G6.

2. For first announcement of physiognotrace, see *Aurora. General Advertiser*, December 28, 1802, and *Gazette of the United States*, December 28, 1802. Saint Mémin, *Aurora. General Advertiser*, January 7, 1803. See Charles Willson Peale to Rembrandt and Rubens Peale, April 1, 1803 in Miller, Hart, and Ward,

1988, p. 517. See Charles Willson Peale to John Isaac Hawkins, August 28, 1806, in Miller, Hart, and Ward, 1988, p. 981.

3. For mention of 8,880 silhouettes, see Charles Willson Peale, *Autobiography,* typescript, in L. B. Miller, 1980, IIC, p. 319. See also Hart and Ward, 1988, in Miller and Ward, 1991, p. 224. Hart and Ward's estimates of the size of Peale's audience may be inflated, since they assume each visitor paid only twenty-five cents. Yet those who paid to see both the main collections and the mastodon paid seventy-five cents. The total audience size after 1802 was, therefore, probably considerably lower than they estimate. For the claim of silhouettes in every household, see Charles Willson Peale to John Isaac Hawkins, December 17, 1805, in Miller, Hart, and Ward, 1988, p. 916. For Raphaelle Peale's claim of 100,000 silhouettes, see *Philadelphia Repository and Weekly Register,* April 14, 1804.

4. The date of Moses Williams's manumission is based on Peale's tax assessments in Philadelphia County Tax Assessment Ledgers, New Market Ward and South Ward. For silhouette commission at one-sixteenth of a dollar, see *Aurora. General Advertiser,* July 11, 1803. For charge of eight cents per sitting, see Charles Willson Peale, "Guide to the Philadelphia Museum" (Philadelphia: Peale Museum Press, April, 1805), in Miller, Hart, and Ward, 1988, p. 763. For a general discussion of attitudes toward freed slaves in early Philadelphia, see Nash, 1988, pp. 66–99.

5. The identification of "Mr. Shaw's blackman" is further complicated by the difficulty in determining who Mr. Shaw was. The silhouette collection at the Library Company of Philadelphia also includes a likeness of J. Shaw. Philadelphia directories offer alternative identifications for J. Shaw: James Shaw, carpenter; John Shaw, Commander in the Navy; John Shaw, grocer; Joshua Shaw, laborer; and Rev. Joseph Shaw, pastor of the Associate Church. Robinson, 1803 and 1808.

6. For Peale's identification of silhouettes with women, see *Aurora. General Advertiser,* October 18, 1803. Regarding vanity, see Charles Willson Peale to Rembrandt and Rubens Peale, April 1, 1803, in Miller, Hart, and Ward, 1988, p. 517. Explaining the popularity of the physiognotrace, Peale wrote, "such is the love we have of our pretty faces." Charles Coleman Sellers wrote, "At first, Peale could only see evidence of human vanity in the rush for silhouettes" (C. C. Sellers, 1969a, p. 306).

7. These statistics account for three boxes of silhouettes, which are mounted on folded sheets of black construction paper. They do not include the silhouette albums discussed below.

8. See Vlach, 1988, pp. 136–38. Just how seriously Philadelphia's Quakers took these restrictions deserves further study, since Quakers were the subjects of many of Peale's oil paintings.

9. See Ewers, 1966, pp. 1–26. According to ethnologist John C. Ewers, "these so-called Missouri and Mississippi chiefs ranged from chiefs of outstanding importance in their tribes to young men of little reputation and of no political position among their own people." See also Charles Willson Peale to Thomas Jefferson, February 8, 1806, in Miller, Hart, and Ward, 1988, pp. 935–36. Regarding Lavater, see Miller, Hart, and Ward, 1988, pp. 478–79 n. 1; and B. M. Stafford, 1985, pp. 329–63.

10. See Joan K. Stemmler, "The Physiognomical Portraits of Johann Caspar Lavater," *The Art Bulletin,* v. 75, no. 1, March 1993, pp. 151–68. See also Johann Caspar Lavater, *Essays on Physiognomy . . .,* translated by Henry Hunter, with engravings by Thomas Holloway, 3 vols. (London: printed for John Murray et al., 1789–98). Especially appropriate are Lavater's Fragment 11, "Of Silhouettes," v. 2, pp. 176–238, and Fragment 17, "Of the Study of Physiognomy . . .," v. 2, pp. 389–432. In the latter essay Lavater writes that through the study of silhouettes, the student of physiognomy "will possess the knowledge of the whole face of man: he will be able to read in it, as in an opened book" (Lavater, v. 2, p. 407). This brief passage echoes Peale's interest in the "open book of nature," an eighteenth-century trope featured in Peale's engraved ticket of admission (figure 8).

11. This argument is based on the study of four albums that survive in Philadelphia public collections: two at the Library Company of Philadelphia, and one each at the Historical Society of Pennsylvania and the Philadelphia Museum of Art. Anne A. Verplanck, in her dissertation in progress, has accounted for twelve such albums, suggesting that the compilation of silhouette albums was probably more common than previously supposed (Letter from Anne A. Verplanck to the author, April 14, 1993). Silhouette albums and collections documented other social units, as well. At the Winterthur Museum, for example, there is an album of silhouettes that includes the portraits of many early Philadelphia physicians. At the Alexandria-Washington Masonic Lodge, there are thirty-four identically framed silhouettes that were cut by Isaac Todd to honor the members active when George Washington's name was officially added to their lodge's title in 1804. I thank John P. Riddell, custodian of the Replica Room at The George Washington Masonic National Memorial, for this information.

12. This album is catalogued as Book C in the Perot Collection at the Historical Society of Pennsylvania, Philadelphia.

13. See Perot Collection, Book C, Historical Society of Pennsylvania, Philadelphia.

14. See Abigail, Patience, and Sarah Marshall as sisters, from Marshall, n.d., p. 41. See Joseph and Thomas Morris and their families, in Moon, 1898, v. 2, pp. 574 and 575.

15. See Moon, 1898, v. 2, pp. 574–75.

16. Children of Benjamin Marshall, in Marshall, n.d., p. 19. Children of Christopher Marshall, Jr., in Marshall, pp. 30 and 33. Children of Mary Parrish Collins, in Boyd, 1935, p. 74. Children of Elizabeth Parrish Phile, in Boyd, 1935, p. 75. Children of Isaac Parrish, in Boyd, 1935, pp. 130–31.

17. Children of Isaac Tyson, in Evans, Tyson, Bartlett, et al., 1976, pp. 73–74. On the relatives of Elizabeth Thomas, see Thomas, 1877, pp. 27, 32, and 67–68. On Elizabeth Wethered and Evan Ellicott, see Evans, 1976, pp. 52 and 53.

18. For birth date of Henrietta Tyson, see Evans, 1976, p. 74.

19. The inscription on the back of the album reads, "Silhouettes originally belonging to Mary Ann Marshall." Because the subjects relate most closely to Isaac and Patience Tyson and because their arrangement reflects the structure of their families, Mary Ann Marshall could not have compiled the album. It seems likely that the book descended to Mary Ann Marshall after the death of either Patience in 1834 or Isaac in 1864. See *Guide to the Manuscript Collections of the Historical Society of Pennsylvania* (Philadelphia: Historical Society of Pennsylvania, 1991), entry no. 1886. A codicil to the will of Mary Ann Marshall, dated September 19, 1881, names T. Morris Perot executor. Mary Ann Marshall Estate Papers, Historical Society of Pennsylvania (C. C. Sellers, 1964, pp. 395 and 401).

20. For relationship between portraiture and remembrance after death, see *Charleston Courier* (reprinted from a Philadelphia newspaper), April 22, 1808; and *Poulson's American Daily Advertiser*, October 10, 1801.

21. See Fritsch, 1912, p. 360.

Chapter 5: Subscribers to Annual Admission Tickets

1. This chapter is based on a systematic analysis of the 401 subscribers in 1794, and a more impressionistic understanding of subsequent years. The year selected is significant for several reasons. First, it is the year Peale began recording the names of subscribers. Second, it is the year that Peale adopted a more learned display context for the museum by moving into the Hall of the American Philosophical Society. Third, it is the last year that the struggle over the theater was fought with great intensity.

2. For ticket price of one dollar, see *Pennsylvania Packet*, July 21, 1788; for ticket prices of two, five, and six dollars, see *Subscriptions for Tickets in Peale's Museum* (henceforth *Subscriptions*), 1794–1833, ms. vol., Historical Society of Pennsylvania; for price of ten dollars, see *Poulson's American Daily Advertiser and Daily Advertiser*, November 2, 1819. The price increase in 1819 took place under Rubens Peale's management. For three-, six-, and twelve-month tickets in 1823 and daytime limitation in 1798, see *Subscriptions;* for day or evening tickets available, see *Relf's Philadelphia Gazette and Daily Advertiser*, October 2, 1817. Day and evening visiting patterns are from the bar graph of income figures in the timeline (1814–29) at the exhibit "Mermaids, Mummies, and Mastodons: The Evolution of the American Museum," Peale Museum, Baltimore. For a review of the exhibit, see Gary Kulik, *The Journal of American History*, v. 78, no. 1, June 1991, pp. 255–59.

3. For door-to-door sales, see C. C. Sellers, 1980a, p. 54; and Miller, Hart, and Ward, 1988, p. 26 n. 5. For assistance from the Board of Visitors, see Miller, Hart, and Ward, 1988, p. 26. For distribution through other businesses and individuals, 1798, see the end of the *Subscriptions* book. For Peale as agent for Green's lecture tickets, see *Aurora. General Advertiser*, February 18, 1805, and *Aurora. General Advertiser*, April 17, 1805; for Wilson's *Ornithology*, see *Aurora. General Advertiser*, November 23, 1808.

4. For Wilson's debt to Peale, see Schofield, 1989, pp. 34–35; and C. C. Sellers, 1980a, pp. 203–6. For Wilson's donations, see *Memoranda of the Philadelphia Museum:* birds, October 1811, p. 56, and November 30, 1812, p. 64; nests and eggs, July 14, 1808, p. 32; bird skins, December 28, 1810, p. 53; and minerals, December 30, 1808, p. 37 and June 6, 1809, p. 41. For a general discussion of book subscriptions, see Mark V. Barrow, Jr., and Roy E. Goodman, *Broadsides and Other Ephemera in Science, Technology, and*

Medicine, 1700–1900: An Annotated Catalogue of the American Philosophical Society Library Collection, typescript draft of a forthcoming book. I thank Roy Goodman for sharing this material. See also Sarah L. C. Clapp, "The Beginnings of Subscription Publication in the Seventeenth Century," *Modern Philology,* v. 29, no. 2, November 1931, pp. 199–224; Pat Rogers, "Book Subscriptions among the Augustans," *The Times Literary Supplement,* London, no. 3693, December 15, 1972, pp. 1539–40; and Welch, 1988.

5. For moving picture offer, *Pennsylvania Packet,* July 9, 1790. For lectures, 1799–1800, see *Aurora. General Advertiser,* November 5, 1799; and 1800–1801, see *Aurora. General Advertiser,* November 26, 1800. In the first season, the tickets allowed lecture-goers free admission to the collections during the lecture season, and in the second season the tickets were extended for an entire year. "Friends of Science" inscription begins the *Subscriptions* volume.

6. For Jesse Roberts, see *Subscriptions,* March 6, 1797; Benjamin Owren [July 10, 1800]; Jacob Baush, July 25, 1800; Ann Dick [1802]; Julia, Samuel, and Benjamin Rush, Jr. [1803]; John Parry, December 4 [1807]; Theodore Gratz, July 21, 1823; and David Gratz, January 22, 1823.

7. For Lambdin, see *Subscriptions* [January] 23, [1823]. The labels are in the collection of the Peabody Museum of Archaeology and Ethnology, Harvard University. Lambdin's museum was first announced in the Pittsburgh newspaper *Hesperus,* August 2, 1828, reproduced in Sargent, 1984, p. 105. For Wernwag, see *Subscriptions* [October 24, 1823]; Hart, 1986, pp. 351 and 353, in Miller and Ward, 1991, p. 255; and Miller, Hart, and Ward, 1988, p. 179.

8. For Peale's election to the American Philosophical Society, see *Pennsylvania Packet,* July 25, 1786; for his tenure as curator, see American Philosophical Society, 1986; for the building fund subscribers, see *Pennsylvania Packet,* November 1, 1786. For Hominy Club, see C. C. Sellers, 1969a, pp. 96–98. For Whig Society, see Miller, Hart, and Appel, 1983, pp. 226–28; Constitutional Society, p. 282; and Pennsylvania militia, pp. 192–93 n. 191. For Emigrant Society, see *Aurora. General Advertiser,* April 11, 1795.

9. For Delaware and Schuylkill Canal Co., see *Aurora. General Advertiser,* January 8, 1803; for Schuylkill and Susquehanna Co., *Aurora. General Advertiser,* January 6, 1803. For Democratic Republican activity, see *Aurora. General Advertiser,* May 25, 1805 (Passmore); *Aurora. General Advertiser,* August 15, 1805 (Smiley); and *Aurora. General Advertiser,* October 25, 1804 (Thackara). For Society of Cincinnati, see *General Advertiser,* July 7, 1791. For Hibernian Society, see *Aurora. General Advertiser,* March 22, 1809; for Sons of St. George, see Simpson, 1859, p. 91; for German Society, see *Pennsylvania Mercury,* January 1, 1788, indexed in the Hannah Roach Card File. For prison relief society, see *General Advertiser,* January 12, 1791; and for Guardians of the Poor, see *Aurora. General Advertiser,* September 7, 1802. For Sunday schools, see *General Advertiser,* March 26, 1791; and for Bible Society, see *Aurora. General Advertiser,* February 8, 1809. For Dancing Assembly, see *General Advertiser,* November 18, 1790.

10. Washington's and Adams's signatures from the *Subscriptions* book are illustrated in C. C. Sellers, 1980a, p. 72; and in Richardson et al., 1983, p. 145. The book is open to that page in the permanent exhibition "Finding Philadelphia's Past: Visions and Revisions," Historical Society of Pennsylvania, Philadelphia. I thank Linda Stanley for arranging with the exhibitions department to allow me to see the manuscript volume out of the display case. The inference of Peale's manipulation of the subscriptions derives from extant invitations to prominent visitors, such as Charles Willson Peale to Edmond-Charles Genêt, minister plenipotentiary from France, May 1793, in Miller, Hart, and Ward, 1988, pp. 48–49; and Charles Willson Peale to Joseph Priestley, scientist and Unitarian theologian, June 26, 1794, in Miller, Hart, and Ward, 1988, pp. 96–97.

11. I have adhered to Blumin's categories: "The high nonmanual category includes merchants of various kinds, brokers, professionals, and high-ranking public officials. It includes gentlemen and gentlewomen as well. The low nonmanual category includes storekeepers of all kinds, grocers, innkeepers, real estate agents, sea captains, manufacturers, clerks, accountants, and minor public officials. The high manual category includes all artisans, and the low manual category includes laborers, sailors, carters, stevedores, and a variety of other unskilled manual occupations" (Blumin, 1989, table 2.1 and p. 44, note to table 2.1). I have made adjustments according to Blumin's observation that "school teachers, doctors and lawyers with small practices, ministers to congregations of ordinary people—also stood outside and below the urban elite on the social scale" (Blumin, 1989, p. 37). Because I have no information on the size of the doctors' and lawyers' practices or the nature of the clergy's congregations, I have used an economic standard. All professionals with accumulated wealth below the 50th percentile, relative to other subscribers, were moved down the socioeconomic scale to the low nonmanual category. It should be noted that in his study of the working class, Billy G. Smith categorizes cordwainers and tailors in the "lower sort" (B. G. Smith, 1990, p. 6), whereas

Blumin counts them in the high manual group. Peale's subscribers in 1794 included four tailors and one cordwainer. Following is the breakdown by occupation of the Peale subscribers in table 1. High nonmanual (total, 195): U.S. representatives (67); merchants (32); appointed officials, federal and state (23); U.S. senators (20); doctors (9); clergymen (8); gentlemen (8); attorneys (5); elected officials, city and county of Philadelphia (4); elected officials, state (4); scriveners, conveyancers, and brokers (4); diplomats (3); scientists (3); bankers (2); U.S. executive officers (2); dentists (1). Low nonmanual (total, 80): clerks (12); merchants (10); ironmongers (9); doctors (7); clergymen (6); grocers (6); shopkeepers (6); medical students, University of Pennsylvania (5); attorneys (3); educators (3); sea captains (3); appointed officials, city and county of Philadelphia (2); inn keepers (2); scriveners, conveyancers, and brokers (1); elected officials, city and county of Philadelphia (1); gentlemen (1); manufacturers and distillers (1); U.S. representatives (1). High manual (total, 38): leather and cloth workers (10); wood workers (9); metal workers (6); printers and booksellers (4); apothecaries (3); painters and printmakers (2); surveyors (2); agriculturalists (1); bakers (1). Low manual (total, 0).

12. For an overview of Peale's efforts to obtain public funding, see Ruth Helm, "Peale's Museum: Politics, Idealism, and Public Patronage in the Early Republic," in Alderson, 1992, pp. 67–77.

13. The eleven subscribers who held public office and whose portraits hung in Peale's Museum by 1794 were John Adams, Elias Boudinot, Alexander Hamilton, Henry Knox, Thomas McKean, James Madison, Thomas Mifflin, Robert Morris, John Page, Samuel Smith, and George Washington. Peale later added portraits of Henry Dearborn (1796 or 1797), Rufus King (1818), James Monroe (1818), all of whom were congressmen and subscribers in 1794 (C. C. Sellers, 1952). Portrait subjects are arranged alphabetically in Sellers, whose catalogue notes designate those portraits that were executed for the museum. For Mifflin, see [Charles Willson Peale], "An Historical Catalogue of Peales' Collection of Paintings" (Philadelphia: Richard Folwell, 1795), pp. 4–5.

14. The interrelationships and importance of commerce, agriculture, and manufactures are discussed in the introduction to this book.

15. For more information on the individuals dealt with collectively here, consult the appendix. See John Swanwick, in Miller, Hart, and Appel, 1983, p. 420 n. 8.

16. Individual mechanics are named in the appendix. For Peale's request for donations of American manufactures, *Aurora. General Advertiser,* November 17, 1808. For Thackara's encyclopedia, see *Aurora. General Advertiser,* March 7, 1797. For Young's encyclopedia, see *Aurora. General Advertiser,* December 13, 1802. For Young as philanthropist, see H. Simpson, 1859, p. 90. See also R[ay] P[almer] B[aker], "Frederick Graff," *DAB,* v. 4, pp. 467–68. For an example of mutual benefits, a printer named John Ormrod subscribed to an annual ticket, and Peale later had Ormrod print a broadside for the museum. See broadside entitled "Skeleton of the Mammoth," printed by John Ormrod, in Miller, Hart, and Ward, 1988, p. 378.

17. In part, the relative absence of farmers and planters may reflect the focus on urban sources, especially city directories and tax lists in identifying Peale's subscribers. See E[dward] H[opkins] J[enkins], "John Adlum," *DAB,* v. 1, p. 109; see also C. C. Sellers, 1969b, pp. 53 and 130. For membership information, see Philadelphia Society for Promoting Agriculture, 1789. Peale's relationship to the agricultural society included sale of firewood and candles and the provision of chimney sweeping services from at least 1806 to 1810 (Philadelphia Society for Promoting Agriculture, v. 3, p. 114, item D; p. 115, item E; p. 118, item C; and p. 120, item 3. The receipts were authorized for payment by George Clymer, who was the vice president of the Philadelphia Society for Promoting Agriculture and a museum subscriber in 1794.

18. Perhaps this visit en masse followed a "general meeting of the clergy," one of which was reported in connection with the theater controversy *(General Advertiser,* December 30, 1793). The best biographical source on these ministers is Sprague, 1857–69. For citations to specific entries on Peale's subscribers, refer to the appendix to this chapter. Anti-theater ministers, *General Advertiser,* December 27, 1793; pro-theater ministers, *General Advertiser,* December 17, 1793 and *General Advertiser,* December 30, 1793. Henry Hill, *General Advertiser,* January 1, 1794. Quaker membership is ascribed through Hinshaw and Marshall, 1938, v. 2. Nicholas Collin, *General Advertiser,* December 30, 1793; Miller, Hart, and Ward, 1988, p. 49; and *Poulson's American Daily Advertiser,* December 17, 18, 19, 20, 23, and 24, 1800.

19. For "Philanthropos," see *General Advertiser,* December 31, 1793. For degrees held by these ministers, see Sprague, 1857–69; and degrees and faculty positions held, see University of Pennsylvania, Society of the Alumni, *Biographical Catalogue of the Matriculates of the College . . .* (Philadelphia: printed for the Society, 1894). For report that Magaw steps down so that trustees will not have to choose between him and

John Andrews, see *General Advertiser,* April 14, 1792. For Pilmore mezzotint, see *Pennsylvania Packet,* May 18, 1787, and July 2, 1787; for the series of engravings, see Richardson, 1964.

20. For affiliations with the University of Pennsylvania, see University of Pennsylvania, *Matriculates,* 1894; University of Pennsylvania, *Alumni of the Medical Department,* 1877; and for nongraduates, *Alumni Master File.* For biographical notes on affiliations with the College of Physicians, the Pennsylvania Hospital, and the Philadelphia Dispensary, see "Roll of Fellows of the College of Physicians of Philadelphia, Elected during the Century Ending January, 1887." For mineralogy as a branch of chemistry, see Greene and Burke, 1978, p. 44. Portraits of sitters with skin pigmentation disorders include Charles Willson Peale, *James,* "a person born a Negro . . .," 1791, not located, and Charles Willson Peale, *Miss Harvey, The Albiness,* 1818, not located; horn growths, Charles Willson Peale, *James Gallaway,* 1790, not located; and longevity, Charles Willson Peale, *John Strangeways Hutton,* 1792, private collection and Charles Willson Peale, *Yarrow Mamout,* 1819, Historical Society of Pennsylvania. For accessions of human material, see *Aurora. General Advertiser,* February 14, 1795; and *Memoranda of the Philadelphia Museum,* [August] 18, [1808], p. 33. For Rush's proposal of a gallery of the infirm, see Benjamin Rush to William Smith, August 5, 1802, in Butterfield, 1951, pp. 852–53; I thank David Steinberg for this reference. For medical interest in long life, see William Martin, "American Longevity," 1790–1793, copy book, University of Pennsylvania Archives. Rubens Peale reported the addition of three portraits of physicians to the museum, Charles Willson Peale after Thomas Sully, *Benjamin Rush;* Charles Willson Peale, *Caspar Wistar;* and Charles Willson Peale after Rembrandt Peale, *James Woodhouse* (see *Poulson's American Daily Advertiser,* February 16, 1818).

21. See Rodney H. True, "François André Michaux, The Botanist and Explorer," *Proceedings of the American Philosophical Society,* v. 78, no. 2, December 10, 1937, p. 315; William J. Robbins and Mary Christine Howson, "André Michaux's New Jersey Garden and Pierre Paul Saunier, Journeyman Gardener," *Proceedings of the American Philosophical Society,* v. 102, no. 4, August 1958, pp. 351–70. See also Brooke Hindle, "Witherspoon, Rittenhouse, and Sir Isaac Newton," *The William and Mary Quarterly,* 3d series, v. 15, no. 3, July 1958, pp. 365–72; J. Barry Love, "The Miniature Solar Systems of David Rittenhouse," *The Smithsonian Journal of History,* v. 3, no. 4, Winter 1968–69, pp. 1–16; Brooke Hindle, ed., *The Scientific Writings of David Rittenhouse* (New York: Arno, 1980). For Boudinot's gift to Princeton, see Simpson, 1859, p. 110. On Zaccheus Collins, see Ronald L. Stuckey, "The First Public Auction of an American Herbarium including an Account of the Fate of the Baldwin, Collins, and Rafinesque Herbaria," *Taxon,* v. 20, no. 4, August 1971, pp. 443–59; American Philosophical Society, *Year Book 1985;* and Academy of Natural Sciences, *Members and Correspondents of the Academy of Natural Sciences of Philadelphia. 1877.* See Thomas D. Cope and H. W. Robinson, "The Astronomical Manuscripts which Charles Mason Gave to Provost the Reverend John Ewing During October 1786," *Proceedings of the American Philosophical Society,* v. 96, no. 4, August 1952, pp. 417–23. See Joseph Samuel Hepburn, "Notes on the Early Teaching of Chemistry in the University of Pennsylvania, the Central High School of Philadelphia, and the Franklin Institute of Pennsylvania," *Journal of Chemical Education,* v. 19, 1932, pp. 1577–91.

22. For specific citations on Joseph Sharpless, Benjamin Tucker, and John C. Moller, see the appendix. For ticket sale to school, see *Subscriptions,* [November] 30, [1825].

23. For the social significance of taverns, see Thompson, 1989. For Oellers's Hotel as a ballroom, see Henry Wansey, *Henry Wansey and His American Journal,* edited by David John Jeremy, *Memoirs of the American Philosophical Society,* v. 82, p. 104. For Peale's statement that "strangers" make up the majority of his audience, see *Aurora. General Advertiser,* January 27, 1800.

24. Table 2 was constructed from the aggregate data in the appendix. This study considered the twelve wards that made up the city of Philadelphia. Consideration of the additional thirteen townships and districts that constituted Philadelphia County would have produced more assessments for Peale subscribers. The percentile assigned to the average wealth for an occupation is based on a comparison to the median income of each decile, and may appear inconsistent for assessments of individuals. For example, David Rittenhouse's personal wealth (1,161 pounds) is in the 80th percentile or second decile, but falls below the median wealth for that group. Median wealth (in pounds) for each decile of Peale's subscribers is as follows:

Percentile	Median Wealth	Percentile	Median Wealth
90th	3,355	40th	66
80th	1,532	30th	46
70th	728	20th	20
60th	294	10th	0
50th	110	Zero	0

Peale was assessed for 401 pounds, ranking him just below the fifty-second subscriber. In other words, Peale's accumulated taxable wealth placed him above more than two-thirds of his subscribers in 1794. This located him economically just below attorney Jared Ingersoll and just above United States Senator Ralph Izard. For observation of relative social position of middling ranks, see Blumin, 1989, p. 33.

25. Categories of assessment were real estate, personal (occupational tax), slaves and servants, plate, riding equipment, horses, and cows. This distorts the property of the middling and the wealthy downward because it does not include the inventory of their shops, nor does it include their personal property other than objects made of precious metal (plate) (B. G. Smith, 1990, pp. 224–29). For the 1774 statistic on home ownership, see Warner, 1968, p. 9. Henry Wansey notes that many United States Congressmen lived at Oellers's Hotel (Wansey, 1970, p. 103). For Bingham's additional property holdings, see *Philadelphia Tax Assessment Ledgers,* ms. vols., Philadelphia City Archives, Middle Ward, 1794, pp. 43 and 46; New Market Ward, 1794, pp. 8, 37, 38, 41, 63, 64, and 84; and South Ward, pp. 12 and 23.

26. Slaveholding subscribers assessed in Philadelphia: John Beale Bordley, James Calbraith, Benjamin Chew, Benjamin Chew, Jr., Ralph Izard, George Latimer, Thomas Lloyd Moore, John Nixon, David Rittenhouse, Edward Shippen, William Turner, and Christian Wiltberger. Indentured servant holding subscribers assessed in Philadelphia: John Andrews, Clement Biddle, John D. Blanchard, John Caldwell, John Ewing, Miers Fisher, Thomas Fitzsimons, Edward Fox, Ashbel Green, Adam Hains, John Hall, Alexander Hamilton, Henry Hill, Henry Knox, William Lane, Mordecai Lewis, Peter Lohra, David McCormick, George Meade, Samuel Meredith, Thomas Mifflin, Robert Morris, Frederick A. Muhlenberg, John Mullowny, Michael Roberts, and Richard Wistar. Assumed slaveholders: Pierce Butler, John Edwards, John Hunter, Nathaniel Macon, James Monroe, Josiah Parker, Andrew Pickens, and Benjamin Williams. For officers of the abolition society, see *General Advertiser,* February 3, 1791.

27. For walking city, see Blumin, 1989, p. 20. Riding equipment and horse ownership were established through the tax ledgers.

28. For American Philosophical Society membership, see American Philosophical Society, 1986, and the membership card file in the library of the society. For University of Pennsylvania affiliation, see University of Pennsylvania, *Matriculates,* 1894; University of Pennsylvania, *Alumni of the Medical Department,* 1877; and University of Pennsylvania, *Alumni Master File.*

29. For a discussion of the patrons who supported Peale in London, see Robert J. H. Janson-LaPalme, "Generous Marylanders: Paying for Peale's Study in England," in Miller and Ward, 1991, pp. 11–27. For members of the Board of Visitors and Directors, see *General Advertiser,* March 16, 1792. For Columbianum founders, see "The Constitution of the Columbianum, or American Academy of the Fine Arts" (Philadelphia: Francis and Robert Bailey, 1795), pp. 14–15. For Philip P. Price and the rival Columbianum, see *Aurora. General Advertiser,* February 26, 1795. For Pennsylvania Academy founders, see Pennsylvania Academy of the Fine Arts, Charter, December 26, 1805, in L. B. Miller, 1980, IIA/37C11–D6 and IIA (Add.)/4E14–F8. For George Clymer as first president of the Academy, see C. C. Sellers, 1952, p. 56. Private portrait subjects and museum portrait subjects were established through C. C. Sellers, 1952, and C. C. Sellers, 1969b.

30. The signatures of Frances[?] or Francis[?] Possils and Ann. Flower remain ambiguous in terms of gender. For signatures of Elizabeth and Margaret Marshall, see *Subscriptions,* [December 9], 1794; for Margaret Meredith, see [June 20, 1794]; for Abigail Parent, see December 1, 1794; For Mrs. Smiley, see June 20, 1794; for Frances[?] or Francis[?] Possils, see September 29, 1794; for Ann. Flower, see April 1794; and for Deglos and his wife, see [July 23], 1794. "Mrs. Meredith" was Margaret Cadwalader Meredith, the wife of Samuel Meredith. See J[ohn] H. F[rederick], "Samuel Meredith," *DAB,* v. 6, p. 548.

31. Alternatively, the purchase of more than one ticket by an individual may have been a means of more generously patronizing the museum. For purchases by Benjamin Chew and Benjamin Chew, Jr., see *Subscriptions,* January 29, 1794; H. Simpson, 1859, pp. 202 and 203–4; and J[ames] C. B[allagh], "Benjamin Chew," *DAB,* v. 2, pp. 64–65. For Bordley as the stepfather of Mifflin, see Miller, Hart, and Ward, 1988, p. 612 n. 2. For James and Joseph Bringhurst, Jr., see Hinshaw and Marshall, 1938, v. 2, p. 340. For Charles Marshall, Jr., see *Subscriptions,* [July 16], 1794. Also see Hinshaw and Marshall, 1938, v. 2, p. 393; and *Philadelphia Tax Assessment Ledger,* South Ward, 1796, p. 25, ms. vol., Philadelphia City Archives. For partnership of Charles Marshall and Christopher Marshall, Jr., apothecaries, see Hardie, 1794. For Marshall family, see Marshall, n.d., pp. 2, 29, 30, and 33. For Stagg and Peale as brothers-in-law, see Miller, Hart, Ward, and Emerick, 1991, p. 70 n. 1.

32. Distance traveled by Peale's subscribers was established by placing the names of 278 subscribers for whom addresses could be identified on an enlarged map of Philadelphia. The 1795 city directory helped to locate addresses between specific blocks. For instance, Zaccheus Collins lived at 60 North Third Street, which was on the west side of Third Street, between Arch and Race Streets (Hogan, 1795). The number of complete blocks was then counted to the two addresses of Peale's Museum in 1794, corner of Third and Lombard Streets and corner of Fifth and Chestnut Streets. In several cases, the number of blocks is only an approximation, since the 1795 directory was less specific for addresses south of Walnut Street. This affects the results minimally, since addresses in various parts of the city lead to patterns of differential distance between the two museum locations. For example, addresses northeast of Philosophical Hall were typically two blocks closer to that location, while addresses southeast of the Lombard Street address were usually six blocks closer to that location. Full blocks counted from east to west were Front Street, Second Street, Third Street, Fourth Street, Fifth Street, Sixth Street, Seventh Street, Eighth Street, Ninth Street; and from north to south were Callowhill Street, Vine Street, Race Street, Arch Street, Market Street, Chestnut Street, Walnut Street, Spruce Street, Pine Street, Lombard Street, Cedar Street, Shippen Street, Plumb Street, German Street, Catherine Street, Queen Street, and Christian Street. This is problematic because the streets are not equal distances apart and because the streets south of Spruce Street are closer together than those north of Spruce.

33. For discussions of the character of Philadelphia's neighborhoods, see Blumin, 1989, pp. 46–50; and Warner, 1968, pp. 11–13.

34. Neighbors or cohabitants who purchased tickets on the same day: William M. Biddle and James Gallaher, *Subscriptions,* January 16, 1794; John Fries and Michael Roberts, January 20, 1794; John Beale Bordley and John F. Mifflin, January 20, 1794; William Bingham and Walter Stewart, January 29, 1794; John Brown, Thomas Lloyd Moore, and John Penn, January 30, 1794; Clement Biddle and Sharp Delany, February 4, 1794; Jasper Cope and Edward Bartlett, July 14, 1794; Nicholas King and Joshua John Moore, July 23, 1794; and Isaac C. Jones and William F. Stokes, September 3, 1794. Neighbors or cohabitants who purchased tickets separately: Charles Heath, July 4, 1794, and Andrew Graydon, August 6, 1794; William Marshall, January 20, 1794, and Benjamin Mifflin, December 25, 1794; Richard Hill Morris, July 31, 1794, and Samuel P. Griffitts, January 29, 1794; Stephen Moylan, August 6, 1794, and George Meade, January 30, 1794; Rowland Parry, September 1, 1794, and Benjamin Harbeson, Jr., July 7, 1794; Joseph Mussi, July 22, 1794, and Thomas Passmore, September 24, 1794; Robert Morris, January 10, 1794, and David McCormick, February 19, 1794; and Amable Brasier, October 19, 1794, and Henry Toland, July 31, 1794. Although the coincidence of neighbors buying tickets on the same day probably indicates that visiting the museum was a shared social experience for some patrons, it may also indicate that Peale continued door-to-door sales after 1790.

Chapter 6: Donors of Minerals, Natural Resources, and American Manufactures

1. See Charles Willson Peale to Stephen Elliott, February 14, 1809, in Miller, Hart, and Ward, 1988, pp. 1179–80. The calculation is as follows: 4 minerals per shelf × 3.5 shelves per panel × 4 panels vertically × 3 shelves horizontally × 7 cases. For enumeration of minerals and other collections, see C. C. Sellers, 1969a, p. 346.

2. For early collection, see Cutler, 1888, v. 1, p. 261; for gift of minerals from Franklin, see Miller, Hart,

and Ward, 1988, p. 39 n. 3; for Board of Visitors' recommendation, see *General Advertiser,* March 16, 1792; for Peale's intentions, see Charles Willson Peale to the Board of Visitors of the Philadelphia Museum, [June 1792], in Miller, Hart, and Ward, 1988, p. 37; and for support from a committee of the Board of Visitors, see "Minutes of Committee," July 12, 1792, in Miller, Hart, and Ward, 1988, p. 38.

3. For Peale's requests for minerals, see *General Advertiser,* March 11, 1793 and February 24, 1794.

4. For recent acquisitions, see *Aurora. General Advertiser,* February 14, 1795; and for Chambers's connection with Loudon Iron Works, see Bining, 1938, p. 60.

5. For Daniel Buckley, see Beal, 1969, p. 24; Walker, 1966, pp. 40, 51, and 52; Bining, 1938, p. 193; *Memoranda of the Philadelphia Museum,* [July 18, 1808], p. 32, [September 24, 1808], p. 35, and [December 1811], p. 57; *Aurora. General Advertiser,* July 27 and October 12, 1808; Walter Hugins, "Hopewell Furnace: The Story of a 19th-Century Ironmaking Community," in Lewis and Hugins, 1983, pp. 38–39; and *Subscriptions for Tickets in Peale's Museum* (henceforth *Subscriptions*), 1794–1833, ms. vol., Historical Society of Pennsylvania.

6. For need to develop manufactures, see Alexander Hamilton, *Report on Manufactures,* presented to the House of Representatives of the United States, January 15, 1790, in Henry Cabot Lodge, ed., *The Works of Alexander Hamilton,* 12 vols. (New York and London: G. P. Putnam's Sons, The Knickerbocker Press, 1904), v. 4, pp. 70–198; Coxe, 1787; and Hutcheson, 1938. For Hamilton and Coxe as museum supporters, see *Subscriptions,* [January 20] and January 15, 1794, respectively. For a plan for the manufacturing society, see *Aurora. General Advertiser,* June 19, 1802; for a public toast to manufactures, see *Aurora. General Advertiser,* May 15, 1809.

7. The following citations are from the *Aurora. General Advertiser:* legislation to limit British imports, October 28, 1806; call for response to British attack on the *Leopard,* July 2, 1807; modification to Non-Importation Act, March 9, 1808; Non-Intercourse Act, February 27, 1809; Constitution of the Philadelphia Premium Society, June 9, 1808; Maryland Association for the Encouragement of Domestic Manufactures, established in Baltimore, September 4, 1809; Articles of Association of the Columbia Manufacturing Society, established in Washington, July 22, 1808; Carolina Society for the Promotion of Domestic Manufactures, established at Charleston, September 8, 1809; Peale's request for American manufacturers, November 17, 1808; and public toast, May 29, 1809. North, 1966, pp. 37–38.

8. For the role of Peale's donors in the ceramics industry, see Myers, 1980, pp. 53, 62, and 87–88. For their donations, see *Memoranda of the Philadelphia Museum,* [September 12, 1808], p. 34, [September 16, 1808], p. 35; [June] 8, [1809], p. 41, and March 2, [1815], p. 75; and *Aurora. General Advertiser,* October 12, 1808. Other sources on Binny, Ronaldson, and Trotter include Barber, 1893, p. 111; Spargo, 1926, pp. 177–80, 190, and 215; Ramsay, 1939, pp. 175 and 227; Maddock, 1962, p. 70; and Myers, 1980, pp. 6, 7, 11, 14, 17, and 56.

9. For donations from local potters, see Branin, 1988, pp. 36, 97, 98; Myers, 1980, pp. 61–62; for donations from Branch Green, see *Memoranda of the Philadelphia Museum,* [May] 22, [1808], p. 30 and [February] 4, [1809], p. 39; *Aurora. General Advertiser,* July 27, 1808; Maddock, p. 72; for donations from Thomas Vickers, see *Memoranda of the Philadelphia Museum,* [December 28, 1810], p. 53, [September 14, 1811], p. 56; for European ceramics received, see *Memoranda of the Philadelphia Museum,* [March 28, 1805], p. 2, and [May 4, 1814], p. 73. Further information on Green may be found in W. Oakley Raymond, "Remney Family: American Potters," pt. II, *Antiques,* v. 32, no. 2, September 1937, p. 133; Ramsay, 1939, p. 175; Robert J. Sim and Arthur W. Clement, "The Cheesequake Potteries," *The Magazine Antiques,* v. 45, no.3, March 1944, p. 123; and Myers, 1980, pp. 14, 15, and 16. The bibliography on Thomas and John Vickers includes Barber, 1971, p. 103 and Spargo, 1974, pp. 162, 214, and 215.

10. For "Franklin" on textiles, see *Aurora. General Advertiser,* July 27, 1802; July 29, 1802; August 3, 1802; and August 21, 1802. For Tench Coxe, see Hutcheson, 1938, pp. 143–89. For Humphreys, see S. T. W[illiams], "David Humphreys," *DAB,* v. 5, pp. 373–75; Cifelli, 1982, pp. 103–23; for cloth manufactured by Humphreys, see *Memoranda of the Philadelphia Museum,* [December] 3, [1808], and *Aurora. General Advertiser,* January 2, 1809. For Philadelphia Domestic Society, see *Aurora. General Advertiser,* June 9 and July 26, 1808; for alum from Thomas Bedwell, see *Memoranda of the Philadelphia Museum,* [April 24, 1805], p. 3; for uses of alum, see Chambers, 1728, v. 1, p. 67; and Harold E. Gillingham, "Calico and Linen Printing in Philadelphia," *The Pennsylvania Magazine of History and Biography,* v. 52, no. 2, 1928, p. 107.

11. See Charles Willson Peale to Rembrandt Peale, November 17, 1809, in Miller, Hart, and Ward, 1988, p. 1239; and Charles Willson Peale to Rembrandt Peale, February 3, 1810, in Miller, Hart, Ward,

and Emerick, 1991, pp. 3 and 8 n. 3, and pp. 8 and 10 n. 9; see also "Chromic Yellow," *The American Mineralogical Journal,* v. 1, no. 2, n.d. [after August 1, 1810], p. 125; Charles Willson Peale to Rembrandt Peale, February 3, 1810, in L. B. Miller, 1980, IIA/48E1–2; Greene and Burke, 1984, p. 33. For donations of the mineral and the paint product, see *Memoranda of the Philadelphia Museum,* [October 26, 1809], p. 42.

12. For Hamilton's obituary, see *Poulson's American Daily Advertiser,* August 1 and 2, 1820. For Hamilton, see also United States, Works Projects Administration, *Index to Records of Aliens' Declarations of Intention and/or Oaths of Allegiance, 1789–1880,* 11 vols. ([Harrisburg]: Sponsored by the Pennsylvania Historical Commission, [1940?]), v. 5, p. 44; and Philadelphia Wills, 1820–25, in *Collections of the Genealogical Society of Pennsylvania,* v. 80, 1904, p. 4999; for gifts from Hamilton, see *Memoranda of the Philadelphia Museum,* [July] 12, [1807], p. 24, and November 18, [1807], p. 25; and *Aurora. General Advertiser,* October 12, 1807, and January 7, 1808. A review of accessions records at the Pennsylvania Academy of the Fine Arts indicates that Hamilton left at least three works to the academy: Nicolas Boschaert, *Flower Piece,* n.d., oil on canvas mounted on wood, 29.5 inches × 24.5 inches, Nicolas Boschaert, *Flower Piece,* n.d., oil on canvas mounted on wood, 28 inches × 25 inches, and J. Horemans, *A Country School,* n.d., medium and dimensions not recorded. All three paintings have since been deaccessioned. This information was provided by the registrar's office at the academy.

13. For Jefferson's gift from the Lewis and Clark Expedition, see *Memoranda of the Philadelphia Museum,* [December 29, 1809], p. 45. For portraits of Lewis, Clark, Jessup, Titian Peale, and Jefferson, see C. C. Sellers, 1952, p. 127, no. 481; p. 54, no. 142; pp. 111–12, no. 418; p. 169 no. 679; and pp. 110–11, no. 413. Peale also painted Stephen Long, Thomas Say, and William Baldwin from the Long Expedition party (C. C. Sellers, 1952, p. 130, no. 492; p. 191, no. 773; and p. 26, no. 16). For the Marquis d'Yrujo, see *Aurora. General Advertiser,* July 1, 1800, and Miller, Hart, and Ward, 1988, p. 376 n. 5. The only other major gift of wood specimens consisted of 237 examples of the wood native to Brazil, given by Thomas Bulkley *(Memoranda of the Philadelphia Museum,* [June] 15, [1805], p. 6).

14. For Peale's first use of Linnaeus and Chambers, see Miller, Hart, and Appel, 1983, p. 533 n. 186; for minerals arranged according to Kirwan, see Charles Willson Peale, "Guide to the Philadelphia Museum" (Philadelphia: Museum Press, April, 1805), in Miller, Hart, and Ward, 1988, p. 762; also see Linnaeus, 1766–68; Chambers, 1728; Scott, 1753; Kirwan, 1784; Cleaveland, 1816; and Greene and Burke, 1978, p. 37. Throughout this chapter, Greene and Burke have been relied upon for identifying publications by Peale's scientific donors and for understanding the importance of these figures in the history of science.

15. See Charles Willson Peale to Angelica Kauffman Peale Robinson, October 16, 1808, in Miller, Hart, and Ward, 1988, p. 1150; R[eijer] Hooykas, "René-Just Haüy," in Gillispie and Holmes, 1972, v. 6, pp. 178–83; *Memoranda of the Philadelphia Museum,* [December 30, 1808], p. 38, and [March 12, 1810], pp. 49–50; and Greene and Burke, 1978, pp. 12–13 and 15. Mineral names were translated using Allan, 1808, pp. 3, 4, and 45. Peale owned a copy of Allan's *Synonymns. Memoranda of the Philadelphia Museum,* [February 8, 1810], p. 49. For portraits of Haüy and his French colleagues, see *Aurora. General Advertiser,* November 17, 1808.

16. See R[eijer] Hooykas, "René-Just Haüy," in Gillispie and Holmes, 1972, v. 6, pp. 178–79; Greene and Burke, 1978, pp. 17–18; Haüy, 1801; René-Just Haüy, *Traité élémentaire de physique,* 2 vols., (Paris, 1803); Haüy, 1808, pp. 241–70; and Haüy, 1809. Donations of Haüy's publications are recorded in *Memoranda of the Philadelphia Museum,* [December 30, 1808], p. 38 and [June, 1810], p. 50.

17. For the occupations of Zaccheus Collins, Charles Wister, Solomon Conrad, and Mahlon Dickerson, see Robinson, 1808, and Robinson, 1810. For the occupation of Reuben Haines, see Miller, Hart, and Ward, 1988, p. 1234 n. 4. I thank Jeff Groff at Wyck for information on Haines's mineral cabinet. For Stephen Elliott, Miller, Hart, and Ward, 1988, p. 864 n. 7; 942 n. 4; 1144–45 n. 1; and Charles Willson Peale to Stephen Elliott, April 15, 1806, in Miller, Hart, and Ward, 1988, p. 957. Membership in the American Philosophical Society was determined through its card file, and in the Academy of Natural Sciences, *Members and Correspondents of the Academy of Natural Sciences of Philadelphia. 1877.*

18. Cloud's blowpipe was actually an improvement upon the invention of Robert Hare, Jr. For material on Cloud and Hare, see Greene and Burke, 1978, pp. 26–28 and 36–37; Miller, Hart, and Ward, 1988, p. 1142 nn. 9 and 10; and Samuel Moore to Andrew Jackson, November 25, 1835, in L. B. Miller, 1980, IXA/5B2. For purchase of the blowpipe, see Current Expenditures, September 1, 1808, in L. B. Miller, 1980, XIA/5B3; for announcements of acquisition and demonstration of the blowpipe, see *Aurora. General Advertiser,* October 12, 1808; January 2, 1809; January 14, 1809; June 5, 1809; and October 18,

1809; for demonstrations by Cloud, see Charles Willson Peale to Rubens Peale, October 18, 1809, in Miller, Hart, and Ward, 1988, p. 1230; Charles Willson Peale to Rubens Peale, October 25, 1809, in Miller, Hart, and Ward, 1988, p. 1232; and Charles Willson Peale to Rembrandt Peale, October 28, 1809, in Miller, Hart, and Ward, 1988, p. 1234. For a discussion of gold discovered in North Carolina, see "Carolina Gold," *The American Mineralogical Journal,* v. 1, no. 2, n.d. [after August 1, 1810], p. 125. For minerals donated by Cloud, see *Memoranda of the Philadelphia Museum,* [September] 16, [1808], p. 34, and October 12, 1808; and *Aurora. General Advertiser,* October 12, 1808, and January 2, 1809.

19. See Green and Burke, 1978, p. 44. For medical training for Coxe, see F[rancis] R[andolph] P[ackard], "John Redman Coxe," *DAB,* v. 2, p. 486; for Seybert, see C[ourtney] R. H[all], "Adam Seybert," *DAB,* v. 9, p. 2; for Silliman, see C[harles] H. W[arner], "Benjamin Silliman," *DAB,* v. 9, pp. 163–64; for Woodhouse, see E[dgar] F[ahs] S[mith], "James Woodhouse," *DAB,* v. 10, pp. 401–2; and for Bruce, see J[ames] M. P[halen], "Archibald Bruce," *DAB,* v. 2, p. 180. Other donors of minerals designated with the title doctor: Dr. William Barnwell, Dr. Samuel Betton, Dr. Samuel Bleight, Dr. Cuthburt, Dr. R. E. Griffith, Dr. E. L. Lauten, Dr. McCorkle, Dr. Samuel Miller, Dr. F. Piper, Dr. Swift, Dr. Tebbs, Dr. Trimble, and Dr. White.

20. For academic affiliations for Woodhouse, see E[dgar] F[ahs] S[mith], "James Woodhouse," *DAB,* v. 10, pp. 401–2; for Coxe, see "Professorship of Chemistry in the University of Pennsylvania," *Medical and Philosophical Register,* v. 6, no. 3, 1809, p. 136; for Bruce, see J[ames] M. P[halen], "Archibald Bruce," *DAB,* v. 2, p. 180; and for Haüy, see R[eijer] Hooykas, "René-Just Haüy," in Gillispie and Holmes, 1972, v. 6, p. 178.

21. For material on Silliman, see C[harles] H. W[arner], "Benjamin Silliman," *DAB,* v. 9, pp. 160–63; *Memoranda of the Philadelphia Museum,* [January] 22, [1808], p. 28; *Aurora. General Advertiser,* February 8 and April 5, 1808; Greene and Burke, 1978, pp. 24–26. For contemporary notice of the Weston meteorite, see Benjamin Silliman and James L. Kingsley to John Vaughan, February 18, 1808, "Memoir on the Origin and Composition of the Meteoric Stones which Fell from the Atmosphere, in the County of Fairfield, and State of Connecticut, on the 14th of December 1807," and Benjamin Silliman, "Chemical Examination of the Stones which Fell at Weston (Connecticut) December 14th, 1807," *Transactions of the American Philosophical Society,* o.s., v. 6, pt. 2, 1809, pp. 324 and 334–35; James Woodhouse, "Account of the Meteor which Was Seen at Weston, in the State of Connecticut, on the 14th of December, 1807; With an Analysis of the Stones," *The Philadelphia Medical Museum,* vol. 5, no. 2, 1808, p. 133. For competition over this discovery, see C. M. Brown, 1989, pp. 221–29. Brown argues the importance of this discovery to Silliman's reputation, and shows that Silliman competed with James Woodhouse for credit. "Silliman resolved at once to go to Philadelphia to secure his claim to scientific proprietorship of the stone" (C. M. Brown, 1989, p. 223).

22. See James Woodhouse, "Experiments and Observations on the Lehigh Coal," *The Philadelphia Medical Museum,* vol. 1, no. 4, 1805, pp. 441–44; *Memoranda of the Philadelphia Museum,* May 3, 1805, p. 6; and Greene and Burke, 1978, p. 24.

23. See James Woodhouse, "An Account of the Perkiomen Zinc Mine, with an Analysis of the Ore. In a Letter to the Editor," *The Philadelphia Medical Museum,* v. 5, no. 2, 1808, pp. 133–36. Adam Seybert, "Facts to Prove that Blende, or the Sulphuret of Zinc, May Be Worked with Advantage in the United States. In Answer to the Question, 'Can this Ore be Worked to Advantage in the United States?'," *The Philadelphia Medical Museum,* v. 5, no. 4, 1808, pp. 209–16; for Seybert, see C[ourtney] R. H[all], "Adam Seybert," *DAB,* v. 9, pp. 2–3; James Woodhouse, "Woodhouse's Reply to Seybert's Strictures on His Essay Concerning the Perkiomen Zinc Mine," *The Philadelphia Medical Museum,* v. 6, no. 1, 1809, pp. 44–54; for Woodhouse's donation, see *Memoranda of the Philadelphia Museum,* [February] 15, [1808], p. 28. Archibald Binny and James Ronaldson, owners of a letter foundry, donated a second specimen of the ore later in the year. See *Memoranda of the Philadelphia Museum,* September 16, 1808, p. 35; *Aurora. General Advertiser,* July 27 and October 12, 1808; Robinson, 1807; and Greene and Burke, 1978, p. 24.

24. See Adam Seybert, "A Catalogue of Some American Minerals, Which Are Found in Different Parts of the United States," *The Philadelphia Medical Museum,* v. 5, no. 3, 1808, pp. 152–59, and v. 5, no. 4, 1808, pp. 256–68; Greene, 1984, p. 218; and Greene and Burke, 1978, p. 31. For Seybert's contributions, see *Memoranda of the Philadelphia Museum,* [March] 27, [1807], p. 21 and [November 18, 1807], p. 25; *Aurora. General Advertiser,* April 23, 1807, and January 7, 1808. See also Greene and Burke, 1978, pp. 29–30 and 39. Silvain Godon also contributed minerals related to his geological mapping projects and publications. See Silvain Godon, "Mineralogical Observations, Made in the Environs of Boston, in the Years

1807 and 1808," *Memoirs of the American Academy of Arts and Sciences,* v. 3, no. 1, 1809, pp. 127–54, and Silvain Godon, "Observations to Serve for the Mineralogical Map of the State of Maryland," *Transactions of the American Philosophical Society,* o.s., v. 6, pt. 2, 1809, pp. 319–23. For Godon's contributions from these projects, see *Memoranda of the Philadelphia Museum,* [December 29, 1808], p. 37, February 4, [1809], p. 39, May 8, [1809], p. 40, and [January 31, 1810], p. 48; and *Aurora. General Advertiser,* January 2, 1809.

25. For donors as publishers, see F[rancis] R[andolph] P[ackard], "John Redman Coxe," *DAB,* v. 2, p. 487; C[harles] H. W[arner], "Benjamin Silliman," *DAB,* v. 9, pp. 163–64; and J[ames] M. P[halen], "Archibald Bruce," *DAB,* v. 2, p. 180. "Prospectus of a periodical work, to be entitled, *The American Mineralogical Journal,* conducted by Archibald Bruce," *Medical and Philosophical Register,* v. 6, no. 4, 1809, pp. 175–76. Also on Bruce, see Greene and Burke, 1978, p. 57. For receipt of Coxe's publication, see *Memoranda of the Philadelphia Museum,* [March] 6, [1806], p. 13 and for Bruce's, see *Memoranda of the Philadelphia Museum,* [December 5, 1810], p. 52; June 12, [1811], p. 55; and January 6, 1812, p. 59.

26. See Greene and Burke, 1978, pp. 32–33; Silvain Godon, "Mineralogical Observations, Made in the Environs of Boston, in the Years 1807 and 1808. Inclosed with a Letter to the Hon. John Davis, Esq. F.A.A. and by Him Communicated," *Memoirs of the American Academy of Arts and Sciences,* v. 3, pt. 1, 1809, pp. 127–54; *Aurora. General Advertiser,* December 3, 1808, March 22, 1809, and April 11, 1809; Charles Willson Peale to Stephen Elliott, February 14, 1809, in Miller, Hart, and Ward, 1988, p. 1178.

27. See Robinson, 1807; Young Ladies' Academy of Philadelphia, "Syllabus of Lectures, Containing the Application of the Principles of Natural Philosophy, and Chemistry, to Domestic and Culinary Purposes. Composed for the Use of the Young Ladies' Academy, in Philadelphia" (Philadelphia: printed for Andrew Brown, Principal of the said academy, 1787), p. iii; and Greene and Burke, 1978, p. 14.

28. See Charles Willson Peale to Rubens Peale, October 25, 1809, Miller, Hart, and Ward, 1988, pp. 1232 and 1233; Charles Willson Peale to Rubens Peale, October 18, 1809, Miller, Hart, and Ward, 1988, pp. 1230 and 1232 n. 5; Miles and Abrahams, 1957; Miles, 1968; broadside, reproduced in Miles and Abrahams, 1957, p. 450; and *Aurora. General Advertiser,* October 24, 1811, and October 24, 1812. Contributions of minerals and related items from women include "Sand from the Desarts of Arabia" by Mrs. Mary Heston, "beautiful specimen[s] of Chrystal & perites from Bath" by Mrs. Dilwin, and "A Number of Minerals" by Mrs. Musser of Lancaster. See *Memoranda of the Philadelphia Museum,* November 17, [1806], p. 19, [May 30, 1807], p. 23, and [March 12, 1810], p. 49; and *Aurora. General Advertiser,* October 12, 1807.

Chapter 7: Donors of Artifacts of Human Difference

1. See Lillian B. Miller, "Charles Willson Peale: A Life of Harmony and Purpose," in Richardson, Hindle, and Miller, 1983, pp. 170–233. Charles Coleman Sellers developed Peale's role as benevolent patriarch by punctuating the artist's biography with accounts of his loving and protecting relationships to three wives and seventeen children, eleven of whom reached adulthood (C. C. Sellers, 1969a). See also John Adams to Abigail Adams, August 29, 1776, in C. C. Sellers, 1952, p. 157. For an extended discussion of this painting, see Steinberg, 1993, pp. 200–277.

2. See Charles Willson Peale, "An Essay, To Promote Domestic Happiness," 1812, in L. B. Miller, 1980, IID/29B13–D4; and Miller, Hart, Ward, and Emerick, 1991, pp. 139, 140, and 143–45.

3. Although Lloyd convincingly demonstrated the tension between Charles Willson Peale and Raphaelle Peale, she overstated her case by making the outrageous claim that Peale intentionally poisoned his son (Lloyd, 1988).

4. For eagle and chicken exhibit, see *Claypoole's American Daily Advertiser,* January 6, 1797. For snake, squirrel, and bird, see *Poulson's American Daily Advertiser,* June 21, 1810. Rubens's grouping of animals repeated the combination offered for view by an earlier itinerant animal keeper in Philadelphia in 1799. See *Claypoole's American Daily Advertiser,* December 11, 1799.

5. For the African bow, see Charles Willson Peale, "The Bow," *American Museum,* v. 6, 1789, pp. 205–6, in L. B. Miller, 1980, IID/1A12–B3; and Charles Willson Peale, *Diary,* August 1, 1789, in Miller, Hart, and Appel, 1983, pp. 565–66, including n. 24. For contemporary response to this exhibit, see Bernard, 1887, pp. 200–201.

6. See John Thomas Carré to Charles Willson Peale, 1793, in Miller, Hart, and Ward, 1988, p. 80.

7. See Charles Willson Peale to Rembrandt Peale, October 28, 1809, in L. B. Miller, 1980, IIA/48A11, and typescript, IIA/48B5. For theater violence, see *General Advertiser*, October 25, 1794. For Fourth of July celebrations, see *General Advertiser*, June 29, 1791; *General Advertiser*, July 6, 1791; *General Advertiser*, July 20, 1791; and *General Advertiser*, July 30, 1793. For an example of violence during a Fourth of July celebration as an example of political factionalism in Pennsylvania, see *Aurora. General Advertiser*, July 8, 1805.

8. See C. C. Sellers, 1975, in Miller and Ward, 1991, pp. 119–29 (quote on p. 120). For "Supporter," see *Gazette of the United States*, July 7, 1800.

9. Peale's public announcement of Wayne's gift was noted in the *Aurora. General Advertiser*, June 20, 1796. On Wayne's successful campaign in the Northwest, see Wiley Sword, *President Washington's Indian War: The Struggle for the Old Northwest, 1790–1795* (Norman: University of Oklahoma Press, 1985) and Knopf, 1960. For Pickering quote, see Sword, 1985, p. 325. Josiah Harmar, the general who preceded Wayne in command of the forces in Ohio, donated to the museum an ivory crucifix from the Miami Town. See *General Advertiser*, May 26, 1791.

10. Peale's announcement of these ten wax figures invoked the theme of harmony by reminding his readers of Red Pole and Blue Jacket's role in the treaties signed in 1796, following the chance encounter of enemy chiefs at his museum. However, the fact that the other figures exemplified racial types, rather than individuals, and that Peale described the figures in racially charged terms—"North American Savage," "Savage of South America," and "sooty African"—distanced them as exotic. See *Aurora. General Advertiser*, August 14, 1797; and *Aurora. General Advertiser*, September 29, 1797 to July 16, 1798. William Cobbett, editor of *Porcupine's Gazette*, satirized Peale's advertisement, suggesting that "the sooty African" was not such a phenomenal addition to the museum. Cobbett apparently refers to the growing number of free blacks in Philadelphia. See *Porcupine's Gazette*, October 3, 1797. Charles Coleman Sellers understood this as a purely politically motivated attack on a Democratic Republican (Peale) by a Federalist (Cobbett) (C. C. Sellers, 1969a, pp. 284–85). Blue Jacket's speech to the Shawnees in 1790 is quoted in Sword, 1985, p. 99. Reference to the annuity promised to Blue Jacket by Wayne appears in Sword, 1985, p. 318.

11. Charles Willson Peale to Thomas Jefferson, January 29, 1808, quoted in C. C. Sellers, 1975, in Miller and Ward, 1991, pp. 127–28.

12. See "Bluejacket, the Famous Shawnee Chief," *Transactions of the Kansas State Historical Society*, v. 10, 1907–8, pp. 397–98. I thank Duane H. King for encouraging me to consider this dimension of the exhibits.

13. For orangutan advertisement, see *Claypoole's American Daily Advertiser*, April 13, 1799; and Charles Willson Peale, "A Walk through the Philadelphia Museum," [1805–6], p. 7, in L. B. Miller 1980, IID27.

14. See Jefferson, 1787, pp. 70–71.

15. See John Redman Coxe, "Account of an Albino," *The Philadelphia Museum*, v. 1, 1805, pp. 151–56.

16. For repetition of Peale's account of James, see *General Advertiser*, November 1, 1791; *National Gazette*, October 31, 1791; *Virginia Gazette and Alexandria Advertiser*, November 10, 1791; *The Maryland Gazette, or the Baltimore General Advertiser*, November 11, 1791; and *Universal Asylum and Columbian Magazine*, v. 7, 1791, pp. 409–10. For a modern reprint of this item, a letter on the subject of the case study of James from Charles Willson Peale to Robert Patterson, October 7, 1791, and notes on the question of race, racism, and slavery, see Miller, Hart, and Appel, 1983, pp. 619–21. For contemporary interest in changes in skin pigmentation, see the description of Harry Moss, in *Aurora. General Advertiser*, July 13, 1796; and the display by Abraham Wright of a man whose skin changed from brown to white, *Aurora. General Advertiser*, August 24, 1796.

17. For notice of the portrait of Miss Harvey, by Charles Willson Peale, see *Poulson's American Daily Advertiser*, May 13, 1818; and *The Union*, May 20, 1818. See also Gall, 1981, p. 43.

18. Drawing of a flower by Sarah Rogers, donated by William Hamilton of Woodlands, *Memoranda of the Philadelphia Museum*, [April 30, 1807], p. 22 and *Aurora. General Advertiser*, October 12, 1807; Cut papers by Martha Ann Honeywell, donated by the artist, *Memoranda of the Philadelphia Museum*, [April] 30, [1807], p. 22 and *Aurora. General Advertiser*, October 12, 1807; Two paintings by Sarah Rogers [donor?], *Memoranda of the Philadelphia Museum*, [November 18, 1807], p. 26 and *Aurora. General Advertiser*, January 7, 1808; landscape painting by Sarah Rogers, donated by the artist, *Memoranda of the Philadelphia Museum*, [February 20, 1810], p. 49. "The Wonder of the World," broadside, Library Company of Philadelphia, sm #AM 1807 Won; *General Advertiser*, January 24, 1791. Also on Honeywell and

Rogers, see Groce and Wallace, 1957, pp. 324 and 545. For advertisements announcing Honeywell in Philadelphia, *Aurora. General Advertiser,* April [25], 1807, and *Aurora. General Advertiser,* June 11, 1807. For Rogers, *Aurora. General Advertiser,* November 24, 1807; *Aurora. General Advertiser,* December 10, 1807; and *Aurora. General Advertiser,* November 18, 1809.

19. The Gallaway notice appears in the *Aurora. General Advertiser,* February 14, 1795. Peale performed a second operation on Gallaway and displayed that horn also (*Aurora. General Advertiser,* August 27, 1795). For another example of a horn in Peale's collection, scar tissue taken from the knee of a forty-five-year-old African-American woman was removed and donated by Anderson Donaphan; see *Memoranda of the Philadelphia Museum,* [March] 5, [1806], p. 13. For fires and housing codes, see *Aurora. General Advertiser,* May 7, 1795; and Scharf and Westcott, 1884, v. 1, pp. 205, 265, 367, 368, 467, 492, 515, 516, 523, 528, and 614. For fire in Savannah, see *Aurora. General Advertiser,* December 15, 1796; in Albany, *Aurora. General Advertiser,* August 14, 1797; and in Philadelphia, *Aurora. General Advertiser,* May 12, 1806. For Peale's offer of a benefit day for the Savannah fire victims, *Aurora. General Advertiser,* December 30, 1796 and for the results, *Aurora. General Advertiser,* January 6, 1797. For Peale's claims that his stoves promoted safe use of fire, see *Aurora. General Advertiser,* November 4, 1797. For a thorough study of Peale's stove and fireplace innovations, see Hart, in Miller and Ward, 1991, pp. 244–48. For Peale's help in obtaining a fire engine for Annapolis, see Charles Willson Peale to John Muir, January 22, 1804, in Miller, Hart, and Ward, 1988, pp. 631–33; and Charles Willson Peale to John Shaw and J. William Alexander, July 22 and 23, 1806, in Miller, Hart, and Ward, 1988, pp. 976–78.

20. For Elizabeth DePeyster Peale's death, see *Aurora. General Advertiser,* February 21, 1804. For the yellow fever epidemic of 1793, see Miller, Hart, and Ward, 1988, pp. 64–65 and 70–72. For Peale's 1797 advertisement on the museum's healthy location, see *Aurora. General Advertiser,* September 29, 1797. For the Quaker petition suggesting divine intervention, see Society of Friends, "Philadelphia, 6th of 12th mo. 1793. A Committee of Friends this Day Attended Each House of the Legislature of this State, with the Following Address and Petition," broadside [Philadelphia, 1793]; for the clergy's version, *General Advertiser,* December 27, 1793. See also Charles Willson Peale to Gabriel Furman, September 16, 1799, in L. B. Miller, 1980, IIA/22F11. On moral living and long life in "Epistle to a Friend" and "An Essay, to Promote Domestic Happiness," see Hart, in Miller and Ward, 1991, p. 240; and C. C. Sellers, 1969a, pp. 308–10 and 364–65.

21. For Peale on Hutton, see *General Advertiser,* September 5, 1792. For Peale on Mamout, see Charles Willson Peale, *Diary,* January 30, 1819, in Miller, Hart, Ward, and Emerick, 1991, pp. 650–52. See also C. C. Sellers, 1947b, pp. 98–102. For accounts of longevity, see *General Advertiser,* October 12, 1790; June 27, 1791; July 25, 1792; and May 10, 1793. With the upper limits of age being pushed by this unidentified man and by the allegedly 134–year-old Yarrow Mamout, a manumitted slave, one questions whether the mysteries of race were among the unstated subthemes.

22. Bruliman's finger was donated by Mr. Plumstead, July, 1790, later recorded in the *Memoranda of the Philadelphia Museum,* [January 31, 1810], pp. 46–48. Hall, 1925. For the perceived immorality of billiards, *General Advertiser,* March 12, 1791, and *General Advertiser,* March 15, 1791. For other museum exhibits on criminality and punishment, see "An Iron Gag, which fits round the head. ~~used in~~ from Georgia. pr: by Norman McLeod Esqr. of Georgia." See *Memoranda of the Philadelphia Museum,* June, [1810], p. 50. The gag was removed from the museum "in consequence of reports." See *Memoranda of the Philadelphia Museum,* September 14, [1810], p. 52. Shortly after Charles Willson Peale's death, the museum added a "Model of a Garotte [which produces death by strangulation] used under the Spanish Constitution for Execution. Made & Pres: by Mr. James E Brooks." See *Memoranda of the Philadelphia Museum,* [October] 23, [1827], p. [131].

23. For Pendergrast's gift, see *Memoranda of the Philadelphia Museum,* May 8, 1817, p. 84. See C. C. Sellers, 1952, for portraits of Columbus, p. 56; Vespucci, pp. 214–15; Magellan, p. 139; and Cortez, p. 57.

24. For the Lewis and Clark materials, see *Memoranda of the Philadelphia Museum,* December 28, 1809, pp. 43–45; *Poulson's American Daily Advertiser,* March 1, 1810; *United States Gazette,* March 2, 1810; and *Aurora. General Advertiser,* March 15, 1810; and Willoughby, 1905. Lewis and Clark met Neeshneparkkeook in 1806, and on May 5 of that year Clark described him as "one of four principal Cheafs of the nation." Clark continued, "to this man we gave a Medal of the Small Size with a likeness of the President. he may be a great Chief but his Countiance has but little inteligence and his influence among his people appears very inconsiderable" (Moulton, 1991, v. 7, p. 213). On May 11, Lewis recorded a meeting with Neeshneparkkeook and the other Nez Perce chiefs, in which the American officers advanced the na-

tional agenda: "as all those cheifs were present in our lodge we thought it a favourable time to repeat what had been said yesterday and to enter more minutely into the views of our government with rispect to the inhabitants of this western part of the continent, their intention of establishing trading houses for their releif, their wish to restore peace and harmony among the natives, the strength power and wealth of our nation &c." (Moulton, 1991, v. 7, p. 242).

25. See Ronda, 1984, p. 4; and *Memoranda of the Philadelphia Museum,* December 28, 1809, pp. 43–45.

26. See *Memoranda of the Philadelphia Museum,* December 28, 1809, pp. 43–45.

27. See *Memoranda of the Philadelphia Museum,* December 28, 1809, pp. 43–45.

28. On Titian Peale's contributions, see *Memoranda of the Philadelphia Museum:* Florida Indian mound contents, May 1, 1818, pp. 92–93; pumice, March 10, 1821, p. 112; and specimens and drawings, March 23, 1821, pp. 112–13. See also Poesch, 1961, pp. 20–35. On Titian's participation in the Long Expedition, see Miller, Hart, Ward, and Emerick, 1991, pp. 694–97; and Haltman, 1992. For Peale's paintings based on Seymour's drawings, see *Memoranda of the Philadelphia Museum,* [February 16, 1822], p. 118.

29. See C. C. Sellers, 1952, for portraits of the following explorers: Baldwin, p. 26 no. 16; Clark, p. 54 no. 142; Jessup, p. 111 no. 418; Lewis, p. 127 nos. 481 and 482; Long, p. 130 no. 492; Peale, p. 169 no. 679; Pike, p. 172 no. 690; and Say, p. 191 no. 773. On the European explorers, see Miller, Hart, Ward, and Emerick, 1991, p. 383 n. 11.

30. For African (Mandingo) bow and arrows, see Charles Wister, *Memoranda of the Philadelphia Museum,* [November] 27, [1807], p. 26, and *Aurora. General Advertiser,* January 7, 1808; African example, Mrs. Babcock, *Memoranda of the Philadelphia Museum,* [1826], p. [128]; South American example, Mrs. Miercken, *Memoranda of the Philadelphia Museum,* [March] 6, [1827], p. [128]; African example, W. De la Roche, *Memoranda of the Philadelphia Museum,* [October] 25, [1827], p. [131]. See gift by George Harrison, recorded in *Memoranda of the Philadelphia Museum,* [October 26, 1805], pp. 9–10 (strikeout text is in original): "Curious portions of Armour from Persia & India. viz. 3 Jackets made of rings of different Metals interwoven, ~~One Crimson velvet Coat of mail~~ A Coat of Mail, composed of Crimson Velvet richly studded with Gold & finished with plates of Steel highly ornamented, on the Breast, back & sides. the whole of this quilted with Cotton, between which and the Velvet, is a curious interlining of large Fish-Scales—the Arms are enclosed from the Elbow in what may be called Boxes of ~~Steel~~ embossed Steel, trimmed with studded Velvet, and fastened on with Buckles. This appears to be part of the Dress of an Emperor or Commander in Chief. Two embossed Helmets with Wire Nettings; Several Elegant & curious Sabres & Daggers. George Harrison, Esquire." Feather helmet and cape, George Washington, *General Advertiser,* August 28, 1792 and C. C. Sellers, 1980, p. 41. African bark clothing, Messr. M[aclure], O[rd], S[ay], and P[eale], *Memoranda of the Philadelphia Museum,* [May 1, 1818], p. 93; bark clothing from the South Pacific, Mr. George Hinsey, *Memoranda of the Philadelphia Museum,* [June 29 and July 7, 1810], p. 51; and bark clothing from the Northwest Coast, Mr. George Caldwell, *Memoranda of the Philadelphia Museum,* October, [1820], p. 102. Chinese woman's shoes, Mr. Jacob Bitterton, *General Advertiser,* August 28, 1792. Hookahs, Mr. Tiffin, *Memoranda of the Philadelphia Museum,* December 2, [1808], p. 37; and *Aurora. General Advertiser,* January 2, 1809. Algerine pocketbook, Mrs. Thompson, Alexandr[ia?], *Memoranda of the Philadelphia Museum,* July 23 [September 9, 1817], p. 88. Medals of Edward Preble, George Armitage, *Memoranda of the Philadelphia Museum,* [June 18, 1807], p. 23 and *Aurora. General Advertiser,* October 12, 1807; and Mr. George Harrison, Secretary of the Navy, *Memoranda of the Philadelphia Museum,* December 10, [1807], p. 26. For a letter from Joel Barlow on his diplomatic success in Algiers, see *Aurora. General Advertiser,* February 10, 1797; for Preble's success in Tripoli and resulting treaty with Tripoli, see *Aurora. General Advertiser,* June 6, 1797.

31. The members of Peale's audience who were officers of the anti-slavery society included Nicholas Collin, Samuel P. Griffitts, John McCrea, Miers Fisher, Richard Wells, and Caleb Lownes; see *General Advertiser,* February 3, 1791. For Native American artifacts as the "record of Christian violence," see Howitt, 1820, pp. 60–61.

Epilogue

1. For the importance of the curtain in this image, see Stein, in Miller and Ward, 1991, pp. 201–3; and Kulik, 1989, p. 3. For the significance of the taxidermy kit and artist's tools in this narrative, see Stein, in

Miller and Ward, 1991, pp. 182, 190, and 191. The link between viewing practices and power has been discussed within the framework of the theoretical concept of "the gaze." In American art scholarship, see, for example, Boime, 1991; and A. Miller, 1993.

2. For the *Rachel Weeping* poem, see *The Freeman's Journal*, December 4, 1782, as quoted in Lloyd, 1982, p. 7.

3. For Gallaway, see *Aurora. General Advertiser*, February 14, 1795. For receipt of the living cow, see *General Advertiser*, May 26, 1791, and for its preservation, see *Aurora. General Advertiser*, February 14, 1795.

4. See Miller, Hart, and Ward, 1988, p. 387.

Selected Bibliography

Academy of Natural Sciences, *Members and Correspondents of the Academy of Natural Sciences of Philadelphia. 1877* (Philadelphia: printed for the Academy, 1877).

Alderson, William T., ed. *Mermaids, Mummies, and Mastodons: The Emergence of the American Museum* (Washington, D.C.: American Association of Museums for the Baltimore City Life Museums, 1992).

Alexander, Edward P. "Early American Museums: From Collections of Curiosities to Popular Education." *The International Journal of Museum Management and Curatorship*, v. 16, no. 4, December 1987, pp. 337–51.

———. *Museums in Motion: An Introduction to the History and Functions of Museums* (Nashville: American Association for State and Local History, 1979).

———. *Museum Masters: Their Museums and Their Influence* (Nashville: American Association for State and Local History, 1983).

Alexander, J[ames] E[dward]. *Transatlantic Sketches, Comprising Visits to the Most Interesting Scenes in North and South America . . .*, 2 vols. (London: Richard Bentley, 1833).

Allan, T[homas]. *An Alphabetical List of the Names of Minerals, at Present Most Familiar in the English, French, and German Languages, with Tables of Analyses* (Edinburgh: Caledonian Mercury Press, 1808).

Altick, Richard D. *The Shows of London* (Cambridge, Mass., and London: Belknap Press of Harvard University Press, 1978).

The American Mineralogical Journal, New York, 1810–14.

American Museum, Philadelphia, 1787–92.

American Philosophical Society. Member Card File (Philadelphia: American Philosophical Society).

———. *Year Book 1985* (Philadelphia: American Philosophical Society, 1986).

Appel, Toby A. "Science, Popular Culture and Profit: Peale's Philadelphia Museum." Paper presented at the International Conference on the History of Museums and Collections in Natural History, London, April 3–6, 1979. *Journal of the Society for the Bibliography of Natural History*, v. 9, pt. 4, April 1980, pp. 619–34.

Appleby, Joyce. *Capitalism and a New Social Order: The Republican Vision of the 1790s* (New York and London: New York University Press, 1984).

Arfwedson, Carl David. *The United States and Canada in 1832, 1833, and 1834*, 2 vols. (1834; reprint, with an introduction by Marvin Fisher, New York and London: Johnson Reprint Corporation, 1969).

Aurora. General Advertiser, Philadelphia, 1794–1827.

Baily, Francis. *Journal of a Tour in Unsettled Parts of North America in 1796 & 1797* (London: Baily Brothers, 1856).

Barber, Edwin Atlee. *Pottery and Porcelain of the United States* (1893; reprint, Watkins Glen, N.Y.: Century House Americana 1971).

Beal, Rebecca. *Jacob Eichholtz 1776–1842: Portrait Painter of Pennsylvania* (Philadelphia: Historical Society of Pennsylvania, 1969).

Becker, Howard S. *Art Worlds* (Berkeley: University of California Press, 1982).

Belknap, Jeremy. "Letter of Rev. Jeremiah Belknap to Rev. Manasseh Cutler, LL.D., 1785." *The Pennsylvania Magazine of History and Biography*, v. 37, no. 4, 1913, pp. 491–98.

Bell, Whitfield J., Jr. "A Box of Old Bones. A Note on the Identification of the Mastodon, 1766–1806." *Proceedings of the American Philosophical Society*, v. 93, no. 2, May 16, 1949, pp. 169–77.

———. "Nicholas Collin's Appeal to American Scientists." *The William and Mary Quarterly*, 3d series, v. 13, no. 4, October 1956, pp. 519–50.

Bernard, John. *Retrospections of America 1797–1811* (New York: Harper & Brothers, 1887).

Bernhard, Karl, Duke of Saxe-Weimar-Eisenach. *Travels through North America, During the Years 1825 and 1826*, 2 vols. (Philadelphia: Carey, Lea & Carey, 1828).

Bibbins, Arthur Barneveld. "Charles Willson Peale's Painting, *The Exhuming of the First American Mastodon.*" *Bulletin of the Geological Society of America*, v. 18, 1906, pp. 650–52.

Bining, Arthur Cecil. *Pennsylvania Iron Manufacture in the Eighteenth Century* (Harrisburg: Pennsylvania Historical Commission, 1938).

Bissett, Richard Lemar. Diary of Richard Lemar Bissett, Independence National Historical Park, Philadelphia, 1801.

[Blane, William Newnham]. *An Excursion Through the United States and Canada During the Years 1822–23. By an English Gentleman.* (1824; reprint, New York: Negro Universities Press, 1969).

Blumin, Stuart M. *The Emergence of the Middle Class: Social Experience in the American City, 1760–1900* (Cambridge: Cambridge University Press, 1989).

Boime, Albert. *The Magisterial Gaze: Manifest Destiny and American Landscape Painting c. 1830–1865* (Washington, D.C., and London: Smithsonian Institution Press, 1991).

Bourdieu, Pierre. "The Aristocracy of Culture," translated by Richard Nice, in Richard Collins, James Curran, Nicholas Garnham, Paddy Scanell, Philip Schlesinger, and Colin Sparks, eds., *Media, Culture and Society: A Critical Reader* (London: Sage Publications, 1986), pp. 164–93.

Boyd, Scott Lee, comp. *The Parrish Family* . . . (Santa Barbara, Calif.: Published by the compiler, 1935).

Branin, M. Lelyn. *The Early Makers of Handcrafted Earthenware and Stoneware in Central and Southern New Jersey* (Rutherford, N.J.: Fairleigh Dickinson University Press, and London and Toronto: Associate University Press, 1988).

Brigham, Clarence S. *History and Bibliography of American Newspapers, 1690–1820* (Worcester, Mass.: American Antiquarian Society, 1947).

Brigham, David R. 'A World in Miniature': Charles Willson Peale's Philadelphia Museum and Its Audience, 1786–1827." Ph.D. diss., University of Pennsylvania, Philadelphia, 1992.

Broadside Collection, Library Company of Philadelphia.

Brown, Alexander. *The Cabells and Their Kin: A Memorial Volume of History, Biography, and Genealogy* (Boston and New York: Houghton, Mifflin and Co., 1895).

Brown, Chandos Michael. *Benjamin Silliman: A Life in the Young Republic* (Princeton, N.J.: Princeton University Press, 1989).

Buckingham, J[ames] S[ilk]. *The Eastern and Western States of America*, 3 vols. (London and Paris: Fisher, Son, & Co., [1842]).

Butterfield, Lyman H. *Letters of Benjamin Rush. Memoirs of the American Philosophical Society*, v. 30, pts. 1 and 2 (Princeton, N.J.: Princeton University Press, 1951).

[Candler, Isaac]. *A Summary of America . . . By an Englishman* (London: printed for T. Cadell, in the Strand, and W. Blackwood, Edinburgh, 1824).

Chambers, E[phraim]. *Cyclopaedia: Or, an Universal Dictionary of Arts and Sciences,* 2 vols. (London: printed for James and John Knapton et al., 1728).

Chartier, Roger. "Culture as Appropriation: Popular Cultural Uses in Early Modern France," in Steven L. Kaplan, ed., *Understanding Popular Culture: Europe from the Middle Ages to the Nineteenth Century* (Berlin, New York, and Amsterdam: Mouton Publishers, 1984).

Cifelli, Edward M. *David Humphreys* (Boston: Twayne Publishers, 1982).

Claypoole's American Daily Advertiser, Philadelphia, 1796–1800.

Cleaveland, Parker. *An Elementary Treatise on Mineralogy and Geology* (Boston: published by Cummings and Hilliard; Cambridge, Mass.: printed by Hilliard and Metcalf, University Press; 1816).

Click, Patricia M. "Enlightened Entertainment: Educational Amusements in Nineteenth-Century Baltimore." *Maryland Historical Magazine,* v. 85, no. 1, Spring 1990, pp. 1–14.

Clifford, James. *The Predicament of Culture: Twentieth-Century Ethnography, Literature, and Art* (Cambridge, Mass., and London: Harvard University Press, 1988).

Cole, Garold L. *Travels in America from the Voyages of Discovery to the Present: An Annotated Bibliography of Travel Articles in Periodicals, 1955–1980* (Norman: University of Oklahoma Press, 1984).

College of Physicians of Philadelphia. "Roll of Fellows of the College of Physicians of Philadelphia, Elected during the Century Ending January, 1887." *Transactions of the College of Physicians of Philadelphia*, 3d series, v. 9, 1887, pp. ccxxxix–cccix.

Colton, Harold Sellers. "Peale's Museum." *The Popular Science Monthly,* v. 75, September 1909, pp. 221–38.

Columbian Magazine, Philadelphia, 1786–92.

Combe, George. *Notes on the United States of North America During a Phrenological Visit in 1838-9-40,* 2 vols. (Philadelphia: Carey & Hart, 1841).

Coxe, Tench. "An Enquiry into the Principles in Which a Commercial System for the United States of America Should Be Founded; to Which Are Added Some Political Observations Connected with the Subject" (Philadelphia: printed and sold by Robert Aitken, 1787).

Craigie, Sir William A., and James R. Hurlburt. *A Dictionary of American English in Historical Principles,* 4 vols. (Chicago: University of Chicago Press, 1938–44).

Crompton, Robert D. "James Trenchard of the 'Columbian' and 'Columbianum.'" *The Art Quarterly*, v. 23, no. 4, Winter 1960, pp. 378–97.

Cutler, Manasseh. *Life, Journals and Correspondence of Rev. Manasseh Cutler, LL.D.*, 2 vols., edited by William Parker Cutler and Julia Perkins Cutler (Cincinnati: Robert Clarke & Co., 1888).

Cutright, Paul Russell. *Lewis and Clark: Pioneering Naturalists* (Urbana, Chicago, and London: University of Illinois Press, 1969).

[DAB] *Dictionary of American Biography*, 10 vols. plus supplements, edited by Allen Johnson and Dumas Malone (New York: Charles Scribner's Sons, 1928–36; reprint, New York: Charles Scribner's Sons, 1964).

Darnton, Robert. "Readers Respond to Rousseau: The Fabrication of Romantic Sensitivity." *The Great Cat Massacre and Other Episodes in French Cultural History* (New York: Basic Books, 1984), pp. 215–56.

Darnton, Robert, and Daniel Roche, eds. *Revolution in Print* (Berkeley, Los Angeles, and London: University of California Press, n.d.).

Davidson, Abraham A. "Catastrophism and Peale's 'Mammoth.'" *American Quarterly*, v. 21, no. 3, Fall 1969, pp. 620–29.

———. "Charles Willson Peale's *Exhuming the First American Mastodon:* An Interpretation," in Frederick Hartt and Patricia Egan, eds., *Art Studies for an Editor: 25 Essays in Memory of Milton S. Fox* (New York: Harry N. Abrams, Inc., 1975), pp. 61–71.

Davidson, Cathy N. *Revolution and the Word: The Rise of the Novel in America* (New York and Oxford: Oxford University Press, 1986).

Davis, John. *Travels of Four Years and a Half in the United States of America During 1798, 1799, 1800, 1801, and 1802,* with an introduction and notes by A. J. Morrison (New York: Henry Holt and Company, 1909).

Davis, Susan G. *Parades and Power: Street Theatre in Nineteenth-Century Philadelphia* (Berkeley: University of California Press, 1988).

Desilver, Robert, ed. *The Philadelphia Index, or Directory for 1823* (Philadelphia: Published by the editor, 1823).

Dillenberger, John. *The Visual Arts and Christianity in America: The Colonial Period through the Nineteenth Century* (Chico, Calif.: Scholars Press, 1984).

DiMaggio, Paul, and Michael Useem. "Cultural Democracy in a Period of Cultural Expansion: The Social Composition of Arts Audiences in the United States," in Jack B. Kamerman and Rosanne Martorella, eds., *Performers and Performances: The Social Organization of Artistic Work* (South Hadley, Mass.: Bergin and Garvey Publishers, Inc., 1983), pp. 199–225.

Donakowski, Conrad L. *A Muse for the Masses: Ritual and Music in an Age of Democratic Revolution, 1770–1870* (Chicago and London: University of Chicago Press, 1972).

Downs, Robert B. *Images of America: Travelers from Abroad in the New World* (Urbana and Chicago: University of Illinois Press, 1987).

Drinker, Elizabeth. Diary of Elizabeth Drinker, Historical Society of Pennsylvania, Philadelphia, 1758–1807.

Duncan, John M. *Travels Through a Part of the United States and Canada in 1818 and 1819,* 2 vols. (Glasgow: printed at the University Press for Hurst, Robinson, & Company, London; Oliver & Boyd, Edinburgh; and Wardlaw & Cunninghame, Glasgow; 1823).

Dunlap and Claypoole's American Daily Advertiser, Philadelphia, 1793–95.

Dunlap's American Daily Advertiser, Philadelphia, 1791–93.

Dunlop, M. H. "Curiosities Too Numerous to Mention: Early Regionalism and Cincinnati's Western Museum." *American Quarterly,* v. 36, no. 4, Fall 1984, pp. 524–48.

Edgerton, Samuel Y., Jr. "*The Murder of Jane McCrea:* The Tragedy of an American Tableau d'Histoire." *The Art Bulletin,* v. 47, no. 4, December 1965, pp. 481–92.

Ellis, Joseph J. *After the Revolution: Profiles of Early American Culture* (New York: W. W. Norton and Co., 1979), pp. 41–71.

Evans, Charles Worthington, Martha Ellicott Tyson, and G. Hunter Bartlett. *American Family History: Fox, Ellicott, Evans;* edited by Harry Lee Hoffman, Jr., and Charlotte Feast Hoffman; foreword by Silvio A. Bedini. (Cockeysville, Md.: Fox, Ellicott, Evans Fund, 1976).

Ewers, John C. "'Chiefs from the Missouri and Mississippi' and Peale's Silhouettes of 1806," *The Smithsonian Journal of History,* v. 1, no. 1, Spring 1966, pp. 1–26.

Faxon, Walter. "Relics of Peale's Museum." *Bulletin of the Museum of Comparative Zoology of Harvard College,* v. 59, no. 3, July 1915, pp. 119–48.

Ferrall, Simon A[nsley]. *A Ramble of Six Thousand Miles Through the United States of America* (London: Effingham Wilson, 1832).

Finch, I. *Travels in the United States of America and Canada . . .* (London: Longman, Rees, Orme, Brown, Green, and Longman, 1833).

Fish, Stanley. *Is There a Text in This Class?: The Authority of Interpretive Communities* (Cambridge, Mass.: Harvard University Press, 1980).

Flint, James. *Letters from America . . .* (Edinburgh: printed for W. and C. Tait; London: printed for Longman, Hurst, Rees, Orme, and Brown, 1822).

Forbes, David W. *Encounters with Paradise: Views of Hawaii and Its People, 1778–1941* (Honolulu: University of Hawaii Press and Honolulu Academy of Fine Arts, 1992).

Ford, Timothy. "Diary of Timothy Ford, 1785–1786," with notes by Joseph W. Barnwell. *The South Carolina Historical and Genealogical Magazine,* v. 13, no. 3, July 1912, pp. 132–47.

Fortune, Brandon Brame. "Portraits of Virtue and Genius: Pantheons of Worthies and Public Portraiture in the Early American Republic, 1780–1820." Ph.D. diss., University of North Carolina, Chapel Hill, 1987.

———. "Charles Willson Peale's Portrait Gallery: Persuasion and the Plain Style," *Word & Image,* v. 6, no. 4, October–December, 1990, pp. 308–24.

Foster, Sir Augustus John. *Jeffersonian America: Notes on the United States of America Collected in the Years 1805–6–7 and 11–12 by Sir Augustus John Foster, Bart.,* edited by Richard Beale Davis (San Marino, Calif.: Huntington Library, 1954; reprint, Westport, Conn.: Greenwood Press, Publishers, 1980).

Foucault, Michel. *The Order of Things: An Archaeology of the Human Sciences* (New York: Vintage Books, 1973).

Franklin, Benjamin. *The Autobiography & Other Writings by Benjamin Franklin,* edited by Peter Shaw (New York: Bantam Books, 1982).

Fritsch, Catherine. "Notes of a Visitor to Philadelphia, Made by a Moravian Sister in 1810," translated by A. R. Beck. *The Pennsylvania Magazine of History and Biography,* v. 36, no. 3, 1912, pp. 346–61.

Gall, Ludwig. "Pennsylvania Through a German's Eyes: The Travels of Ludwig Gall, 1819–1820," translated by Frederic Trautmann. *The Pennsylvania Magazine of History and Biography*, v. 105, no. 1, January 1981, pp. 35–65.

Garvan, Anthony N. B., ed. *The Mutual Assurance Company Papers*, v. 1. *The Architectural Surveys 1784–1794* (Philadelphia: Mutual Assurance Company, 1976).

Gazette of the United States, Philadelphia, 1790–1804.

Geib, George W. "Playhouses and Politics: Lewis Hallam and the Confederation Theater." *Journal of Popular Culture*, v. 5, no. 2, Fall 1971, pp. 324–39.

General Advertiser, Philadelphia, 1790–94.

Gillispie, Charles Coulston, and Frederic L. Holmes, eds. *Dictionary of Scientific Biography*, 18 vols., including supplements (New York: Charles Scribner's Sons, 1970–90).

Greene, John C. *American Science in the Age of Jefferson* (Ames: Iowa State University Press, 1984).

———. "The Founding of Peale's Museum," in Thomas R. Buckman, ed., *Bibliography and Natural History* (Lawrence: University of Kansas Libraries, 1966), pp. 66–72.

Greene, John C., and John G. Burke. *The Science of Minerals in the Age of Jefferson. Transactions of the American Philosophical Society*, v. 68, pt. 4 (Philadelphia: American Philosophical Society, July 1978).

Groce, George C., and David H. Wallace. *The New-York Historical Society's Dictionary of Artists in America 1564–1860* (New Haven, Conn., and London: Yale University Press, 1957).

Haberly, Loyd. "The American Museum from Baker to Barnum." *The New-York Historical Society Quarterly*, v. 43, no. 3, July 1959, pp. 272–87.

———. "The Long Life of Daniel Bowen." *The New England Quarterly*, v. 32, no. 3, September 1959, pp. 320–32.

Hall, Francis. *Travels in Canada, and the United States, in 1816 and 1817* (London: printed for Longman, Hurst, Rees, Orme, and Brown, 1818).

Hall, H. U. "A Link with the Old Peale Museum." *The Museum Journal*, v. 16, no. 1, March 1925, pp. 64–69.

Haltman, Kenneth. "Figures in a Western Landscape: Reading the Art of Titian Ramsay Peale from the Long Expedition to the Rocky Mountains, 1819–1820." Ph.D. diss., Yale University, New Haven, Conn., 1992.

Hamilton, Alexander. *The Works of Alexander Hamilton*, 12 vols., edited by Henry Cabot Lodge (New York and London: G. P. Putnam's Sons, Knickerbocker Press, 1904).

Hardie, James. *The Philadelphia Directory and Register* (Philadelphia: printed for the author by T. Dobson, 1793).

———. *The Philadelphia Directory and Register*, 2d ed. (Philadelphia: Jacob Johnson & Co., 1794).

Harlow, Thompson R. "The Life and Trials of Joseph Steward." *The Connecticut Historical Society Bulletin*, v. 46, no. 4, October 1981.

———. "The Versatile Joseph Steward, Portrait Painter." *The Magazine Antiques*, v. 121, no. 1, January 1982, pp. 303–11.

Harris, Neil. *The Artist in American Society: The Formative Years 1790–1860* (Chicago and London: University of Chicago Press, 1966).

————. *Humbug: The Art of P. T. Barnum* (Boston and Toronto: Little, Brown & Co., 1973).

Hart, Sidney. "'To Encrease the Comforts of Life': Charles Willson Peale and the Mechanical Arts." *The Pennsylvania Magazine of History and Biography,* v. 110, no. 3, July 1986, pp. 323–57.

Hart, Sidney, and David C. Ward. "The Waning of an Enlightenment Ideal: Charles Willson Peale's Philadelphia Museum, 1790–1820." *Journal of the Early Republic,* v. 8, no. 4, Winter 1988, pp. 389–418.

Haüy, René-Just. "Sur l'arragonite." *Annales du Muséum d'Histoire Naturelle,* v. 11, 1808, pp. 241–70.

————. *Tableau comparatif des résultats de la cristallographie et de l'analyse chimique relativement à la classification des minéraux* (Paris: Courcier, 1809).

————. *Traité de mineralogie,* 5 vols. (Paris: Chez Louis, 1801).

Held, Beverly Orlove. "'To Instruct and Improve . . . to Entertain and Please': American Civic Protests and Pageants, 1765–1784." Ph.D. diss., University of Michigan, Ann Arbor, 1987.

Helm, Ruth. "'For Credit, Honor, and Profit': Three Generations of the Peale Family in America." Ph.D. diss., University of Colorado, Boulder, 1991.

Hinshaw, William Wade, and Thomas Worth Marshall, comps. *Encyclopedia of American Quaker Genealogy,* 7 vols. (1938; reprint, Ann Arbor, Mich.: Edwards Brothers, Inc., 1969–77).

Hodgson, Adam. *Remarks During a Journey Through North America in the Years 1819, 1820, and 1821, in a Series of Letters* (New York: J. Seymour, 1823; reprint, Westport, Conn.: Negro Universities Press, 1970).

Hogan, Edmund. *The Prospect of Philadelphia, and Check on the Next Directory* (Philadelphia: Francis and Robert Bailey, 1795).

Howitt, E[manuel]. *Selections from Letters Written During a Tour through the United States, in the Summer and Autumn of 1819* . . . (Nottingham, England: printed and sold by J. Dunn, Market-place, [1820]).

Hudson, Kenneth. *Museums of Influence* (Cambridge, England: Cambridge University Press, 1987).

Hunter, Wilbur Harvey. *The Peale Family and Peale's Baltimore Museum 1814–1830* (Baltimore: Peale Museum, February 1965).

Hunter, Wilbur H., Jr. "The Tribulations of a Museum Director in the 1820s." *Maryland Historical Magazine,* v. 49, no. 3, September 1954, pp. 214–22.

Hutcheson, Harold. *Tench Coxe: A Study in American Economic Development* (Baltimore: Johns Hopkins Press, 1938).

Huth, Hans. "Pierre Eugène DuSimitière and the Beginnings of the American Historical Museum." *The Pennsylvania Magazine of History and Biography,* v. 69, no. 4, October 1954, pp. 315–25.

Independent Gazetteer, Philadelphia, 1786–90.

Jacob, Kathryn Allamong, and Bruce A. Ragsdale, eds. *Biographical Directory of the United States Congress, 1774–1989* (Washington, D.C.: U.S. Government Printing Office, 1989).

James, Reese D. *Old Drury of Philadelphia: A History of the Philadelphia Stage, 1800–1835* (Philadelphia: University of Pennsylvania Press; London: Humphrey Milford, Oxford University Press; 1932).

Janson, Charles William. *The Stranger in America 1793–1806,* edited by Carl S. Driver (1807; reprint, New York: Burt Franklin, 1971).

Jefferson, Thomas. *Notes on the State of Virginia,* edited by William Peden (1787; reprint, New York and London: W. W. Norton & Company, 1982).

John, Richard. "Managing the Mails: The Postal System, Public Policy, and American Political Culture, 1823–1836." Ph.D. diss., Harvard University, Cambridge, Mass., 1989.

Johnson, Claudia D. "That Guilty Third Tier: Prostitution in Nineteenth-Century American Theaters." *American Quarterly,* v. 27, no. 5, December 1975, pp. 575–84.

"Joseph Steward and the Hartford Museum." *Connecticut Historical Society Bulletin,* v. 18, nos. 1 and 2, January–April 1953.

Ker, Henry. *Travels through the Western Interior of the United States, from the Year 1808 up to the Year 1816 . . .* (Elizabethtown, N.J.: printed for the author, 1816).

Kerber, Linda K. *Women of the Republic: Intellect and Ideology in Revolutionary America* (New York and London: W. W. Norton & Company, 1980; reprint, New York and London: W. W. Norton & Company, 1986).

Kielbowicz, Richard B. *News in the Mail: The Press, Post Office, and Public Information, 1700–1860s* (Westport, Conn.: Greenwood Press, 1989).

Kirwan, Richard. *Elements of Mineralogy* (London: printed for P. Elmsly, 1784).

Knopf, Richard C. *Anthony Wayne, A Name in Arms: Soldier, Diplomat, Defender of Expansion Westward of a Nation. The Wayne–Knox–Pickering–McHenry Correspondence* (Pittsburgh: University of Pittsburgh Press, 1960).

Knox, Katharine McCook. *The Sharples: Their Portraits of George Washington and His Contemporaries . . .* (New Haven, Conn.: Yale University Press; London: Humphrey, Oxford University Press; 1930).

Koch, Albert C. *Journey Through a Part of the United States of North America in the Years 1844 to 1846,* translated and edited by Ernst A. Stadler, foreword by John Francis McDermott (Dresden, 1847. Translation, Carbondale and Edwardsville: Southern Illinois University Press, and London and Amsterdam: Feffer & Simons, Inc., 1972).

Kulik, Gary. "Designing the Past: History-Museum Exhibitions from Peale to the Present," in Warren Leon and Roy Rosenzwieg, eds., *History Museums in the United States: A Critical Assessment* (Urbana and Chicago: University of Illinois Press, 1989), pp. 2–37.

Lamberton, E. V. "Colonial Libraries of Pennsylvania." *The Pennsylvania Magazine of History and Biography,* v. 41, no. 3, 1918, pp. 193–234.

Lewis, W. David, and Walter Hugins. *Hopewell Furnace: A Guide to Hopewell Furnace National Historic Site Pennsylvania* (Washington, D.C.: U.S. Department of the Interior, 1983).

Library Company of Philadelphia. Minutes of the Directors, ms., Library Company of Philadelphia.

Lindfors, Bernth. "Circus Africans." *Journal of American Culture,* v. 6, no. 2, Summer 1983, pp. 9–14.

Lingelbach, William E. "The Story of 'Philosophical Hall.'" *Proceedings of the American Philosophical Society,* v. 94, no. 3, June 20, 1950, pp. 185–213.

Linnaeus, Charles. *Systema Naturae,* 4 vols. (Stockholm: printed for Laurence Salve, 1766–68).

Lloyd, Phoebe. "A Death in the Family," *Philadelphia Museum of Art Bulletin,* v. 78, no. 335, Spring 1982, pp. 3–13.

———. "Philadelphia Story." *Art in America,* v. 76, no. 11, November 1988, pp. 154–71, 195–97, 199–201, and 203.

Logan, Robert R. The Robert R. Logan Collection, Historical Society of Pennsylvania, Philadelphia, 1802–9.

Looby, Christopher. "The Constitution of Nature: Taxonomy as Politics in Jefferson, Peale, and Bartram." *Early American Literature,* v. 22, no. 3, 1987, pp. 252–73.

Lyell, Charles. *Travels in North America, in the Years 1841–1842 . . .,* 2 vols. (New York: John Wiley, 1852).

Marryat, Captain Frederick. *Diary in America,* edited with a foreword by Jules Zanger (London: Longman, Orme, Brown, Green, and Longmans, 1839; reprint, Bloomington: Indiana University Press, 1960).

Martin, William. Copy Book of William Martin, ms., University of Pennsylvania Archives and Record Center, Philadelphia, 1757–96.

McClung, Robert M., and Gale S. McClung. "Tammany's Remarkable Gardiner Baker; New York's First Museum Proprietor, Menagerie Keeper, and Promoter Extraordinary." *The New-York Historical Society Quarterly,* v. 42, no. 2, April 1958, pp. 143–69.

Maddock, Archibald M., II. *The Polished Earth: A History of the Plumbing Pottery Fixture Industry in the United States* (Trenton, N.J.: privately printed, 1962).

Margulies, Cecile. "The Natural History Museum: An Historical Sketch." *Field Museum of Natural History Bulletin,* v. 50, no. 10, November 1979, pp. 8–17.

Marshall, Charles, Jr., comp. *Descendants of Christopher Marshall of Dublin, Ireland and Pennsylvania and His Wife Sarah Thomson,* ms. ([Philadelphia]: Genealogical Society of Pennsylvania, n.d.).

May, Henry F. *The Enlightenment in America* (Oxford, London, and New York: Oxford University Press, 1976).

Mease, James. *The Picture of Philadelphia . . .* (Philadelphia: B. & T. Kite, 1811).

[———]. *Picture of Philadelphia . . .* (Philadelphia: E. L. Carey and A. Hart, 1835).

Medical and Philosophical Register, Philadelphia, 1804–11.

Melish, John. *Travels in the United States of America, in the Years 1806 & 1807, and 1809, 1810, & 1811 . . .,* 2 vols. (Philadelphia: Thomas and George Palmer, 1812).

Memoirs of the American Academy of Arts and Sciences, Boston, 1780–1827.

Memoranda of the Philadelphia Museum, ms., Historical Society of Pennsylvania, Philadelphia, 1803–42.

Meyers, Amy R. Weinstein. "Sketches from the Wilderness: Changing Conceptions of Nature in American Natural History Illustration: 1680–1880." Ph.D. diss., Yale University, New Haven, Conn., 1985.

Meyerson, Martin, and Dilys Pegler Winegrad. *Gladly Learn and Gladly Teach: Franklin and His Heirs at the University of Pennsylvania, 1740–1976* (Philadelphia: University of Pennsylvania Press, 1978).

Michaux, François André. *Travels to the Westward of the Allegany Mountains, in the States of the Ohio, Kentucky, and Tennessee, and Return to Charlestown, through the Upper Carolinas . . .,* translated by B. Lambert (London: W. Flint and J. Mawman, 1805).

Miles, Wyndham D. "Public Lectures of Chemistry in the United States." *Ambix: The Journal of the Society for the Study of Alchemy and Early Chemistry,* v. 15, no. 3, October 1968, pp. 136–37.

Miles, Wyndham D., and Harold Abrahams. "The Public Chemistry Lectures of Benjamin Tucker." *Journal of Chemical Education,* v. 34, no. 9, September 1957, pp. 450–51.

Miller, Angela. *The Empire of the Eye: Landscape Representation and American Cultural Politics, 1825–1875* (Ithaca, N.Y., and London: Cornell University Press, 1993).

Miller, Lillian B. *Patrons and Patriotism: The Encouragement of the Fine Arts in the United States 1790–1860* (Chicago and London: University of Chicago Press, 1966).

———, ed. *The Collected Papers of Charles Willson Peale and His Family, 1735–1885.* Microfiche (Millwood, N.Y.: KTO Microform for the National Portrait Gallery, Smithsonian Institution, 1980).

———. "Charles Willson Peale as History Painter: *The Exhumation of the Mastodon.*" *The American Art Journal,* v. 13, no. 1, Winter 1981, pp. 47–68.

———. With an essay by Carol Eaton Hevner. *In Pursuit of Fame: Rembrandt Peale 1778–1860* (Washington, D.C., Seattle, and London: National Portrait Gallery in association with University of Washington Press, 1992).

Miller, Lillian B., Sidney Hart, and Toby A. Appel, eds. *Charles Willson Peale: Artist in Revolutionary America, 1735–1791,* v. 1 (1983) in *The Selected Papers of Charles Willson Peale and His Family,* 3 vols. (New Haven, Conn., and London: Yale University Press, 1983–91).

Miller, Lillian B., Sidney Hart, and David C. Ward, eds. *Charles Willson Peale: The Artist as Museum Keeper, 1791–1810,* v. 2 (1988) in *The Selected Papers of Charles Willson Peale and His Family,* 3 vols. (New Haven, Conn., and London: Yale University Press, 1983–91).

Miller, Lillian B., Sidney Hart, David C. Ward, and Rose S. Emerick, eds. *Charles Willson Peale: The Belfield Years, 1810–1820,* v. 3 (1991) in *The Selected Papers of Charles Willson Peale and His Family,* 3 vols. (New Haven, Conn., and London: Yale University Press, 1983–91).

Miller, Lillian B., and David C. Ward, eds. *New Perspectives on Charles Willson Peale: A 250th Anniversary Celebration* (Pittsburgh: University of Pittsburgh Press, 1991). [Relevant essays published previously are also listed separately.]

Miller, Richard G. *Philadelphia—The Federalist City: A Study of Urban Politics, 1789–1801* (Port Washington, N.Y., and London: Kennikat Press, 1976).

Moon, Robert C. *The Morris Family of Philadelphia: Descendants of Anthony Morris, 1654–1721,* 5 vols. (Philadelphia: Robert C. Moon, 1898–1909).

Mott, Frank Luther. *American Journalism: A History of Newspapers in the United States Through 250 Years, 1690–1940* (New York: Macmillan Company, 1941).

————. *A History of American Magazines,* 5 vols. (Cambridge, Mass.: Harvard University Press, 1930–68).

Moulton, Gary E., ed. *The Journals of the Lewis & Clark Expedition,* 8 vols. (Lincoln and London: University of Nebraska Press, 1983–93).

Mullaney, Steven. *The Place of the Stage: License, Play, and Power in Renaissance England* (Chicago and London: University of Chicago Press, 1988).

————. "Strange Things, Gross Terms, Curious Customs: The Rehearsal of Cultures in the Late Renaissance." *Representations,* v. 1, no. 3, Summer 1983, pp. 40–67.

Myers, Susan H. *Handcraft to Industry: Philadelphia Ceramics in the First Half of the Nineteenth Century.* Smithsonian Studies in History and Technology, no. 43 (Washington, D.C.: Smithsonian Institution Press, 1980).

Nash, Gary B. *Forging Freedom: The Formation of Philadelphia's Black Community, 1720–1840* (Cambridge, Mass.: Harvard University Press, 1988).

Newman, Simon P. "'A Truly American Festival': The Politics of July Fourth Celebrations in the Early Republic." Unpublished paper presented informally to the Philadelphia Center for Early American Studies, February 12, 1991.

————. "Principles or Men? George Washington and the Political Culture of National Leadership, 1776–1801," *Journal of the Early Republic,* v. 12, no. 4, Winter 1992, pp. 477–507.

North, Douglass C. *The Economic Growth of the United States, 1790–1860* (New York: W. W. Norton & Co., Inc., 1966).

Orosz, Joel J. "Curators and Culture: An Interpretive History of the Museum Movement in America, 1773–1870." Ph.D. diss., Case Western Reserve University, Cleveland, Ohio, 1986.

————. *Curators and Culture: The Museum Movement in America, 1740–1870* (Tuscaloosa and London: University of Alabama Press, 1990).

————. "Pierre Eugène DuSimitière: Museum Pioneer in America." *Museum Studies Journal,* v. 1, no. 5, Spring 1985, pp. 8–18.

Pachter, Marc, and Frances Wein, eds. *Abroad in America: Visitors to the New Nation, 1776–1914* (Reading, Mass.: Addison-Wesley Publishing Company, in association with the National Portrait Gallery, Washington, D.C., 1976).

Paxton, John A. *The Philadelphia Directory and Register for 1813* . . . (Philadelphia: B. and T. Kite, 1813).

Peale Family Papers, National Portrait Gallery, Smithsonian Institution, Washington, D.C.

Peale Papers, Historical Society of Pennsylvania, Philadelphia.

Peale-Sellers Papers, American Philosophical Society, Philadelphia.

Pennsylvania Academy of the Fine Arts. *Catalogue of an Exhibition of Portraits by Charles Willson Peale and James Peale and Rembrandt Peale* (Philadelphia: Pennsylvania Academy of the Fine Arts, 1923).

Pennsylvania General Assembly. *Laws of the General Assembly of the Commonwealth of Pennsylvania* (Philadelphia: John Dunlap, 1779; Thomas Bradford, 1786 and 1789; Hall and Sellers, 1794).

————, House of Representatives. *Journal of the House of Representatives of the Commonwealth of Pennsylvania* (Philadelphia: Francis Bailey, [1794]).

————, Senate. *Journal of the Senate of the Commonwealth of Pennsylvania* (Philadelphia: Zachariah Poulson, Jr., [1794]).

Pennsylvania Historical Survey, Division of Community Service Programs, Work Projects Administration. *A Checklist of Pennsylvania Newspapers,* v. 1. Philadelphia County (Harrisburg: Pennsylvania Historical Commission, 1944).

Pennsylvania Packet, Philadelphia, 1786–90.

Peterson, Charles E. "Library Hall: Home of the Library Company of Philadelphia, 1790–1880." *Proceedings of the American Philosophical Society,* v. 95, no. 3, June 12, 1951, pp. 266–85.

Philadelphia County Tax Assessment Ledgers, ms., Philadelphia City Archives.

Philadelphia Gazette, Philadelphia, 1794–1802.

Philadelphia in 1824 . . . (Philadelphia: H. C. Carey and I. Lea, August 1824).

Philadelphia in 1830–1 . . . (Philadelphia: E. L. Carey and A. Hart, 1830).

The Philadelphia Medical Museum, Philadelphia, 1804–11.

Philadelphia Society for Promoting Agriculture. "Laws of the Philadelphia Society for Promoting Agriculture; As Revised and Enacted by the Said Society, February 16th, 1789, with the Premiums Proposed, February 3d, 1789. To Which Is Prefixed, A List of the Members of the Society" ([Philadelphia], 1789).

————. *Manuscripts of the Philadelphia Society for Promoting Agriculture, 1785–1935,* 3 vols., ms., University of Pennsylvania, Van Pelt Library, Rare Book Room.

Poesch, Jessie J. "Mr. Peale's 'Farm Persevere': Some Documentary Views." *Proceedings of the American Philosophical Society,* v. 100, no. 6, December 17, 1956, pp. 545–56.

————. "Germantown Landscapes: A Peale Family Amusement." *Antiques,* v. 72, no. 5, November 1957, pp. 434–39.

————. "A Precise View of Peale's Museum." *Antiques,* v. 78, no. 4, October 1960, pp. 343–45.

————. *Titian Ramsay Peale and His Journals of the Wilkes Expedition, 1799–1885. Memoirs of the American Philosophical Society,* v. 52 (Philadelphia: American Philosophical Society, 1961).

Pollock, Thomas Clark. *The Philadelphia Theatre in the Eighteenth Century, Together with the Day Book of the Same Period* (Philadelphia: University of Pennsylvania Press; London: Humphrey Milford, Oxford University Press; 1933).

Porcupine's Gazette, Philadelphia, 1797–99.

Porter, Charlotte M. *The Eagle's Nest: Natural History and American Ideas, 1812–1842* (University: University of Alabama Press, 1986).

Port Folio, Philadelphia, 1801–27.

Potts, William J[ohn]. "Amusements and Politics in Philadelphia." *The Pennsylvania Magazine of History and Biography,* v. 10, no. 2, 1886, pp. 182–87.

————. "DuSimitière, Artist, Antiquary, and Naturalist, Projector of the First American Museum, with Some Extracts from His Notebook." *The Pennsylvania Magazine of History and Biography,* v. 13, no. 3, 1889, pp. 341–75.

Poulson, Charles A., comp. *Extracts from Various Works of Travel &c., &c., Relating to the City of Philadelphia, 1688–1862,* ms., Library Company of Philadelphia.

Poulson, Zachariah, Jr., comp. *A Chronological Register of the Names of the Members of the Library Company of Philadelphia . . .,* begun ca. 1800, ms. vol., Library Company of Philadelphia.

Poulson's American Daily Advertiser, Philadelphia, 1800–1827.

Powell, J. H. *Bring Out Your Dead: The Great Plague of Yellow Fever in Philadelphia in 1793* (Philadelphia: University of Pennsylvania Press, 1949).

Pratt, Mary Louise. "Interpretive Strategies/Strategic Interpretations: On Anglo-American Reader Response Criticism," in Jonathan Arac, ed., *Postmodernism and Politics* (Minneapolis: University of Minnesota Press, 1986), pp. 26–54.

Pritner, Calvin Lee. "A Theater and Its Audience." *The Pennsylvania Magazine of History and Biography,* v. 91, no. 1, January 1967, pp. 72–79.

Prown, Jules. *John Singleton Copley,* 2 vols. (Cambridge, Mass.: Harvard University Press, 1966).

Radway, Janice A. *Reading the Romance: Women, Patriarchy, and Popular Literature* (Chapel Hill and London: University of North Carolina Press, 1984).

Ramsay, John. *American Potters and Pottery* ([Boston]: Hale, Cushman & Flint, 1939).

Relf's Philadelphia Gazette and Daily Advertiser, Philadelphia, 1803–23.

Richardson, E[dgar] P. "Charles Willson Peale's Engravings in the Year of National Crisis, 1787," *Winterthur Portfolio,* v. 1, 1964, pp. 166–81.

Richardson, Edgar P., Brooke Hindle, and Lillian B. Miller, with a foreword by Charles Coleman Sellers. *Charles Willson Peale and His World* (New York: Harry N. Abrams, 1983).

Rigal, Laura. "An American Manufactory: Political Economy, Collectivity, and the Arts in Philadelphia 1790–1810." Ph.D. diss., Stanford University, Stanford, Calif., 1989.

Riley, Edward M. "The Independence Hall Group." *Transactions of the American Philosophical Society,* n.s., v. 43, pt. 1, March 1953, pp. 7–42.

Roach, Hannah. Hannah Roach Card File, American Philosophical Society, Philadelphia, 1718–1925.

Robinson, James. *The Philadelphia Directory, City and County Register, for 1803* (Philadelphia: William W. Woodward, 1803).

———. *The Philadelphia Directory for 1804* (Philadelphia: John H. Oswald, 1804).

———. *The Philadelphia Directory, for 1807* (Philadelphia: W. Woodhouse, 1807).

———. *The Philadelphia Directory, for 1808* (Philadelphia: W. Woodhouse, 1808).

———. *The Philadelphia Directory for 1810* (Philadelphia: printed for the publisher, 1810).

Ronda, James P. *Lewis and Clark Among the Indians* (Lincoln and London: University of Nebraska Press, 1984).

Rousseau, G[eorge] S., and Roy Porter. *Exoticism in the Enlightenment* (Manchester, England, and New York: Manchester University Press, 1990).

Royall, Anne. *Mrs. Royall's Pennsylvania, Or Travels Continued in the United States,* 2 vols. (Washington: printed for the author, 1829).

Said, Edward W. *Orientalism* (New York: Pantheon Books, 1978).

Sargent, Elizabeth Kennedy. "James Reid Lambdin's Pittsburgh Museum of Natural History and Gallery of the Fine Arts, 1828–1832." Undergraduate tutorial paper, Chatham College, Pittsburgh, 1984.

Scharf, J. Thomas, and Thompson Westcott. *History of Philadelphia, 1609–1884*, 3 vols. (Philadelphia: L. H. Everts & Co., 1884).

Schmiegel, Karol A. "Encouragement Exceeding Expectation: The Lloyd-Cadwalader Patronage of Charles Willson Peale." *Winterthur Portfolio*, v. 12, 1977, pp. 87–102.

Schofield, Robert E. "The Science Education of an Enlightened Entrepreneur: Charles Willson Peale and His Philadelphia Museum, 1784–1827." *American Studies*, v. 30, no. 2, Fall 1989, pp. 21–40.

Schreiber, Lee I. "The Changing Social Climate, 1790–1810 and the Pennsylvania Academy of the Fine Arts." *Journal of American Culture*, v. 2, no. 3, Fall 1979, pp. 361–75.

Scott, George Lewis, ed. *A Supplement to Mr. Chambers's Cyclopaedia: Or, Universal Dictionary of Arts and Sciences*, 2 vols. (London: printed for W. Innys, J. Richardson, et al., 1753).

Sellers, Charles Coleman. *The Artist of the Revolution, The Early Life of Charles Willson Peale* (Hebron, Conn.: Feather and Good, 1939).

———. *Charles Willson Peale, v. 2. Later Life (1790–1827)*, in *Memoirs of the American Philosophical Society*, v. 23, pt. 2 (Philadelphia: American Philosophical Society, 1947a).

———. "Charles Willson Peale and Yarrow Mamout." *The Pennsylvania Magazine of History and Biography*, v. 71, no. 2, April 1947b, pp. 98–102.

———. "The Peale Silhouettes." *American Collector*, v. 17, no. 4, May 1948, pp. 6–8.

———. *Portaits and Miniatures by Charles Willson Peale. Transactions of the American Philosophical Society*, n.s., v. 42, pt. 1 (Philadelphia: American Philosophical Society, June 1952).

———. *Benjamin Franklin in Portraiture* (New Haven, Conn., and London: Yale University Press, 1962).

———. "Joseph Sansom, Philadelphia Silhouettist." *The Pennsylvania Magazine of History and Biography*, v. 88, no. 4, October 1964, pp. 395–438.

———. *Charles Willson Peale* (New York: Charles Scribner's Sons, 1969a).

———. *Charles Willson Peale with Patron and Populace: A Supplement to Portraits and Miniatures by Charles Willson Peale with a Survey of His Work in Other Genres. Transactions of the American Philosophical Society*, n.s., v. 59, pt. 3 (Philadelphia: American Philosophical Society, May 1969b).

———. "'Good Chiefs and Wise Men': Indians as Symbols of Peace in the Art of Charles Willson Peale." *The American Art Journal*, v. 7, no. 2, November 1975, pp. 10–18.

———. *Mr. Peale's Museum: Charles Willson Peale and the First Popular Museum of Natural Science and Art* (New York: W. W. Norton & Company, Inc., 1980a).

———. "Peale's Museum and 'The New Museum Idea.'" *Proceedings of the American Philosophical Society*, v. 124, no. 1, 1980b, pp. 25–34.

Sellers, Horace W[ells]. "Letters of Thomas Jefferson to Charles Willson Peale, 1769–1825." *The Pennsylvania Magazine of History and Biography*, v. 28, no. 2, 1904, pp. 136–54; v. 28, no. 3, 1904, pp. 295–319; and v. 28, no. 4, 1904, pp. 403–19.

Shadwell, Wendy J. "The Portrait Engravings of Charles Willson Peale," in Joan D. Dolmetsch, ed., *Eighteenth-Century Prints in Colonial America: To Educate and Decorate* (Williamsburg, Va.: Colonial Williamsburg Foundation, 1979), pp. 123–44.

Shapiro, Henry D. "Daniel Drake's *Sensorium Commune* and the Organization of the Second American Enlightenment." *The Cincinnati Historical Bulletin*, v. 27, no. 1, Spring 1969, pp. 42–52.

Sifton, Paul Ginsburg. "Pierre Eugène DuSimitière (1737–1784): Collector in Revolutionary America." Ph.D. diss., University of Pennsylvania, Philadelphia, 1960.

Silhouette Collection, Historical Society of Pennsylvania, Philadelphia.

Silhouette Collection, Library Company of Philadelphia.

Silhouette Collection, Library of Congress, Washington, D.C.

Silhouette Collection, National Anthropological Archives, National Museum of Natural History, Smithsonian Institution, Washington, D.C.

Silhouette Collection, Philadelphia Museum of Art.

Simpson, George Gaylord. "The Beginnings of Vertebrate Paleontology in North America." *Proceedings of the American Philosophical Society*, v. 86, no. 1, September 1942, pp. 130–88.

Simpson, George Gaylord, and H. Tobien. "Rediscovery of Peale's Mastodon." *Proceedings of the American Philosophical Society*, v. 98, no. 4, August 1954, pp. 279–81.

Simpson, Henry. *The Lives of Eminent Philadelphians, Now Deceased. Collected from Original and Authentic Sources* (Philadelphia: William Brotherhead, 1859).

Smith, Barbara Clark. *After the Revolution: The Smithsonian History of Everyday Life in the Eighteenth Century* (New York and Washington, D.C.: Pantheon Books, 1985).

Smith, Billy G. *The "Lower Sort": Philadelphia's Laboring People, 1750–1800* (Ithaca, N.Y., and London: Cornell University Press, 1990).

Smith, Murphy D. *Oak from an Acorn: A History of the American Philosophical Society Library, 1770–1803* (Wilmington, Del.: Scholarly Resources, 1976).

Spargo, John. *Early American Pottery and China* (New York: Century Co., 1926; reprint, Rutland, Vt.: Charles E. Tuttle Co., 1974).

Sprague, William B. *Annals of the American Pulpit . . .*, 9 vols. (New York: Robert Carter and Brothers, 1857–69).

Stafford, Barbara Maria. *Body Criticism: Imaging the Unseen in Enlightenment Art and Medicine* (Cambridge, Mass., and London: MIT Press, 1991).

———. "From 'Brilliant Ideas' to 'Fitful Thoughts': Conjecturing the Unseen in Late Eighteenth-Century Art." *Zeitschrift für Kunstgeschichte*, v. 48, no. 3, 1985, pp. 329–63.

Stafford, Cornelius W. *The Philadelphia Directory for 1797* (Philadelphia: William W. Woodward, 1797).

———. *The Philadelphia Directory for 1798* (Philadelphia: William W. Woodward, 1798).

———. *The Philadelphia Directory for 1800* (Philadelphia: William W. Woodward, 1800).

———. *The Philadelphia Directory, for 1801* (Philadelphia: William W. Woodward, 1801).

Stallybrass, Peter, and Allon White. *The Politics and Poetics of Transgression* (Ithaca, N.Y.: Cornell University Press, 1986).

Stein, Roger B. "Charles Willson Peale's Expressive Design: *The Artist in His Museum.*" *Prospects,* v. 6, 1981, pp. 139–85.

Steinberg, David. "The Characters of Charles Willson Peale: Portraiture and Social Identity, 1769–1776." Ph.D. diss., University of Pennsylvania, Philadelphia, 1993.

Stephen, Leslie, and Sidney Lee. *The Dictionary of National Biography,* 21 vols. plus supplements (London: Smith, Elder, & Co. 1885–1901; reprint, London: Oxford University Press, 1963–64).

Stephens, Thomas. *Stephens's Philadelphia Directory for 1796* (Philadelphia: W. Woodward, 1796).

Stewart, Susan. *On Longing: Narratives of the Miniature, the Gigantic, the Souvenir, the Collection* (Baltimore and London: Johns Hopkins University Press, 1984).

Sutcliff, Robert. *Travels in Some Parts of North America, in the Years 1804, 1805, & 1806* (York, England: C. Peacock; London: Darton, Harvey, and Darton; Wm. Phillips; 1811).

The Theatrical Censor, Philadelphia, 1805–6.

Thomas, Lawrence Buckley. *Genealogical Notes: Containing the Pedigree of the Thomas Family, of Maryland* . . . (Baltimore: Lawrence Buckley Thomas, 1877).

Thompson, Peter. "A Social History of Philadelphia's Taverns, 1683–1800." Ph.D. diss., University of Pennsylvania, Philadelphia, 1989.

Torchia, Robert W. "John Neagle, Portrait Painter of Philadelphia." Ph.D. diss., University of Pennsylvania, Philadelphia, 1989.

Transactions of the American Philosophical Society, Philadelphia, 1769–1827.

Trollope, Frances. *Domestic Manners of the Americans* (London: Century Publishing, 1984).

Tudor, Henry. *Narrative of a Tour in North America . . . In a Series of Letters Written in the Years 1831–2,* 2 vols. (London: James Duncan, 1834).

The Union, Philadelphia, 1818–23.

United States Continental Congress. *Journal of the Proceedings of the Congress, Held at Philadelphia, September 5, 1774* (Philadelphia: William and Thomas Bradford, 1774).

United States Gazette, Philadelphia, 1804–18.

University of Pennsylvania, *Alumni Master File,* microfilm, University of Pennsylvania Archives and Record Center, Philadelphia.

———, Society of the Alumni. *Biographical Catalogue of the Matriculates of the College; Together with Lists of the Members of the College Faculty and the Trustees, Officers, and Recipients of Honorary Degrees, 1749–1893* (Philadelphia: printed for the Society, 1894).

———, Society of the Alumni of the Medical Department. *Catalogue of the Alumni of the Medical Department of the University of Pennsylvania, 1765–1877* (Philadelphia: Collins, 1877).

Vlach, John Michael. *Plain Painters: Making Sense of American Folk Art* (Washington, D.C., and London: Smithsonian Institution Press, 1980).

Waldman, Carl. *Who Was Who in Native American History: Indians and Non-Indians from Early Contacts through 1900* (New York, Oxford, and Sydney: Facts on File, 1990).

Walker, Joseph E. *Hopewell Village: The Dynamics of a Nineteenth Century Iron-Making Community* (Philadelphia: University of Pennsylvania Press, 1966).

Wall, A. J. "Wax Portraiture." *The New-York Historical Society Quarterly Bulletin,* v. 9, no. 1, April 1925, pp. 3–26.

Wansey, Henry. *An Excursion to the United States of America in the Summer of 1794,* edited by David John Jeremy. *Memoirs of the American Philosophical Society,* v. 82 (Philadelphia: American Philosophical Society, 1970).

Ward, Barbara McLean, and Gerald W. R. Ward. *Silver in American Life: Selections from the Mabel Brady Garvan and Other Collections at Yale University* (New Haven, Conn.: Yale University Press, 1979).

Ward, David C. "Celebration of Self: The Portraiture of Charles Willson Peale and Rembrandt Peale, 1822–27." *American Art,* v. 7, no. 1, Winter 1993, pp. 9–27.

Warner, Sam Bass, Jr. *The Private City: Philadelphia in Three Periods of Its Growth* (Philadelphia: University of Pennsylvania Press, 1968).

Waterton, Charles. *Wanderings in South America: The North-West of the United States and the Antilles, in the Years 1812, 1816 & 1824, with Original Instructions for the Perfect Preservation of Birds, Etc. for Cabinets of Natural History,* edited by J. G. Wood, with an introduction by David Bellamy (London: n.p., 1825 and 1878; reprint, New York: Hippocrene Books, Inc., and London: Century Publishing, 1984).

Wehtje, Myron F. "Charles Willson Peale and His Temple." *Pennsylvania History,* v. 36, no. 2, April 1969, pp. 161–73.

Welch, Margaret. "John James Audubon and His American Audience: Art, Science, and Nature, 1830–1860." Ph.D. diss., University of Pennsylvania, Philadelphia, 1988.

Wilkinson, Norman B. "Mr. Davy's Diary." *Pennsylvania History,* v. 20, no. 2, April 1953, pp. 123–41, and v. 20, no. 3, July 1953, pp. 258–79.

Willoughby, Charles C. "A Few Ethnological Specimens Collected by Lewis and Clark," *American Anthropologist,* n.s., v. 7, no. 4, 1905, pp. 633–41.

Wilson, James Grant, and John Fiske, eds. *Appleton's Cyclopaedia of American Biography,* 6 vols. (New York: D. Appleton and Company, 1887–89).

Wolcott, John R. "Philadelphia's Chestnut Street Theatre: A Plan and Elevation." *Journal of the Society of Architectural Historians,* v. 30, no. 3, October 1971, pp. 209–18.

Wolf, Bryan Jay. *Romantic Re-Vision: Culture and Consciousness in Nineteenth-Century American Painting and Literature* (Chicago and London: University of Chicago Press, 1982).

Wood, Gordon S. *The Creation of the American Republic, 1776–1787* (New York and London: W. W. Norton & Company, 1969; reprint, New York and London: W. W. Norton & Company, 1972).

[Wright, Frances]. *Views of Society and Manners in America . . . 1818, 1819, and 1820 . . .* (London: printed for Longman, Hurst, Rees, Orme, and Brown, 1821).

Yochelson, Ellis L. "Mr. Peale and His Mammoth Museum." *Proceedings of the American Philosophical Society,* v. 136, no. 4, December 1992, pp. 487–506.

Zolberg, Vera L. "Tensions of Mission in American Art Museums," in Paul J. DiMaggio, ed., *Nonprofit Enterprise in the Arts: Studies in Mission and Constraint* (New York and Oxford: Oxford University Press, 1986), pp. 184–98.

Index

Unless otherwise specified, the term "museum" in this index refers to Peale's Philadelphia Museum. Works of art (in italics) are listed either alphabetically by title or, when applicable, under the heading "portraits."